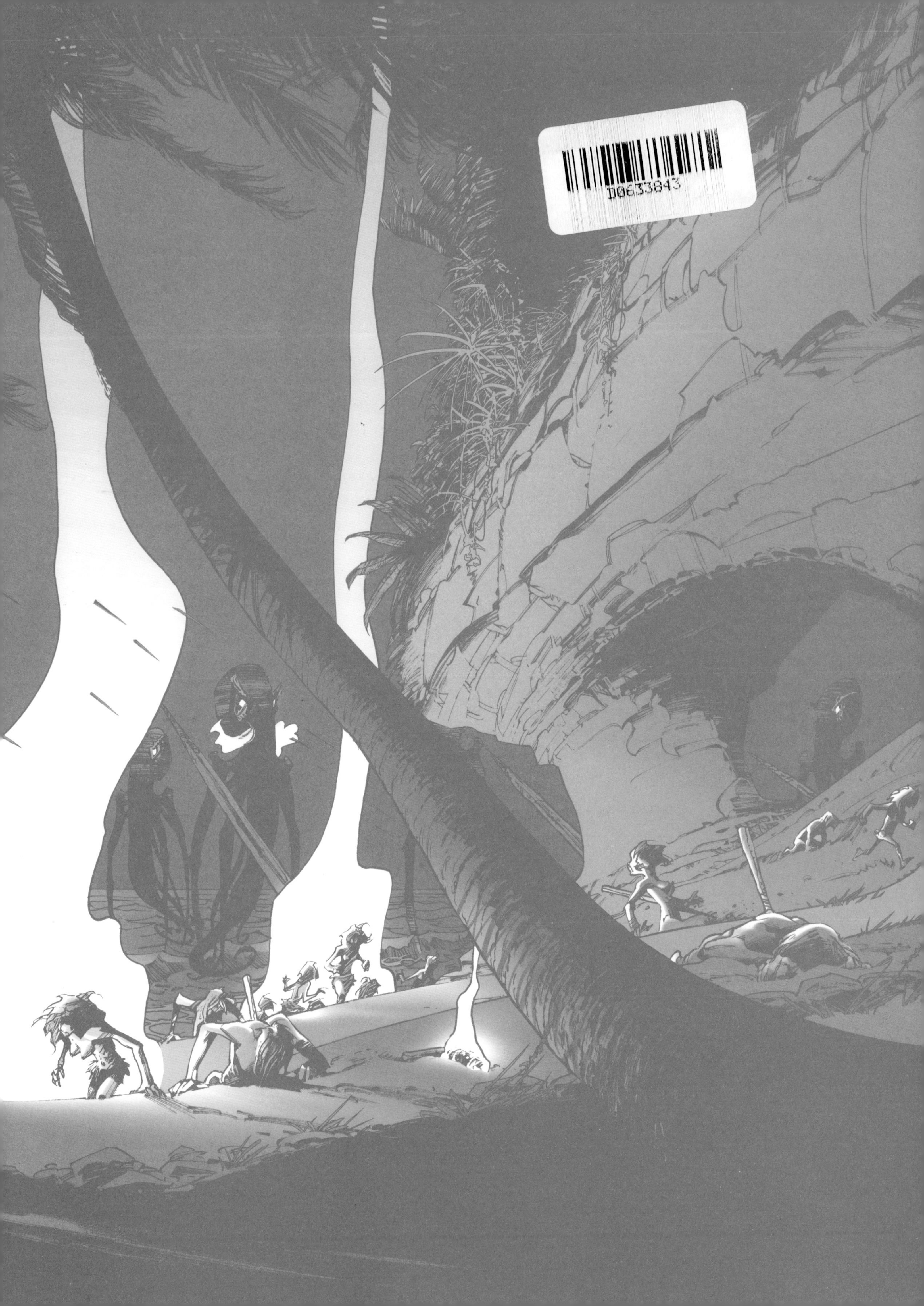

#
NiourK

Story and art by OLIVIER VATINE

DARK HORSE BOOKS

Translated by
BRANDON KANDER and **DIANA SCHUTZ**

Lettering by
CLEM ROBINS

President and Publisher
MIKE RICHARDSON

English Language Edition Editors
KATII O'BRIEN and **JEMIAH JEFFERSON**

Designer
SARAH TERRY

Digital Art Technician
CHRISTINA McKENZIE

Published by Dark Horse Books
A division of Dark Horse Comics, Inc.
10956 SE Main Street | Milwaukie, OR 97222

First US edition: January 2018 | ISBN: 978-1-50670-369-5

10 9 8 7 6 5 4 3 2 1
Printed in China

Advertising Sales: (503) 905-2237 | International Licensing: (503) 905-2377
Comic Shop Locator Service: Comicshoplocator.com

DarkHorse.com | Facebook.com/DarkHorseComics | Twitter.com/DarkHorseComics

NEIL HANKERSON Executive Vice President **TOM WEDDLE** Chief Financial Officer **RANDY STRADLEY** Vice President of Publishing **NICK MCWHORTER** Chief Business Development Officer **MATT PARKINSON** Vice President of Marketing **DAVID SCROGGY** Vice President of Product Development **DALE LAFOUNTAIN** Vice President of Information Technology **CARA NIECE** Vice President of Production and Scheduling **MARK BERNARDI** Vice President of Book Trade and Digital Sales **KEN LIZZI** General Counsel **DAVE MARSHALL** Editor in Chief **DAVEY ESTRADA** Editorial Director **SCOTT ALLIE** Executive Senior Editor **CHRIS WARNER** Senior Books Editor **CARY GRAZZINI** Director of Specialty Projects **LIA RIBACCHI** Art Director **VANESSA TODD** Director of Print Purchasing **MATT DRYER** Director of Digital Art and Prepress **MICHAEL GOMBOS** Director of International Publishing and Licensing

Library of Congress Cataloging-in-Publication Data

Names: Wul, Stefan, author. | Vatine, Olivier, artist. | Schutz, Diana,
  translator. | Robins, Clem, 1955- letterer.
Title: Niourk / Stefan Wul, Olivier Vatine ; translation by Diana Schutz ;
  lettering by Clem Robins.
Other titles: Niourk. English
Description: First US edition. | Burbank, CA : Dark Horse Books, 2018.
Identifiers: LCCN 2017042533 | ISBN 9781506703695 (hardback)
Subjects: LCSH: Graphic novels. | BISAC: COMICS & GRAPHIC NOVELS / Literary.
Classification: LCC PN6747.W85 N5613 2018 | DDC 741.5/944--dc23
LC record available at https://lccn.loc.gov/2017042533

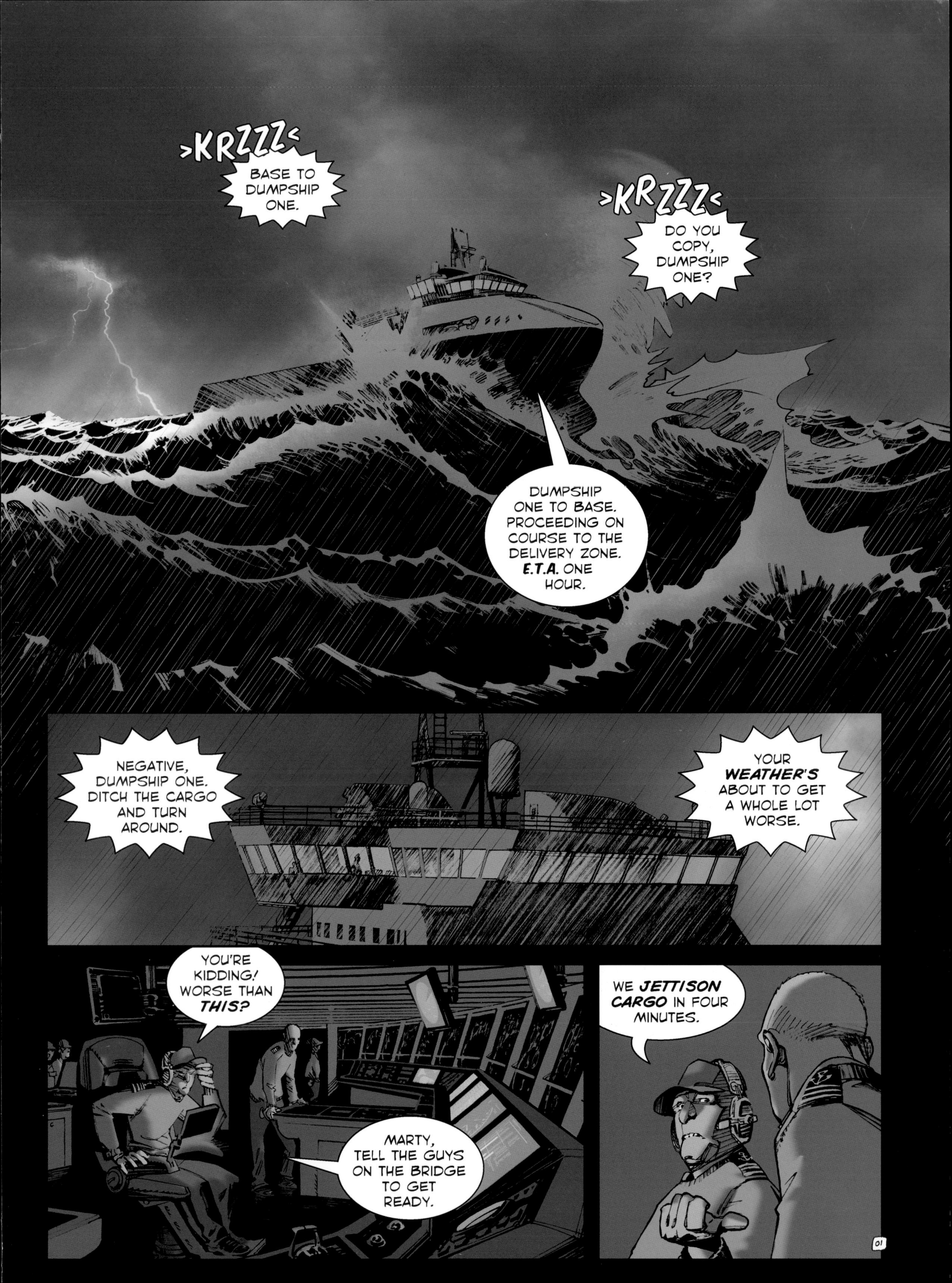
>KRZZZ<
BASE TO DUMPSHIP ONE.
>KRZZZ<
DO YOU COPY, DUMPSHIP ONE?
DUMPSHIP ONE TO BASE. PROCEEDING ON COURSE TO THE DELIVERY ZONE. E.T.A. ONE HOUR.
NEGATIVE, DUMPSHIP ONE. DITCH THE CARGO AND TURN AROUND.
YOUR WEATHER'S ABOUT TO GET A WHOLE LOT WORSE.
YOU'RE KIDDING! WORSE THAN THIS?
MARTY, TELL THE GUYS ON THE BRIDGE TO GET READY.
WE JETTISON CARGO IN FOUR MINUTES.
01

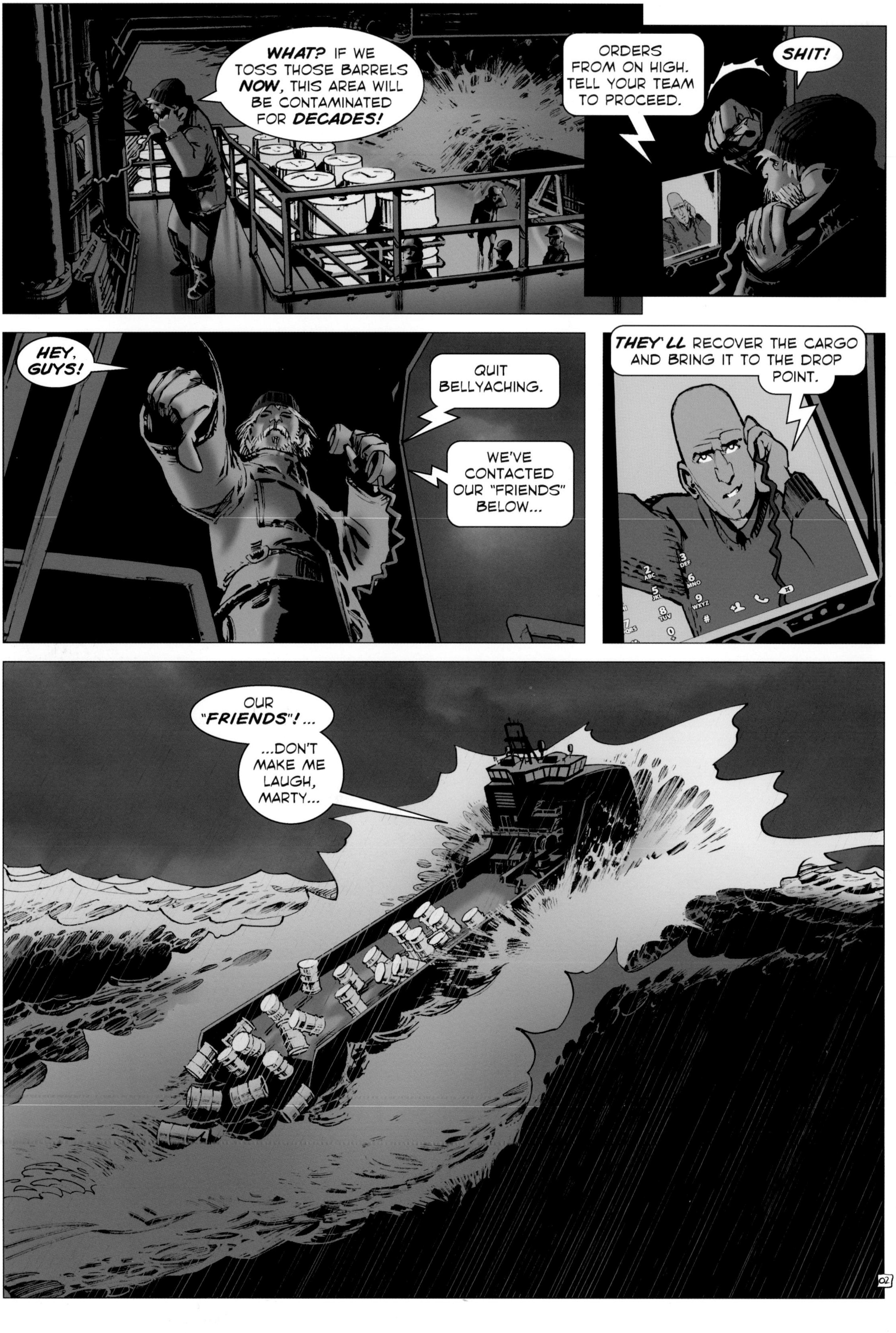
WHAT? IF WE TOSS THOSE BARRELS NOW, THIS AREA WILL BE CONTAMINATED FOR DECADES!
ORDERS FROM ON HIGH. TELL YOUR TEAM TO PROCEED.
SHIT!
HEY, GUYS!
QUIT BELLYACHING.
WE'VE CONTACTED OUR "FRIENDS" BELOW...
THEY'LL RECOVER THE CARGO AND BRING IT TO THE DROP POINT.
OUR "FRIENDS"! ...
...DON'T MAKE ME LAUGH, MARTY...

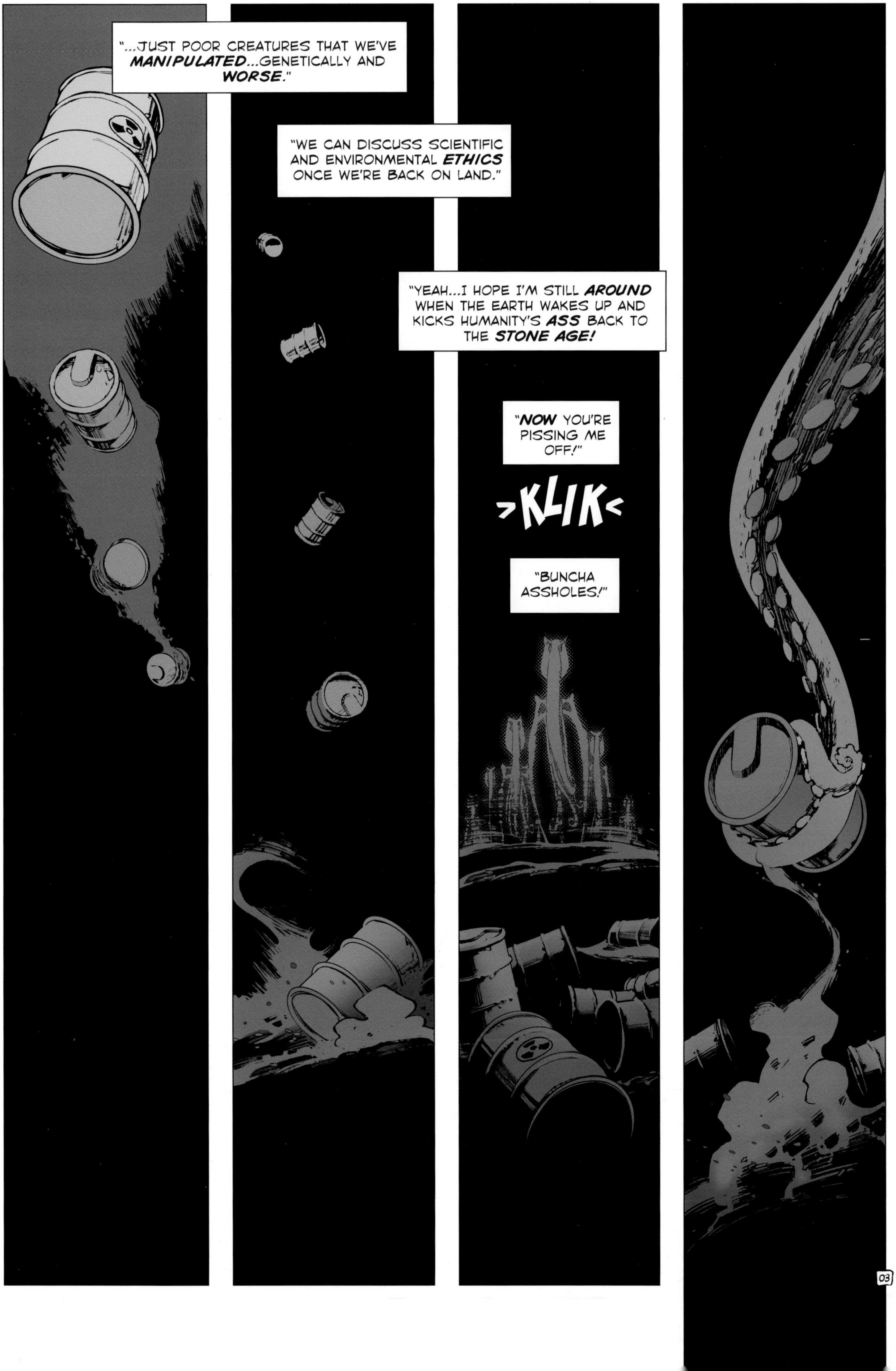
"...JUST POOR CREATURES THAT WE'VE MANIPULATED...GENETICALLY AND WORSE."
"WE CAN DISCUSS SCIENTIFIC AND ENVIRONMENTAL ETHICS ONCE WE'RE BACK ON LAND."
"YEAH...I HOPE I'M STILL AROUND WHEN THE EARTH WAKES UP AND KICKS HUMANITY'S ASS BACK TO THE STONE AGE!
"NOW YOU'RE PISSING ME OFF!"
KLIK
"BUNCHA ASSHOLES!"

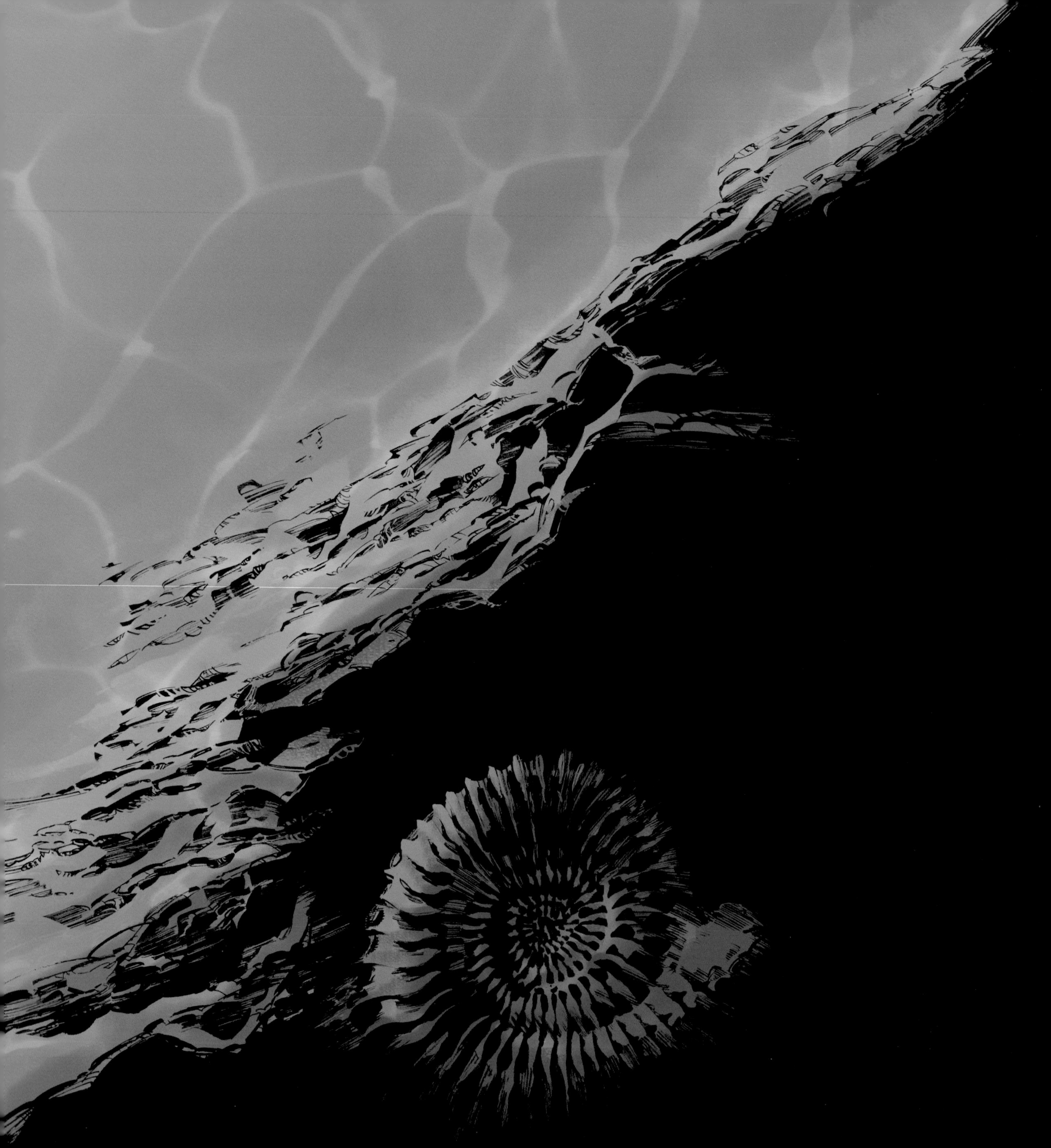

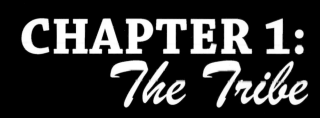

CHAPTER 1: *The Tribe*

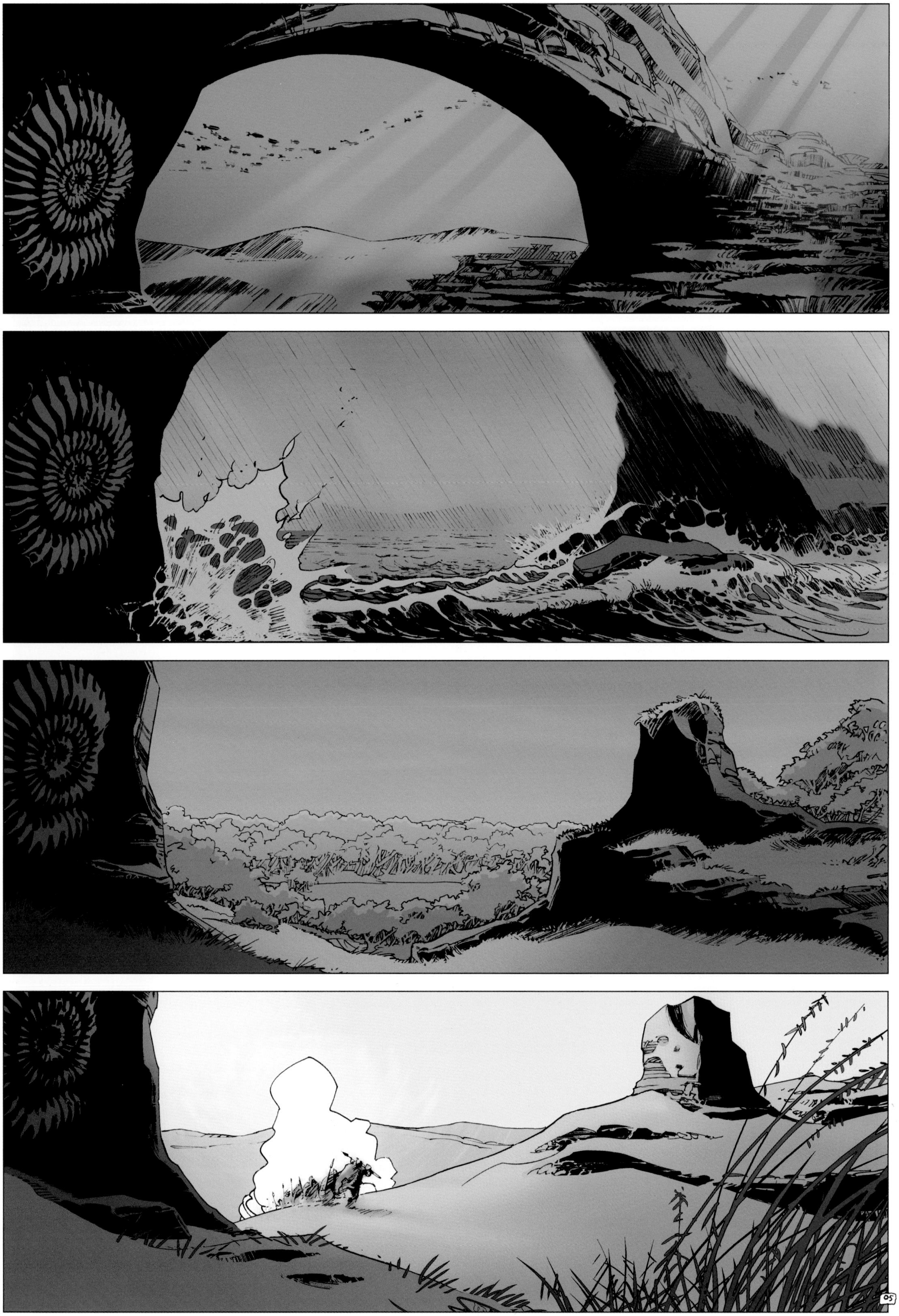

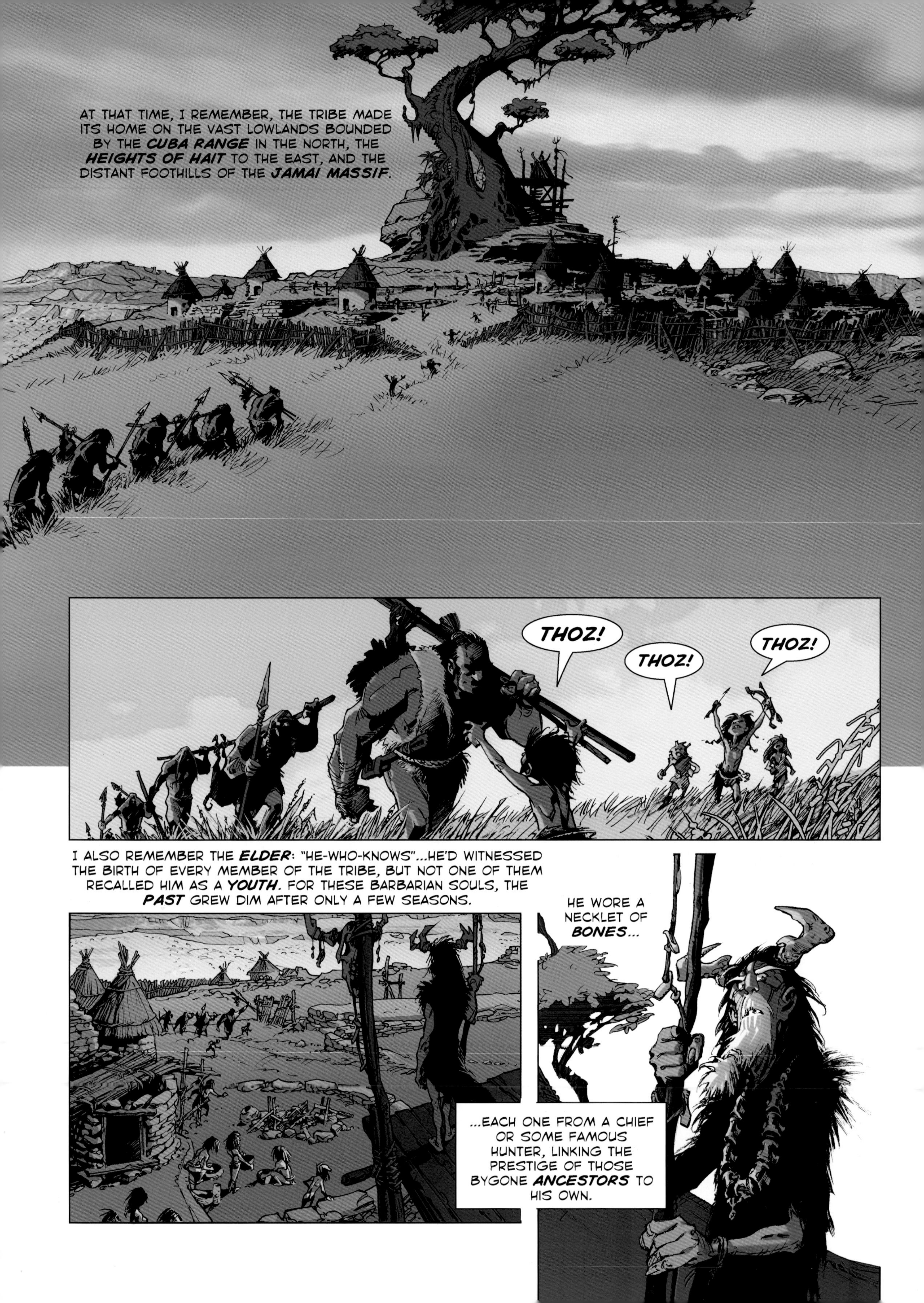
AT THAT TIME, I REMEMBER, THE TRIBE MADE ITS HOME ON THE VAST LOWLANDS BOUNDED BY THE CUBA RANGE IN THE NORTH, THE HEIGHTS OF HAIT TO THE EAST, AND THE DISTANT FOOTHILLS OF THE JAMAI MASSIF.
THOZ!
THOZ!
THOZ!
I ALSO REMEMBER THE ELDER: "HE-WHO-KNOWS"...HE'D WITNESSED THE BIRTH OF EVERY MEMBER OF THE TRIBE, BUT NOT ONE OF THEM RECALLED HIM AS A YOUTH. FOR THESE BARBARIAN SOULS, THE PAST GREW DIM AFTER ONLY A FEW SEASONS.
HE WORE A NECKLET OF BONES...
...EACH ONE FROM A CHIEF OR SOME FAMOUS HUNTER, LINKING THE PRESTIGE OF THOSE BYGONE ANCESTORS TO HIS OWN.

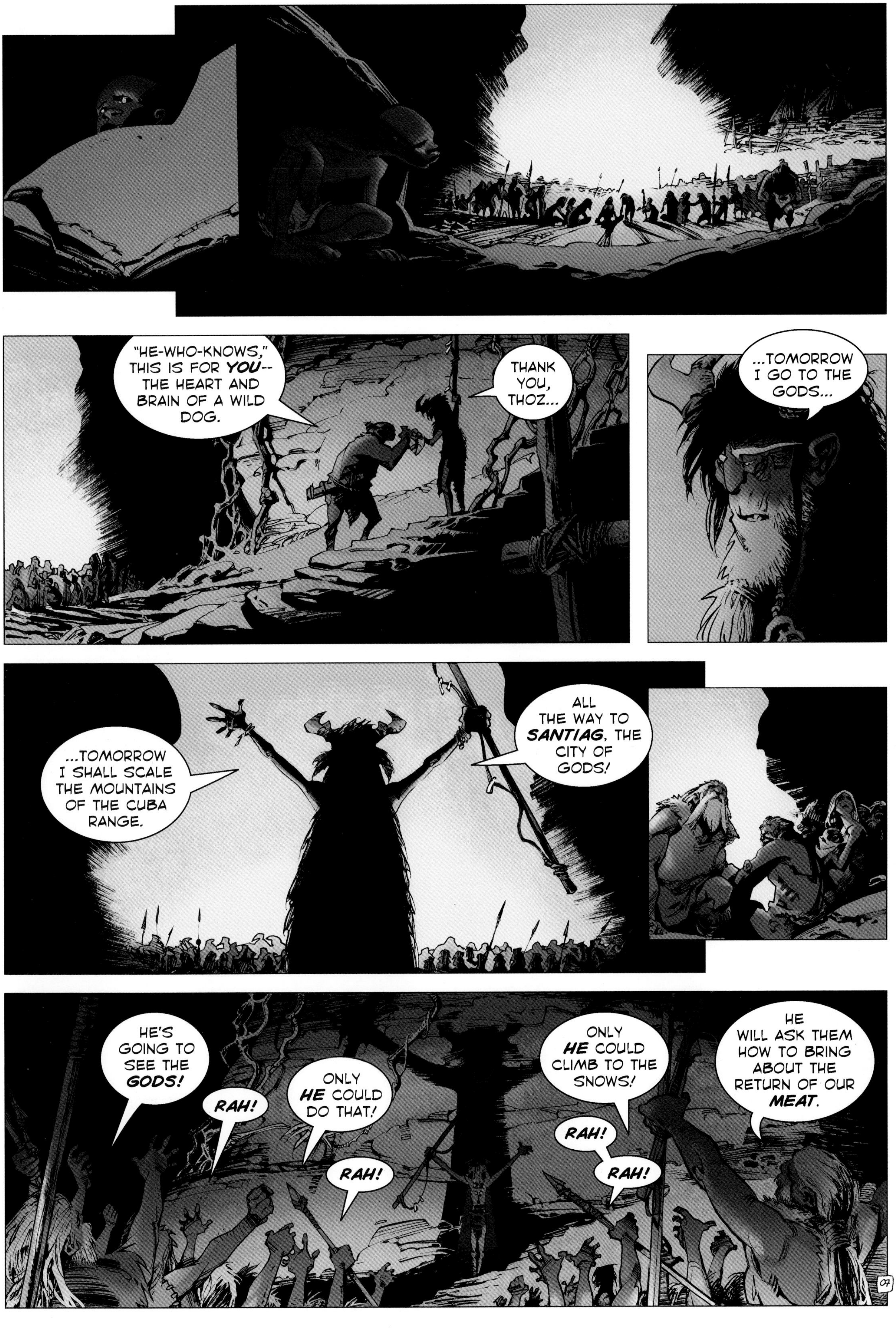
"HE-WHO-KNOWS," THIS IS FOR YOU-- THE HEART AND BRAIN OF A WILD DOG.
THANK YOU, THOZ...
...TOMORROW I GO TO THE GODS...
...TOMORROW I SHALL SCALE THE MOUNTAINS OF THE CUBA RANGE.
ALL THE WAY TO SANTIAG, THE CITY OF GODS!
HE'S GOING TO SEE THE GODS!
RAH!
ONLY HE COULD DO THAT!
RAH!
ONLY HE COULD CLIMB TO THE SNOWS!
RAH!
RAH!
HE WILL ASK THEM HOW TO BRING ABOUT THE RETURN OF OUR MEAT.

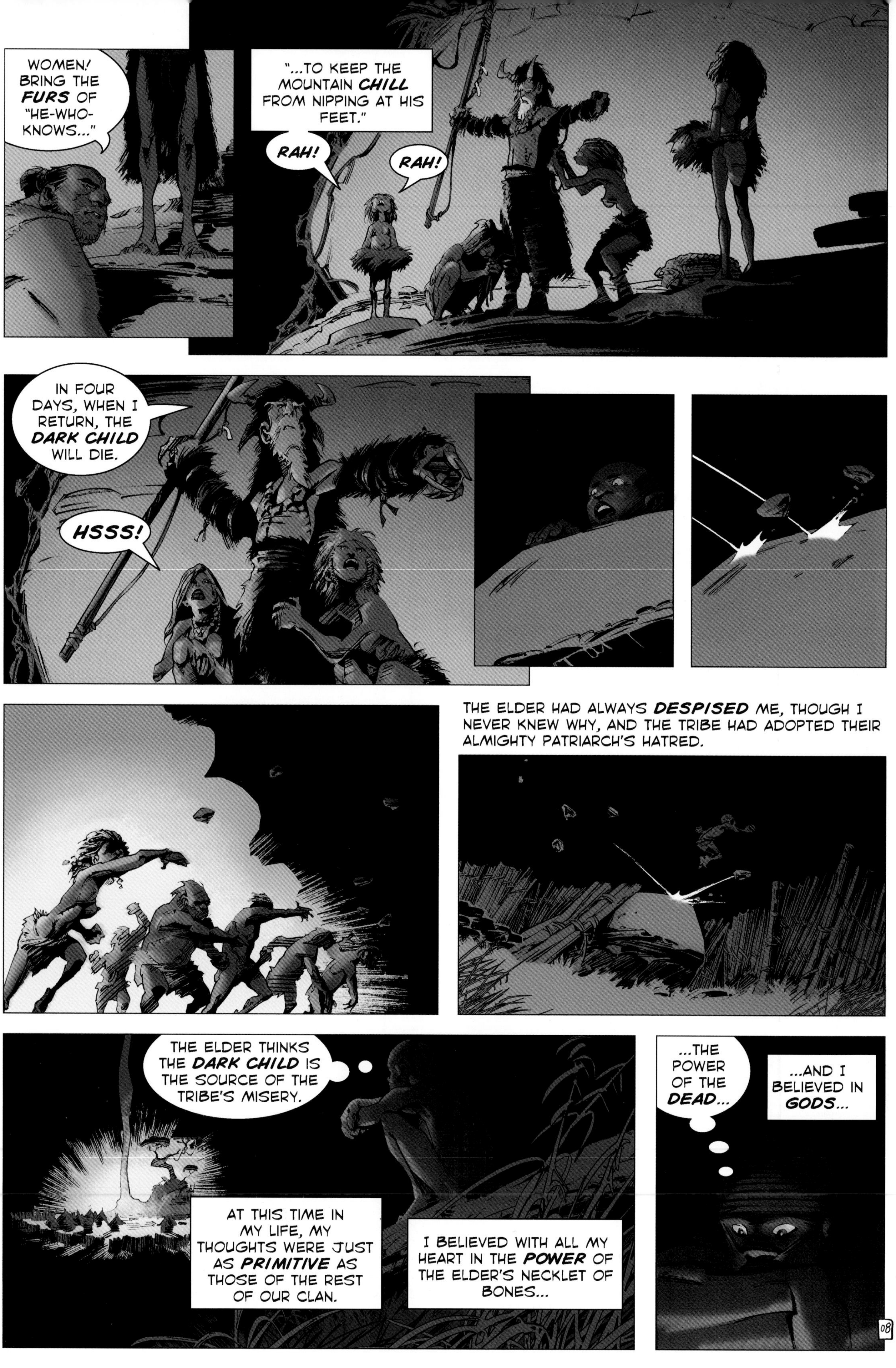

WOMEN! BRING THE FURS OF "HE-WHO-KNOWS..."
"...TO KEEP THE MOUNTAIN CHILL FROM NIPPING AT HIS FEET."
RAH!
RAH!
IN FOUR DAYS, WHEN I RETURN, THE DARK CHILD WILL DIE.
HSSS!
THE ELDER HAD ALWAYS DESPISED ME, THOUGH I NEVER KNEW WHY, AND THE TRIBE HAD ADOPTED THEIR ALMIGHTY PATRIARCH'S HATRED.
THE ELDER THINKS THE DARK CHILD IS THE SOURCE OF THE TRIBE'S MISERY.
AT THIS TIME IN MY LIFE, MY THOUGHTS WERE JUST AS PRIMITIVE AS THOSE OF THE REST OF OUR CLAN.
I BELIEVED WITH ALL MY HEART IN THE POWER OF THE ELDER'S NECKLET OF BONES...
...THE POWER OF THE DEAD...
...AND I BELIEVED IN GODS...

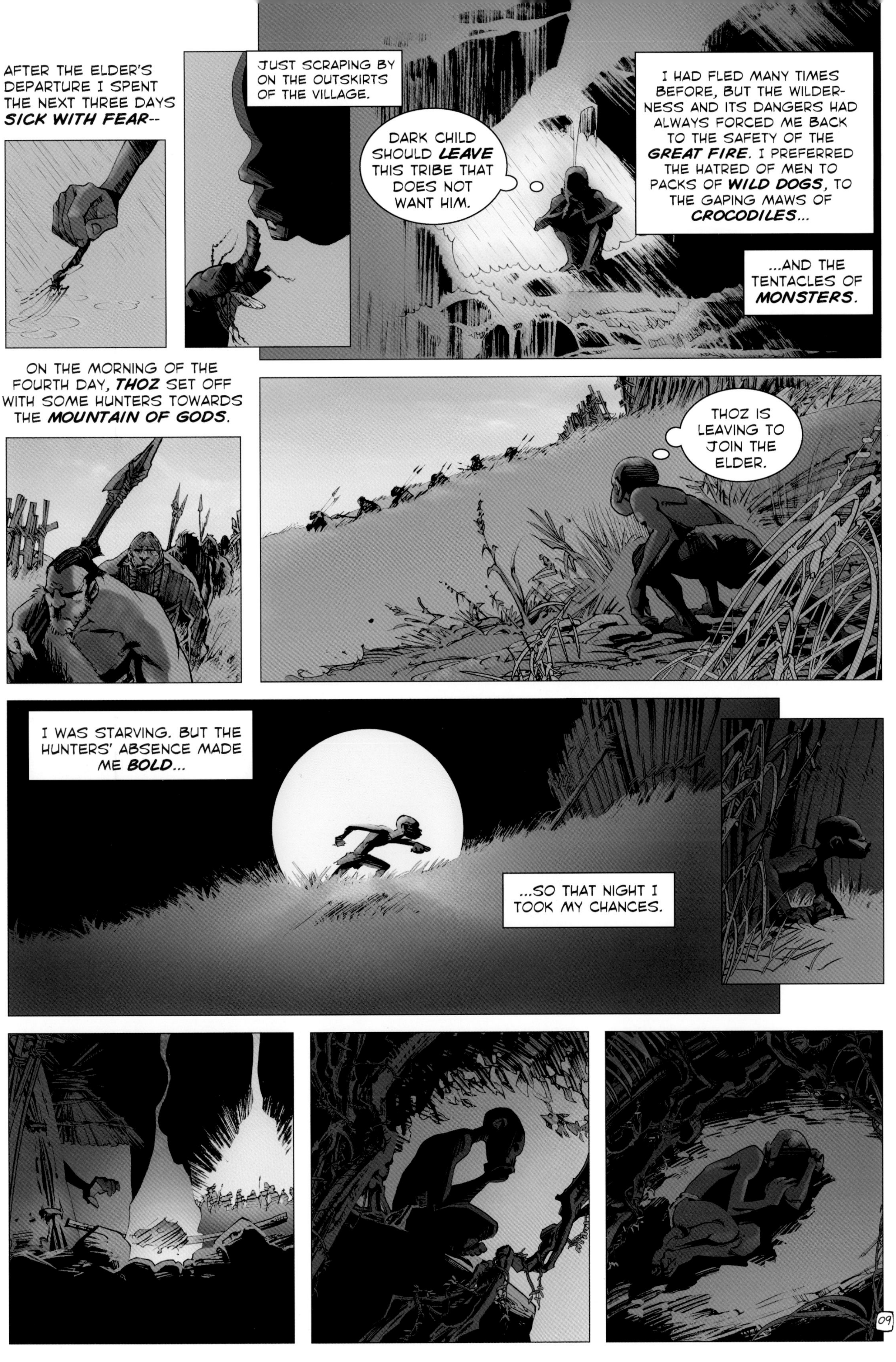

AFTER THE ELDER'S DEPARTURE I SPENT THE NEXT THREE DAYS SICK WITH FEAR--
JUST SCRAPING BY ON THE OUTSKIRTS OF THE VILLAGE.
DARK CHILD SHOULD LEAVE THIS TRIBE THAT DOES NOT WANT HIM.
I HAD FLED MANY TIMES BEFORE, BUT THE WILDERNESS AND ITS DANGERS HAD ALWAYS FORCED ME BACK TO THE SAFETY OF THE GREAT FIRE. I PREFERRED THE HATRED OF MEN TO PACKS OF WILD DOGS, TO THE GAPING MAWS OF CROCODILES...
...AND THE TENTACLES OF MONSTERS.
ON THE MORNING OF THE FOURTH DAY, THOZ SET OFF WITH SOME HUNTERS TOWARDS THE MOUNTAIN OF GODS.
THOZ IS LEAVING TO JOIN THE ELDER.
I WAS STARVING. BUT THE HUNTERS' ABSENCE MADE ME BOLD...
...SO THAT NIGHT I TOOK MY CHANCES.

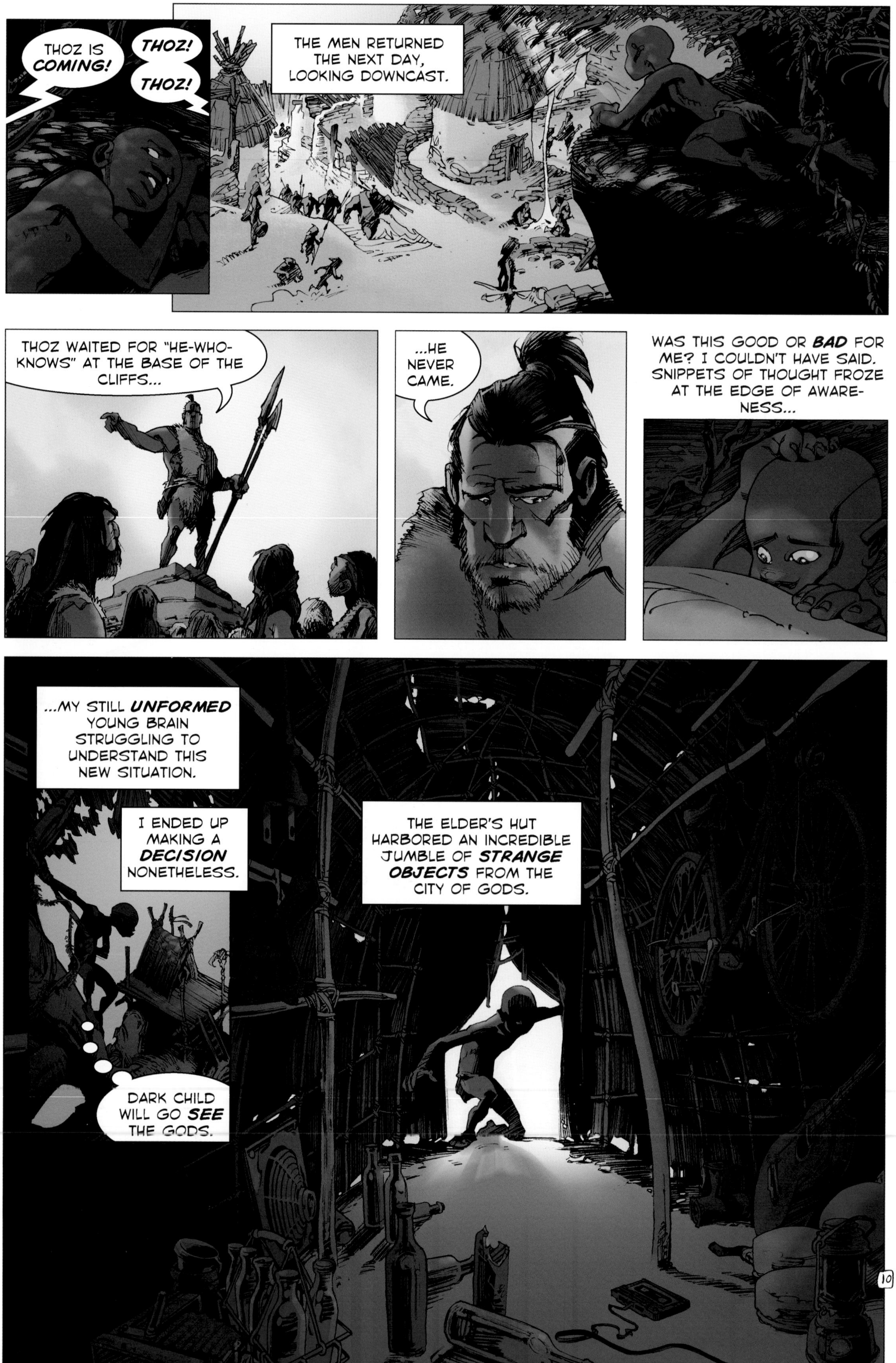
THOZ IS COMING!
THOZ!
THOZ!
THE MEN RETURNED THE NEXT DAY, LOOKING DOWNCAST.
THOZ WAITED FOR "HE-WHO-KNOWS" AT THE BASE OF THE CLIFFS...
...HE NEVER CAME.
WAS THIS GOOD OR BAD FOR ME? I COULDN'T HAVE SAID. SNIPPETS OF THOUGHT FROZE AT THE EDGE OF AWARE-NESS...
...MY STILL UNFORMED YOUNG BRAIN STRUGGLING TO UNDERSTAND THIS NEW SITUATION.
I ENDED UP MAKING A DECISION NONETHELESS.
DARK CHILD WILL GO SEE THE GODS.
THE ELDER'S HUT HARBORED AN INCREDIBLE JUMBLE OF STRANGE OBJECTS FROM THE CITY OF GODS.
10

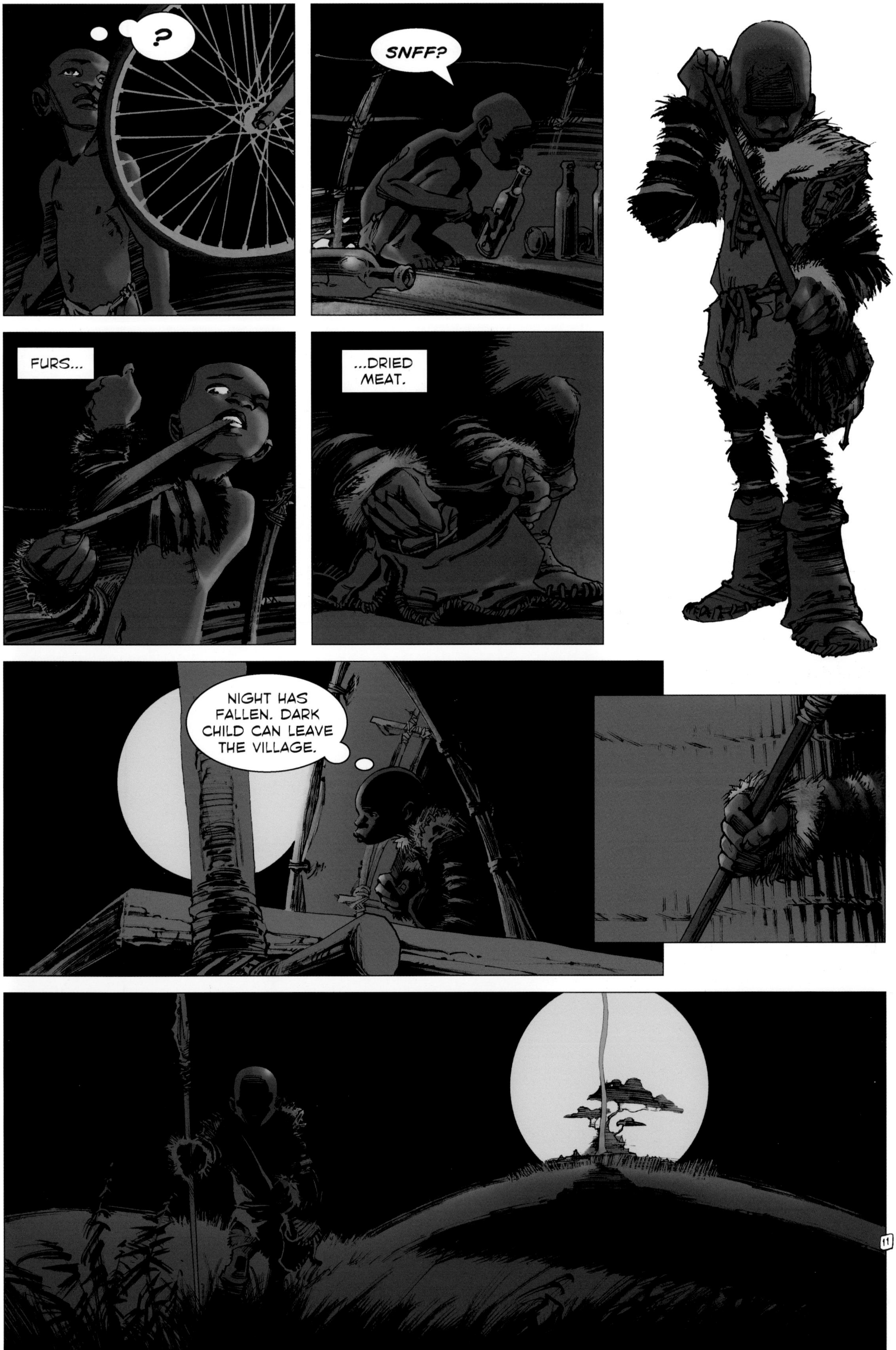
?
SNFF?
FURS...
...DRIED MEAT.
NIGHT HAS FALLEN. DARK CHILD CAN LEAVE THE VILLAGE.

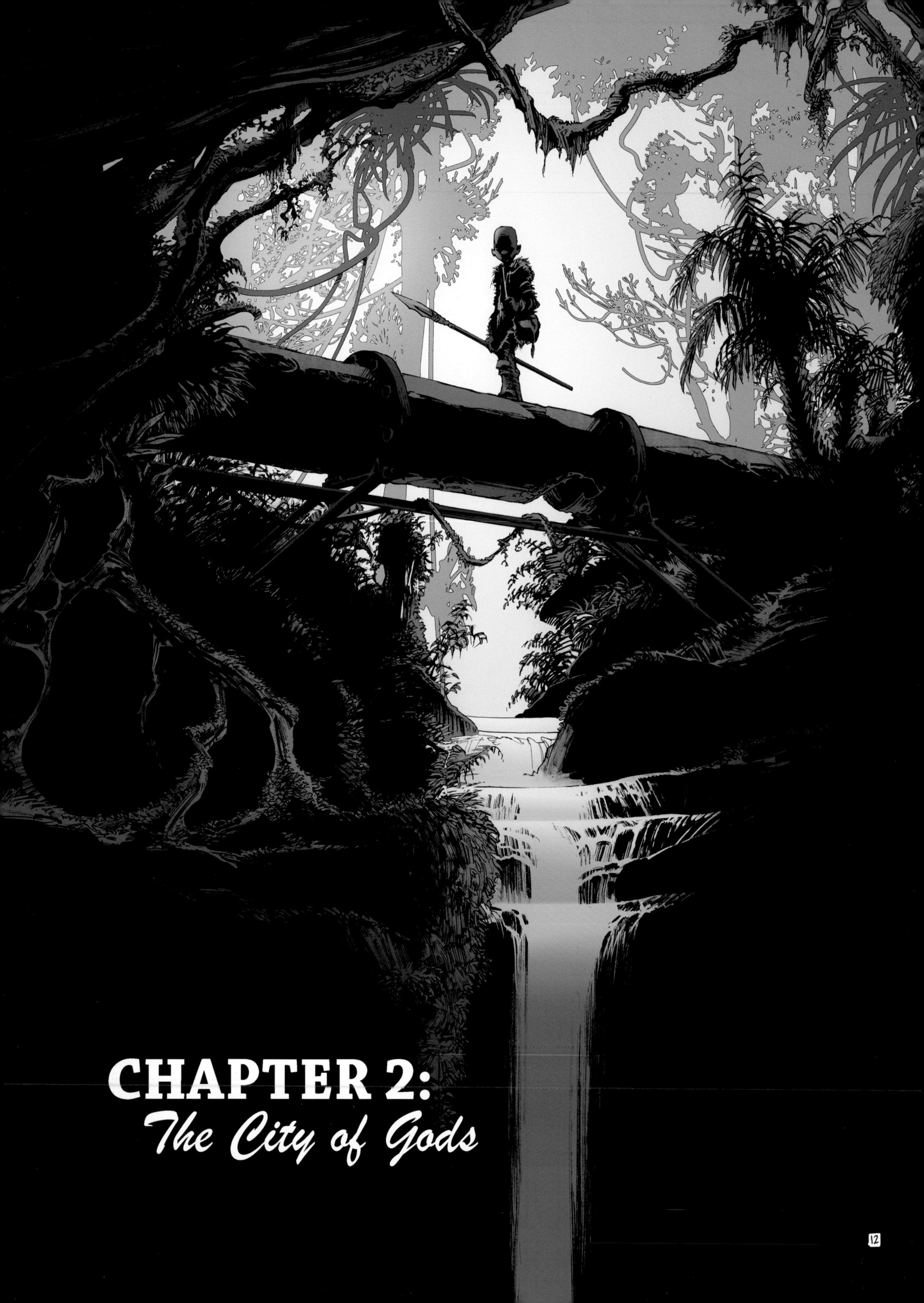

CHAPTER 2:
The City of Gods

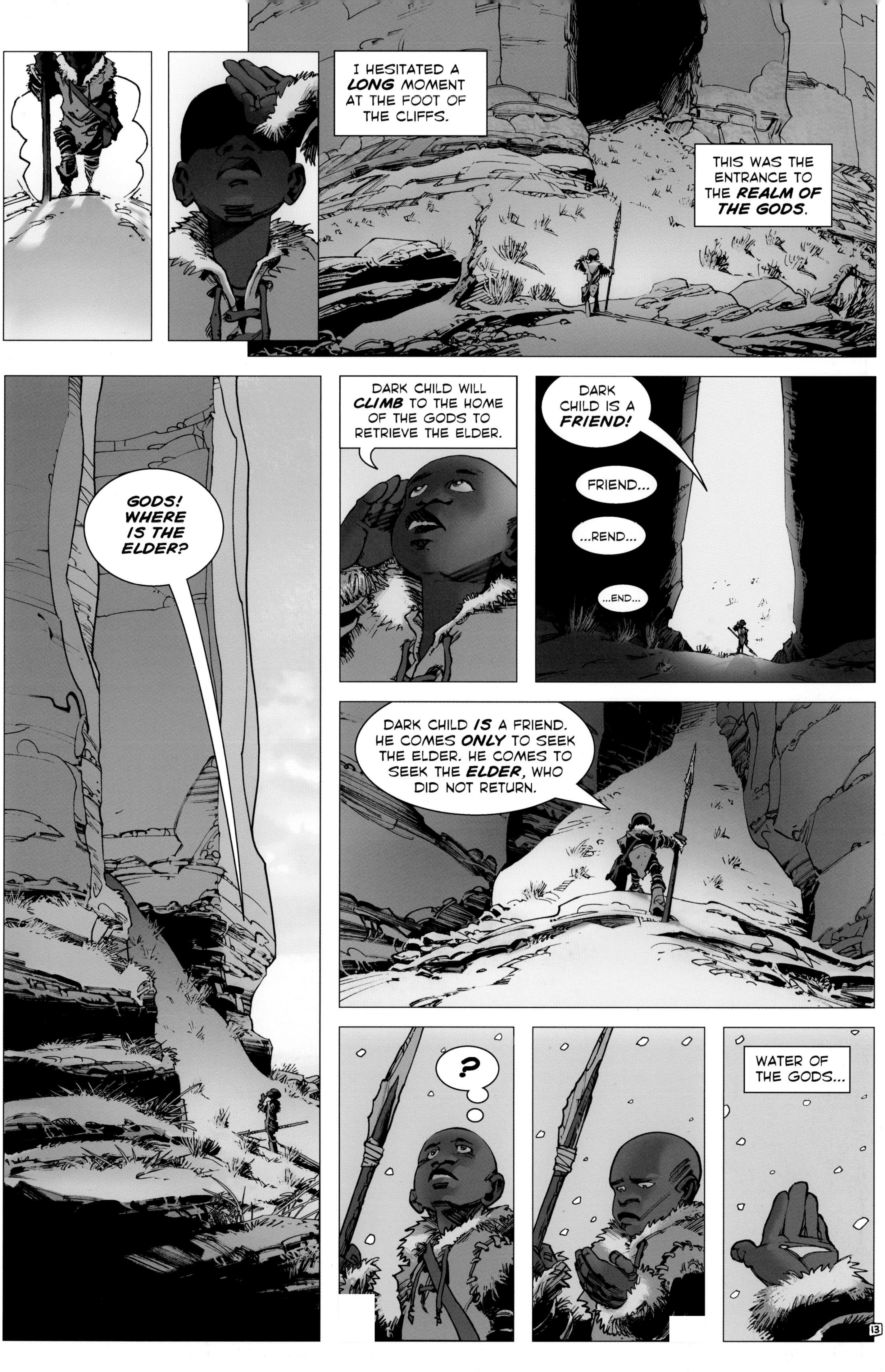
I HESITATED A LONG MOMENT AT THE FOOT OF THE CLIFFS.
THIS WAS THE ENTRANCE TO THE REALM OF THE GODS.
GODS! WHERE IS THE ELDER?
DARK CHILD WILL CLIMB TO THE HOME OF THE GODS TO RETRIEVE THE ELDER.
DARK CHILD IS A FRIEND!
FRIEND...
...REND...
...END...
DARK CHILD IS A FRIEND. HE COMES ONLY TO SEEK THE ELDER. HE COMES TO SEEK THE ELDER, WHO DID NOT RETURN.
?
WATER OF THE GODS...

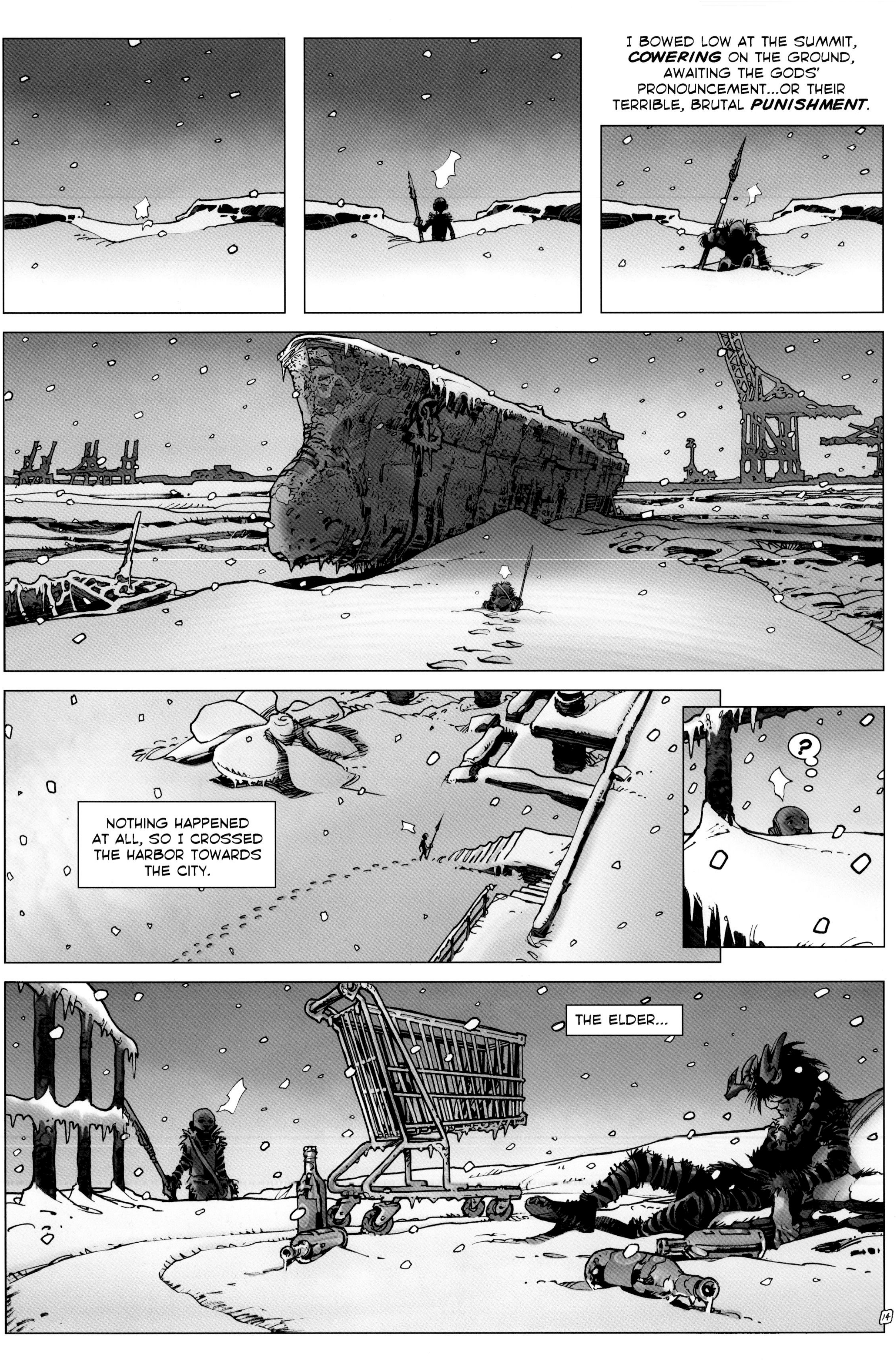
I BOWED LOW AT THE SUMMIT, COWERING ON THE GROUND, AWAITING THE GODS' PRONOUNCEMENT...OR THEIR TERRIBLE, BRUTAL PUNISHMENT.
NOTHING HAPPENED AT ALL, SO I CROSSED THE HARBOR TOWARDS THE CITY.
?
THE ELDER...
14

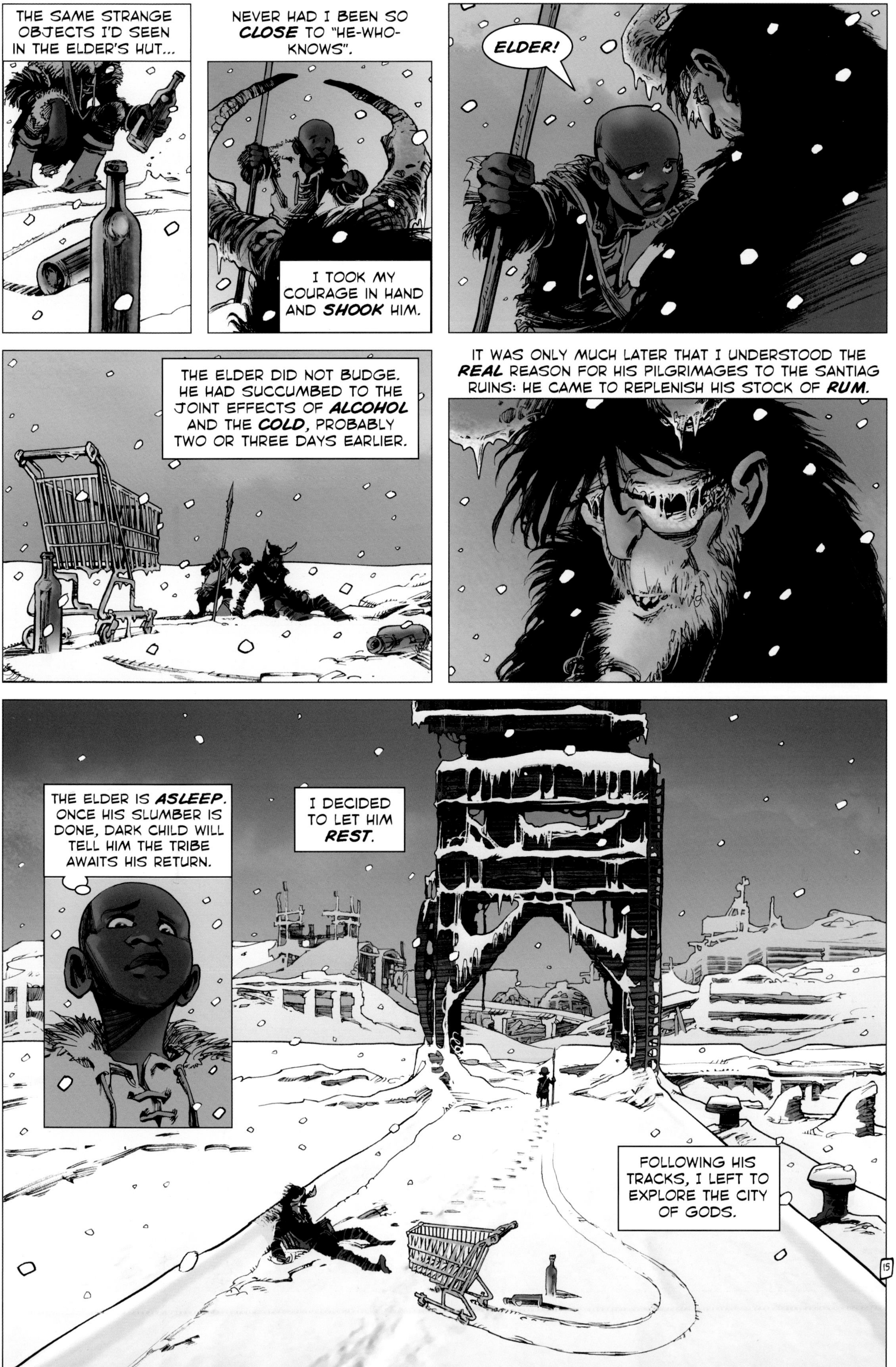
THE SAME STRANGE OBJECTS I'D SEEN IN THE ELDER'S HUT...
NEVER HAD I BEEN SO **CLOSE** TO "HE-WHO-KNOWS".
I TOOK MY COURAGE IN HAND AND **SHOOK** HIM.
ELDER!
THE ELDER DID NOT BUDGE. HE HAD SUCCUMBED TO THE JOINT EFFECTS OF **ALCOHOL** AND THE **COLD**, PROBABLY TWO OR THREE DAYS EARLIER.
IT WAS ONLY MUCH LATER THAT I UNDERSTOOD THE **REAL** REASON FOR HIS PILGRIMAGES TO THE SANTIAG RUINS: HE CAME TO REPLENISH HIS STOCK OF **RUM**.
THE ELDER IS **ASLEEP**. ONCE HIS SLUMBER IS DONE, DARK CHILD WILL TELL HIM THE TRIBE AWAITS HIS RETURN.
I DECIDED TO LET HIM **REST**.
FOLLOWING HIS TRACKS, I LEFT TO EXPLORE THE CITY OF GODS.

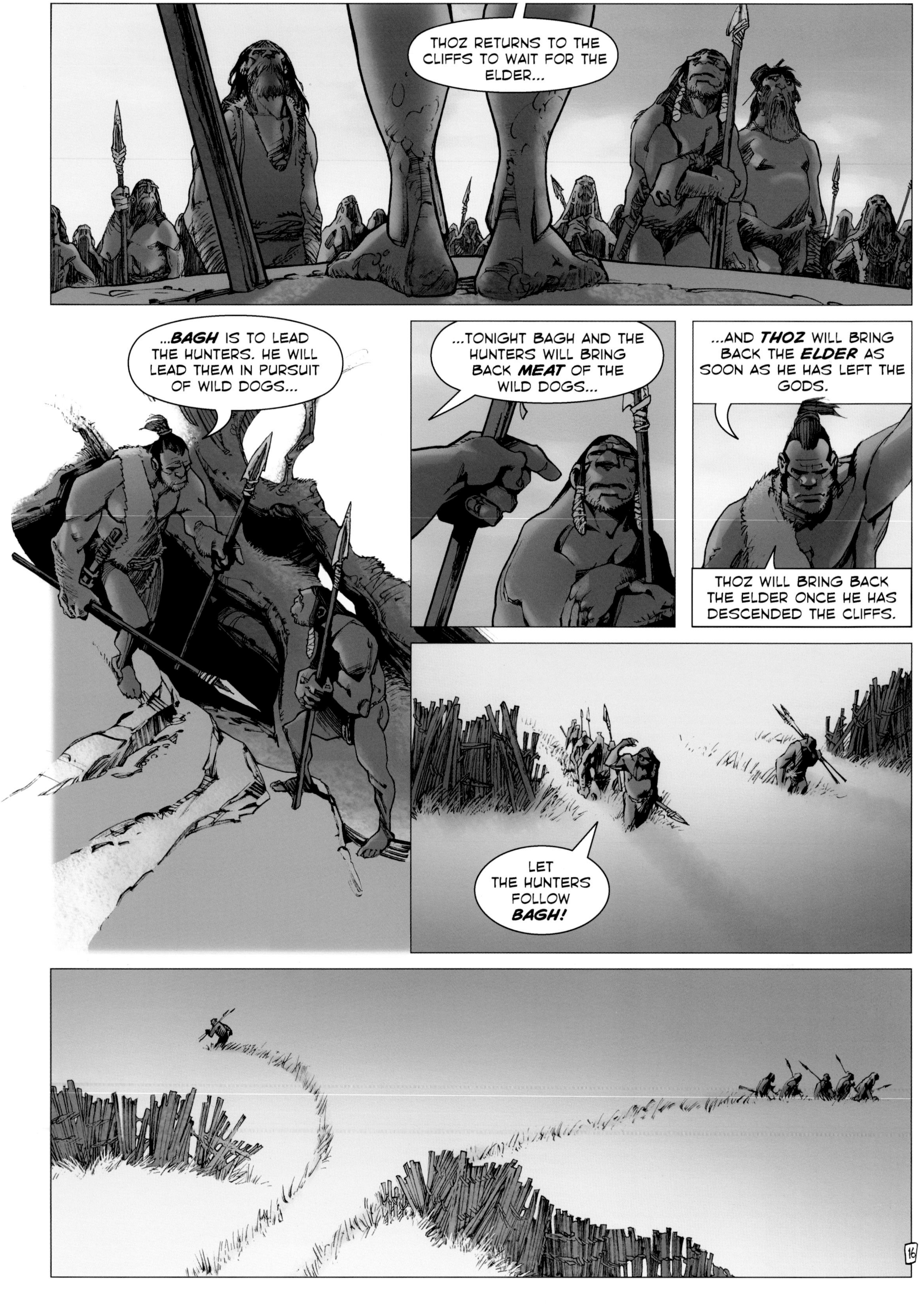
THOZ RETURNS TO THE CLIFFS TO WAIT FOR THE ELDER...
...BAGH IS TO LEAD THE HUNTERS. HE WILL LEAD THEM IN PURSUIT OF WILD DOGS...
...TONIGHT BAGH AND THE HUNTERS WILL BRING BACK MEAT OF THE WILD DOGS...
...AND THOZ WILL BRING BACK THE ELDER AS SOON AS HE HAS LEFT THE GODS.
THOZ WILL BRING BACK THE ELDER ONCE HE HAS DESCENDED THE CLIFFS.
LET THE HUNTERS FOLLOW BAGH!

THE ELDER'S TRACKS LED STRAIGHT TO A SHOPPING CENTER NEAR THE HARBOR.

THIS MIRACULOUSLY **INTACT RELIC** OF ANCIENT CIVILIZATION WAS SO **IMPOSING**, IT LEFT ME DUMBFOUNDED.

A GENTLE WARMTH RIPPLED FROM INSIDE. INNER MAINTENANCE ORGANS STILL **PULSATED** IN THE BOWELS OF THIS BEAST.

I PULLED MYSELF TOGETHER AND ENTERED.

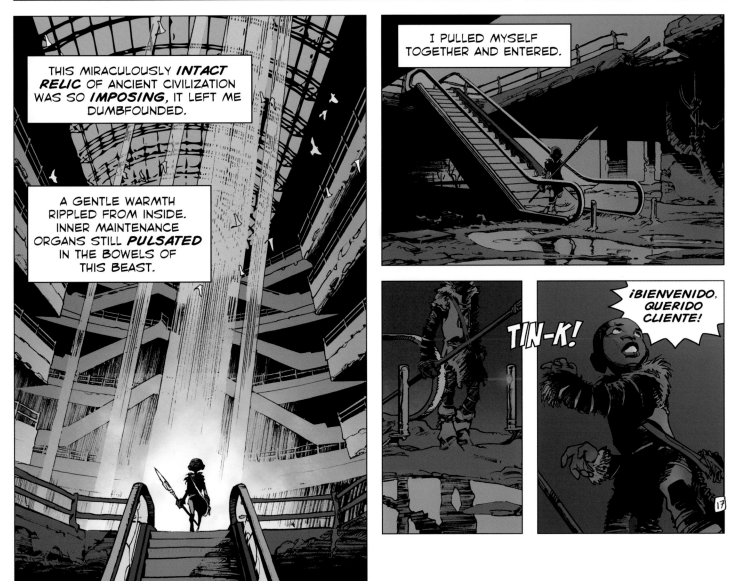

TIN-K!

¡BIENVENIDO, QUERIDO CLIENTE!

17

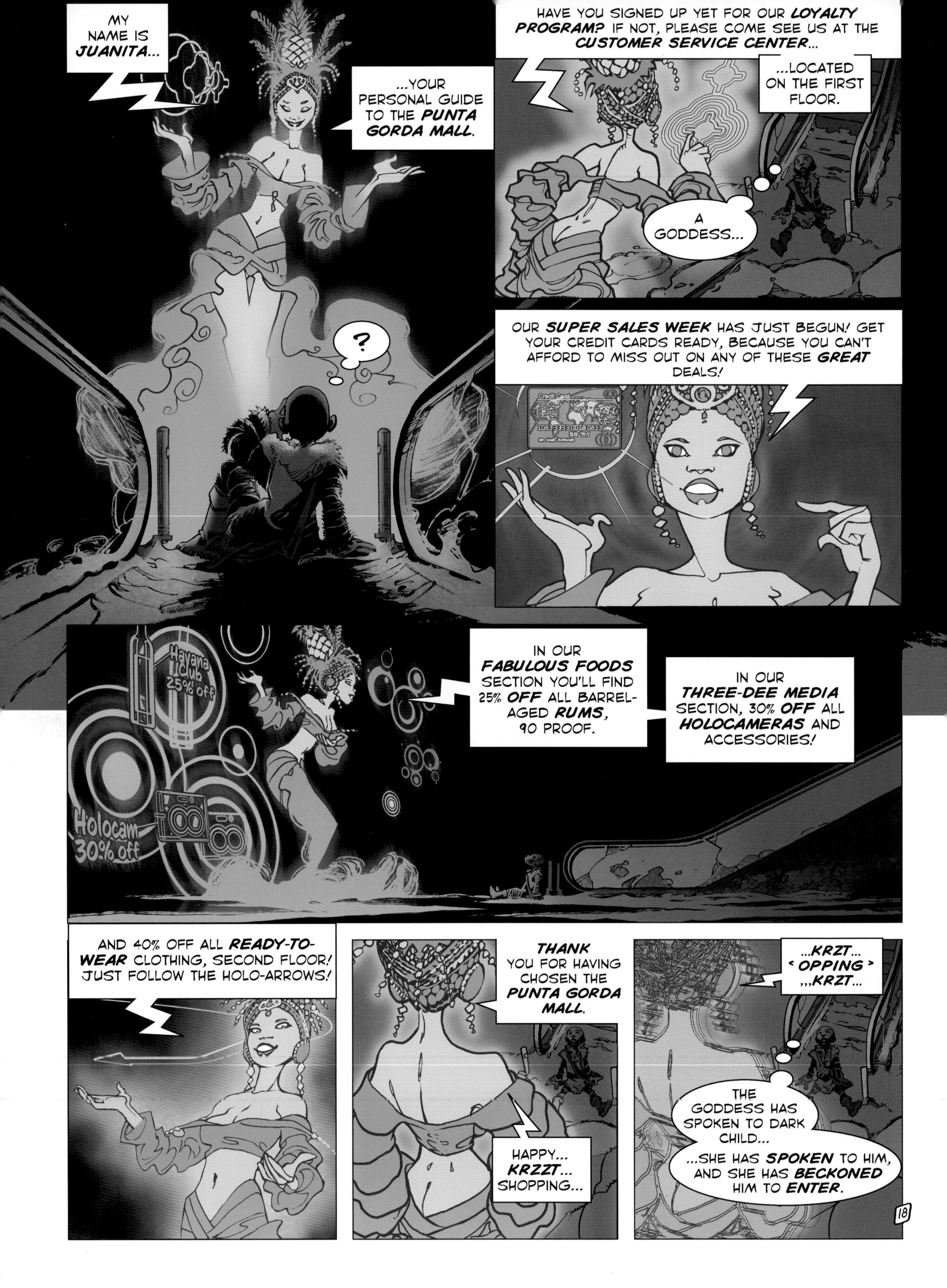

MY NAME IS JUANITA...
...YOUR PERSONAL GUIDE TO THE PUNTA GORDA MALL.
?
HAVE YOU SIGNED UP YET FOR OUR LOYALTY PROGRAM? IF NOT, PLEASE COME SEE US AT THE CUSTOMER SERVICE CENTER...
...LOCATED ON THE FIRST FLOOR.
A GODDESS...
OUR SUPER SALES WEEK HAS JUST BEGUN! GET YOUR CREDIT CARDS READY, BECAUSE YOU CAN'T AFFORD TO MISS OUT ON ANY OF THESE GREAT DEALS!
Credit Card
Havana Club 25% off
Holocam 30% off
IN OUR FABULOUS FOODS SECTION YOU'LL FIND 25% OFF ALL BARREL-AGED RUMS, 90 PROOF.
IN OUR THREE-DEE MEDIA SECTION, 30% OFF ALL HOLOCAMERAS AND ACCESSORIES!
AND 40% OFF ALL READY-TO-WEAR CLOTHING, SECOND FLOOR! JUST FOLLOW THE HOLO-ARROWS!
THANK YOU FOR HAVING CHOSEN THE PUNTA GORDA MALL.
HAPPY... KRZZT... SHOPPING...
...KRZT... ‹OPPING› ,,,KRZT...
THE GODDESS HAS SPOKEN TO DARK CHILD...
...SHE HAS SPOKEN TO HIM, AND SHE HAS BECKONED HIM TO ENTER.

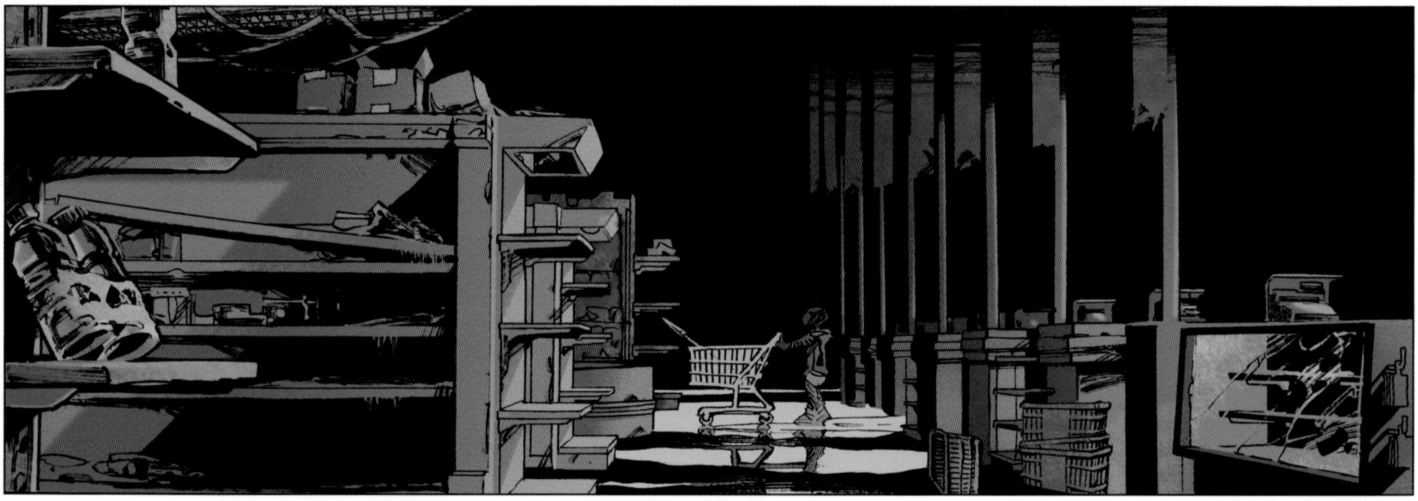

MY HEART WAS FLOODED WITH NEWFOUND JOY! THE ***GODDESS*** HAD WELCOMED ***ME*** INTO THIS SANCTUARY OF GODS.

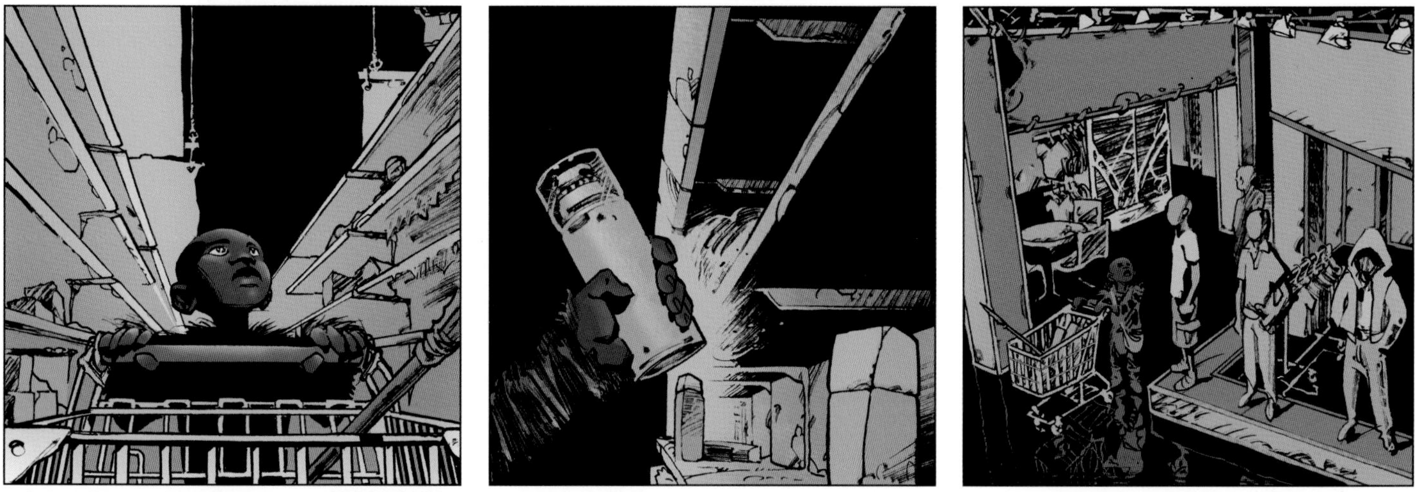

I MUST HAVE SPENT AN ***ETERNITY*** WANDERING THROUGH THE AISLES...

...UNAWARE THAT I WAS FOLLOWING IN THE FOOTSTEPS...

...OF CUSTOMERS WHO'D BEEN ***LOST*** FOR CENTURIES.

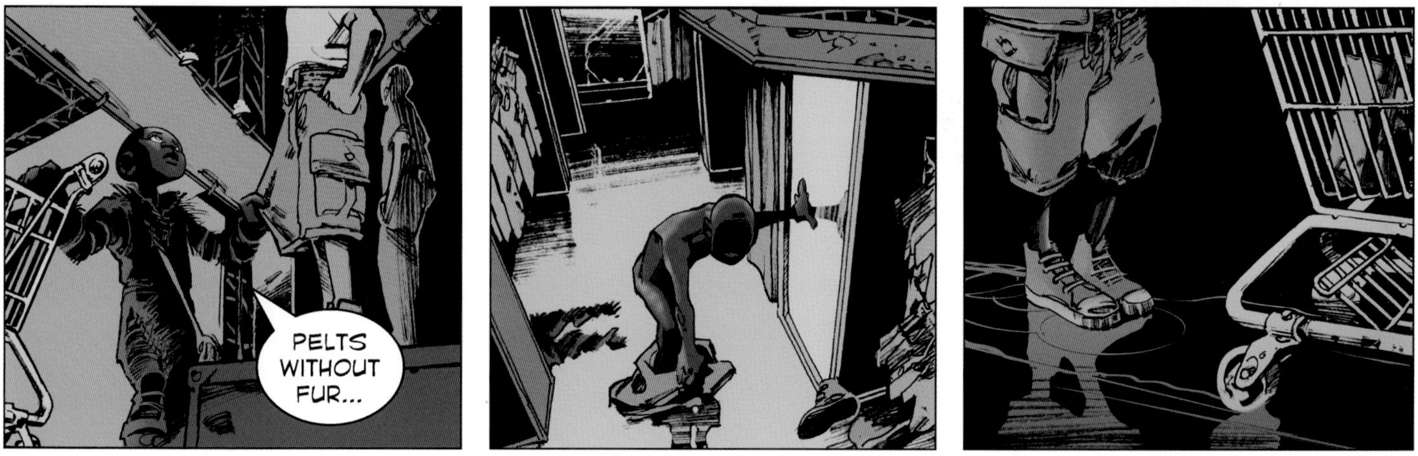
PELTS WITHOUT FUR...

...I STACKED THE CART HIGH WITH UNFATHOMABLE OBJECTS, KNOWING FULL WELL THAT I COULD NEVER GET BACK TO THE PLAINS WITH THIS LITTER OF ***STUFF***.

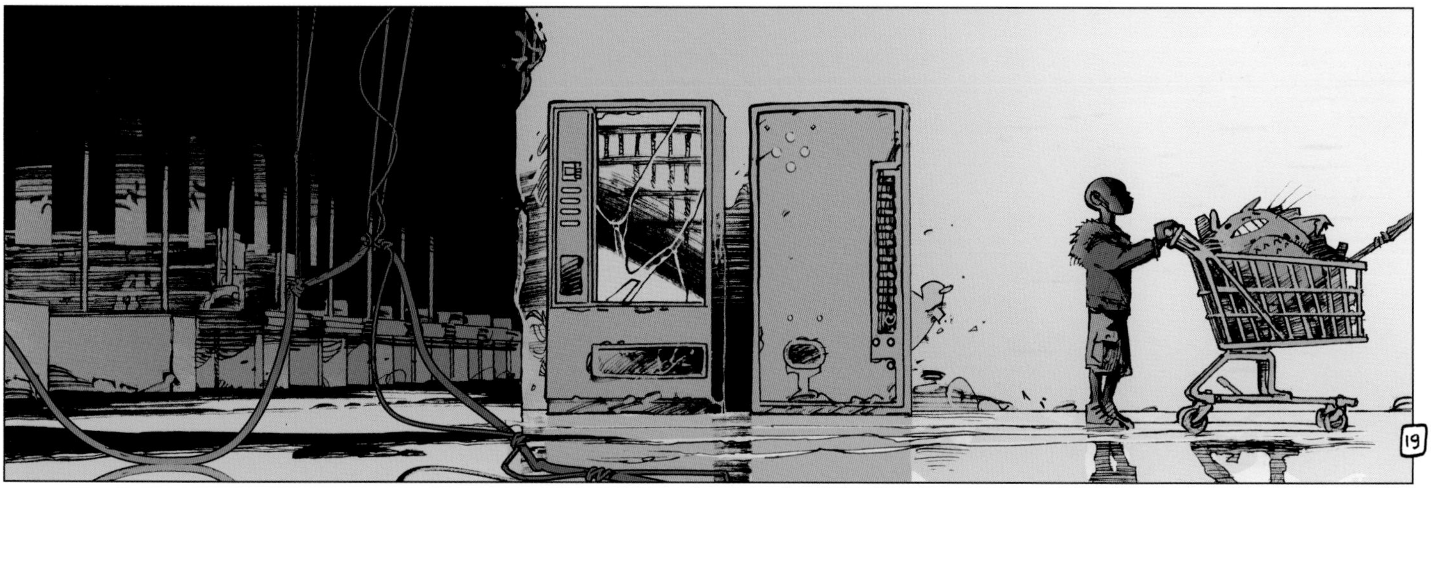

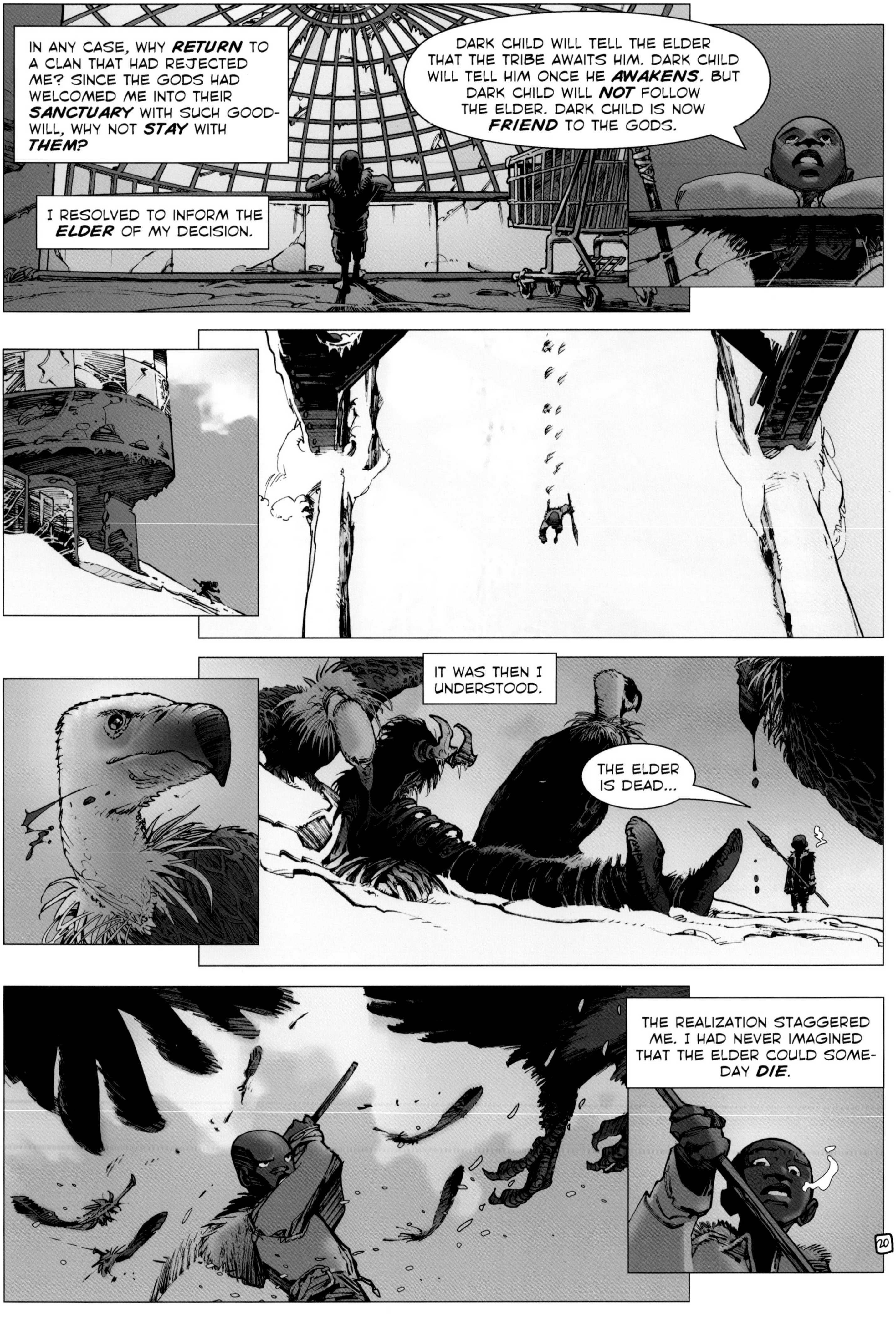

IN ANY CASE, WHY RETURN TO A CLAN THAT HAD REJECTED ME? SINCE THE GODS HAD WELCOMED ME INTO THEIR SANCTUARY WITH SUCH GOOD-WILL, WHY NOT STAY WITH THEM?
I RESOLVED TO INFORM THE ELDER OF MY DECISION.
DARK CHILD WILL TELL THE ELDER THAT THE TRIBE AWAITS HIM. DARK CHILD WILL TELL HIM ONCE HE AWAKENS. BUT DARK CHILD WILL NOT FOLLOW THE ELDER. DARK CHILD IS NOW FRIEND TO THE GODS.
IT WAS THEN I UNDERSTOOD.
THE ELDER IS DEAD...
THE REALIZATION STAGGERED ME. I HAD NEVER IMAGINED THAT THE ELDER COULD SOME-DAY DIE.

BECAUSE *I* HAD DISCOVERED THE ELDER'S DEATH...

...IT WAS UP TO ME TO CARRY OUT THE SAME *RITES* I'D SEEN PER-FORMED BY THE *TRIBE*: NO HUNTER COULD THEN CLAIM TO HAVE FOUND THE ELDER FIRST.

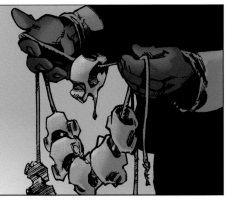

I SPLIT HIS SKULL AND ATE HIS BRAINS RAW, THUS SECURING FOR MYSELF ALL THE ELDER'S *WISDOM* AND *STRENGTH*.

THEN I DUG A *BACKBONE* OUT OF THE ELDER'S CORPSE AND ADDED IT TO HIS NECKLET: THE GREATEST SYMBOL OF HIS *AUTHORITY*.

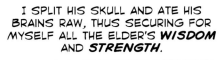

I COULD NOW JUSTIFY MY RETURN TO THE VILLAGE.

DARK CHILD *IS* THE ELDER. THE ELDER *IS* DARK CHILD. THE ELDER IS NO LONGER *DEAD*. HE *LIVES* IN THE BODY OF THE *DARK CHILD*.

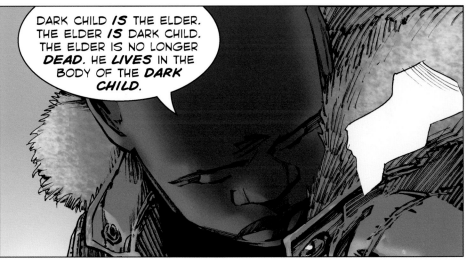

I HAD *BECOME* THE ELDER, AND THE ELDER HAD BECOME *ME*, WHETHER THE HUNTERS APPROVED OR NOT.

BEFORE LEAVING THE HARBOR, I DETOURED TO INSPECT A TOWER THAT HAD INTRIGUED ME WHEN I'D FIRST ARRIVED.

21

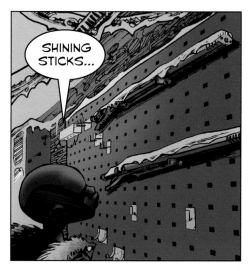

SHINING STICKS...

...THE SHINE OF **METAL**...THE EXOTIC FEEL OF IT **PLEASED** ME.

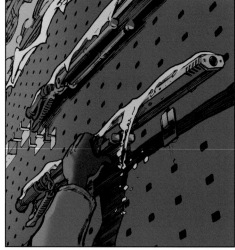

THE **SHINING STICK** IS STRONG! IT WILL SERVE DARK CHILD AS A **MIGHTY CLUB!**

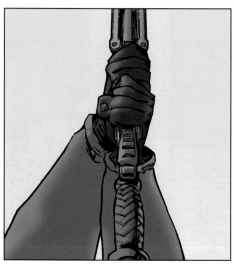

I TOOK THE OBJECT, WITHOUT UNDERSTANDING ITS USE, AND BEGAN MY DESCENT TOWARDS THE TRIBE...

...NO LONGER IN NEED OF THE **GODS' PROTECTION** TO FACE MY FELLOWS.

22

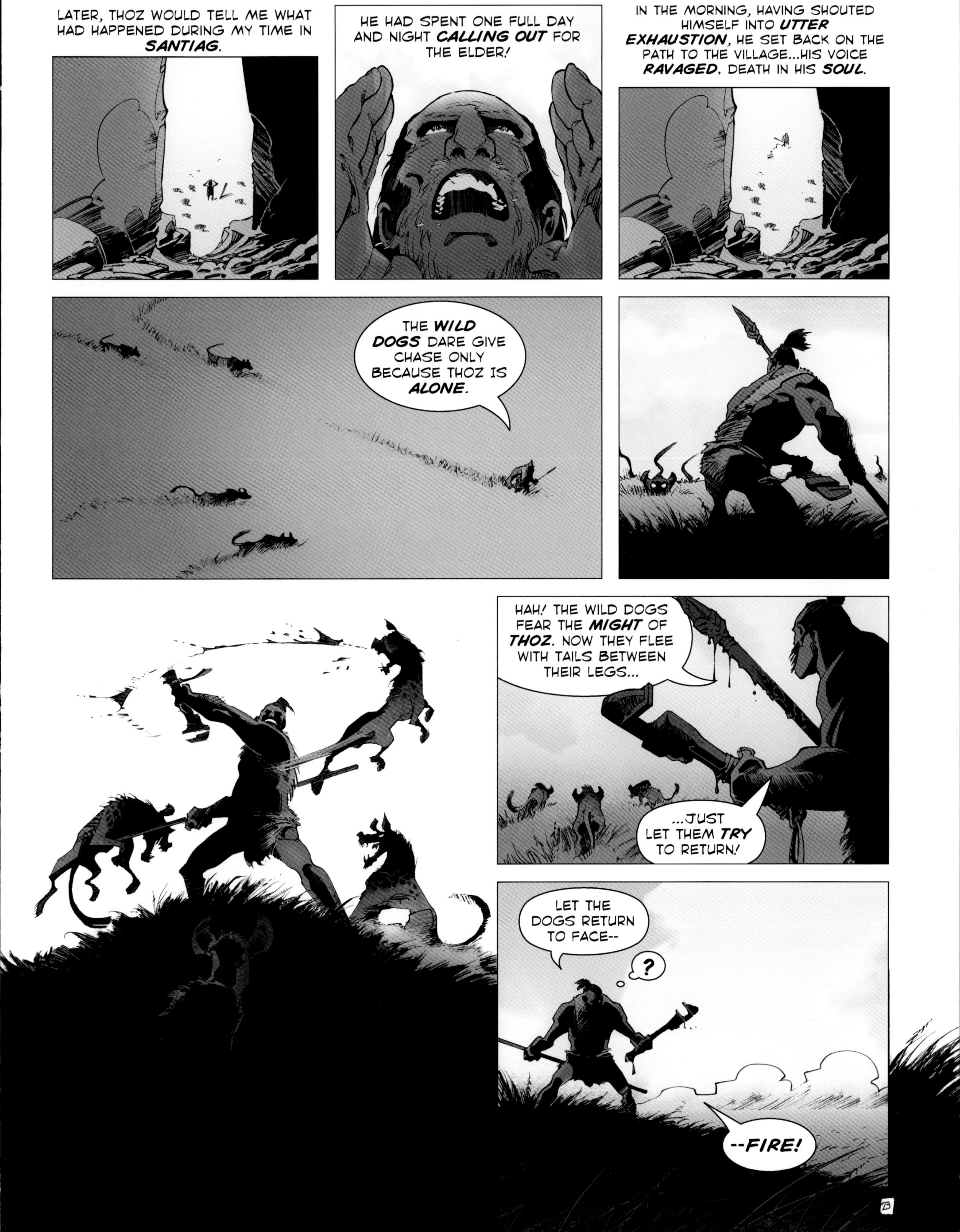
LATER, THOZ WOULD TELL ME WHAT HAD HAPPENED DURING MY TIME IN SANTIAG.
HE HAD SPENT ONE FULL DAY AND NIGHT CALLING OUT FOR THE ELDER!
IN THE MORNING, HAVING SHOUTED HIMSELF INTO UTTER EXHAUSTION, HE SET BACK ON THE PATH TO THE VILLAGE...HIS VOICE RAVAGED, DEATH IN HIS SOUL.
THE WILD DOGS DARE GIVE CHASE ONLY BECAUSE THOZ IS ALONE.
HAH! THE WILD DOGS FEAR THE MIGHT OF THOZ. NOW THEY FLEE WITH TAILS BETWEEN THEIR LEGS...
...JUST LET THEM TRY TO RETURN!
LET THE DOGS RETURN TO FACE--
?
--FIRE!

CHAPTER 3:
Fire of the Gods

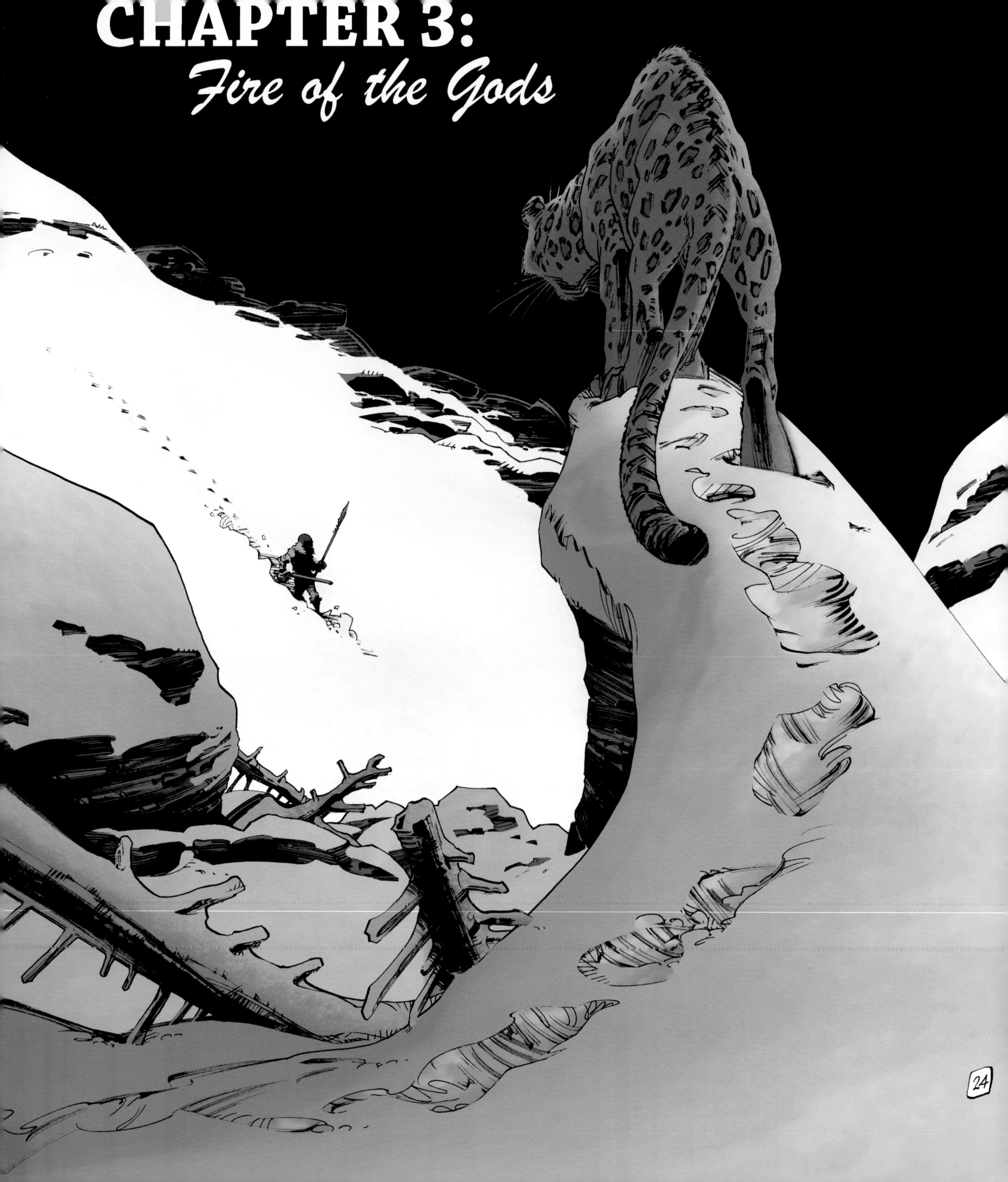

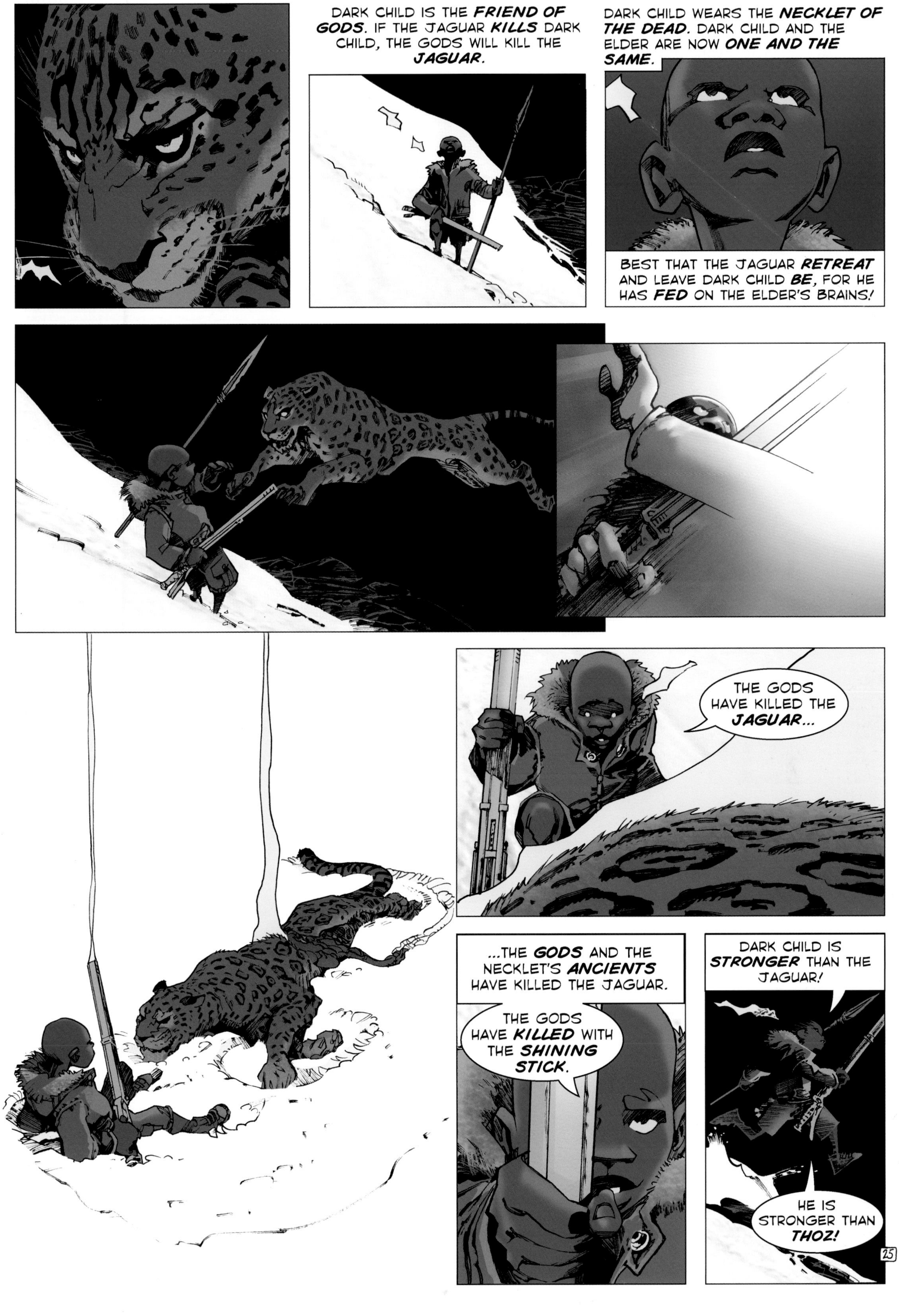
DARK CHILD IS THE FRIEND OF GODS. IF THE JAGUAR KILLS DARK CHILD, THE GODS WILL KILL THE JAGUAR.
DARK CHILD WEARS THE NECKLET OF THE DEAD. DARK CHILD AND THE ELDER ARE NOW ONE AND THE SAME.
BEST THAT THE JAGUAR RETREAT AND LEAVE DARK CHILD BE, FOR HE HAS FED ON THE ELDER'S BRAINS!
THE GODS HAVE KILLED THE JAGUAR...
...THE GODS AND THE NECKLET'S ANCIENTS HAVE KILLED THE JAGUAR.
THE GODS HAVE KILLED WITH THE SHINING STICK.
DARK CHILD IS STRONGER THAN THE JAGUAR!
HE IS STRONGER THAN THOZ!

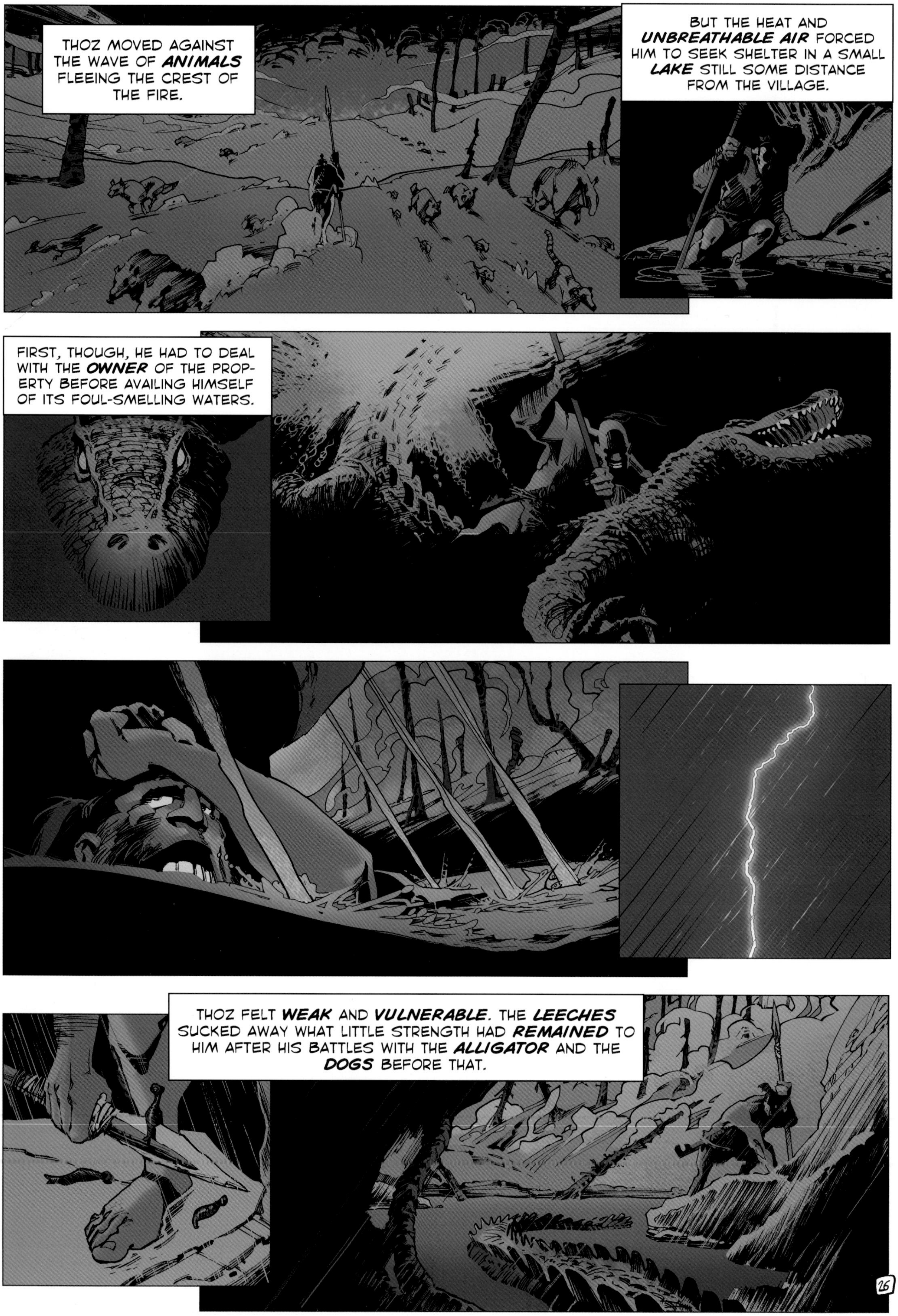
THOZ MOVED AGAINST THE WAVE OF ANIMALS FLEEING THE CREST OF THE FIRE.
BUT THE HEAT AND UNBREATHABLE AIR FORCED HIM TO SEEK SHELTER IN A SMALL LAKE STILL SOME DISTANCE FROM THE VILLAGE.
FIRST, THOUGH, HE HAD TO DEAL WITH THE OWNER OF THE PROPERTY BEFORE AVAILING HIMSELF OF ITS FOUL-SMELLING WATERS.
THOZ FELT WEAK AND VULNERABLE. THE LEECHES SUCKED AWAY WHAT LITTLE STRENGTH HAD REMAINED TO HIM AFTER HIS BATTLES WITH THE ALLIGATOR AND THE DOGS BEFORE THAT.

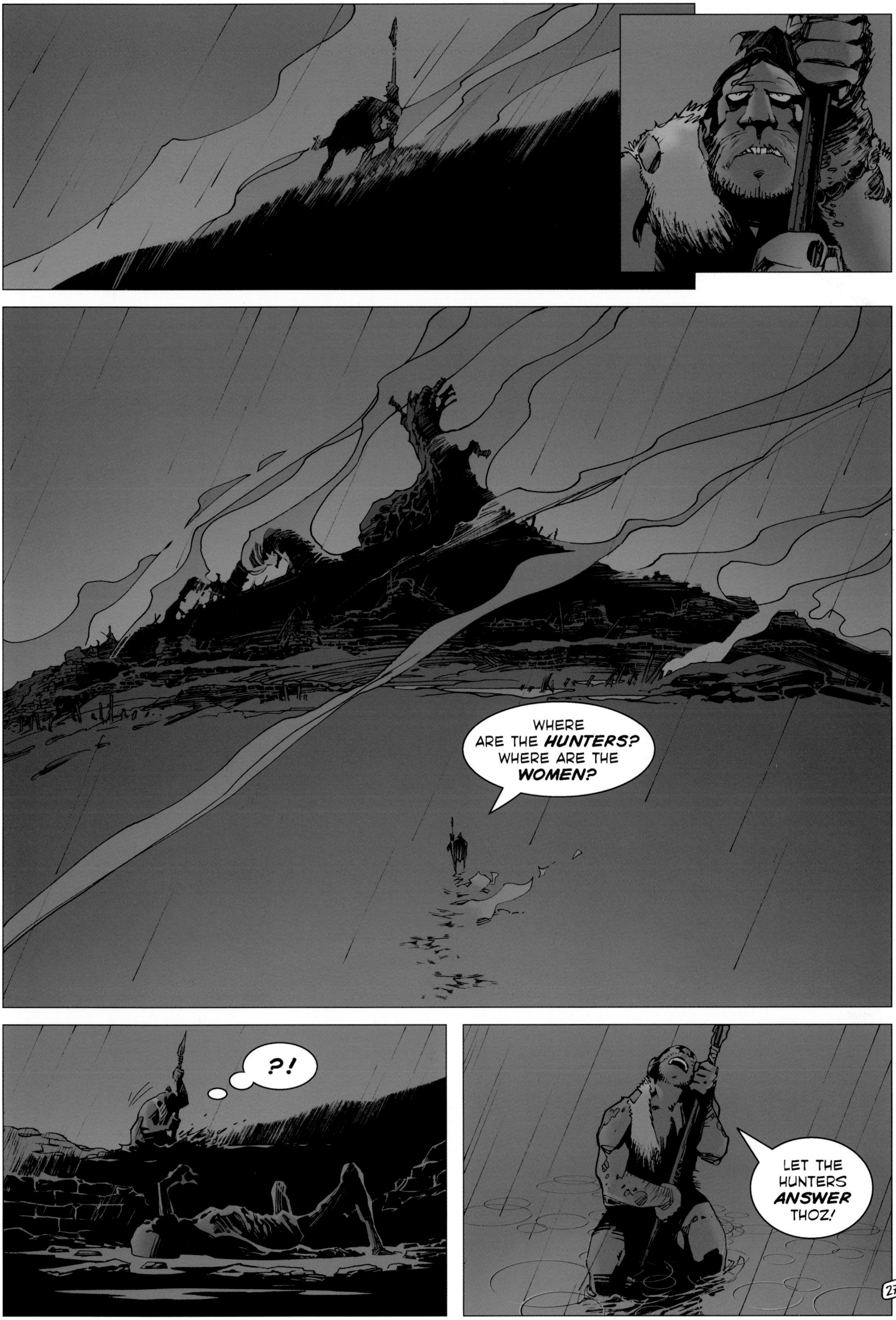

WHERE ARE THE HUNTERS? WHERE ARE THE WOMEN?
?!
LET THE HUNTERS ANSWER THOZ!

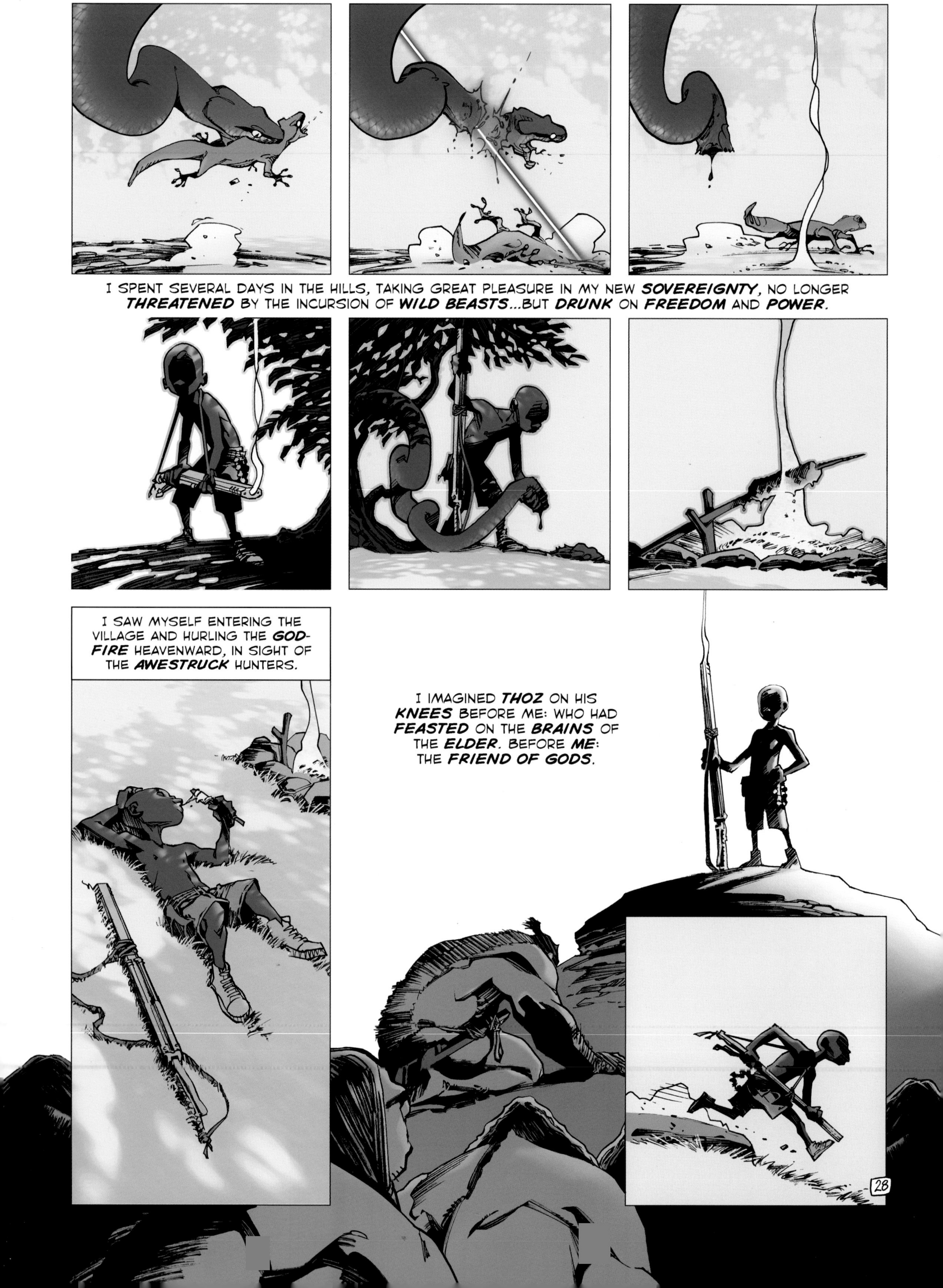

I SPENT SEVERAL DAYS IN THE HILLS, TAKING GREAT PLEASURE IN MY NEW SOVEREIGNTY, NO LONGER THREATENED BY THE INCURSION OF WILD BEASTS...BUT DRUNK ON FREEDOM AND POWER.
I SAW MYSELF ENTERING THE VILLAGE AND HURLING THE GOD-FIRE HEAVENWARD, IN SIGHT OF THE AWESTRUCK HUNTERS.
I IMAGINED THOZ ON HIS KNEES BEFORE ME: WHO HAD FEASTED ON THE BRAINS OF THE ELDER. BEFORE ME: THE FRIEND OF GODS.

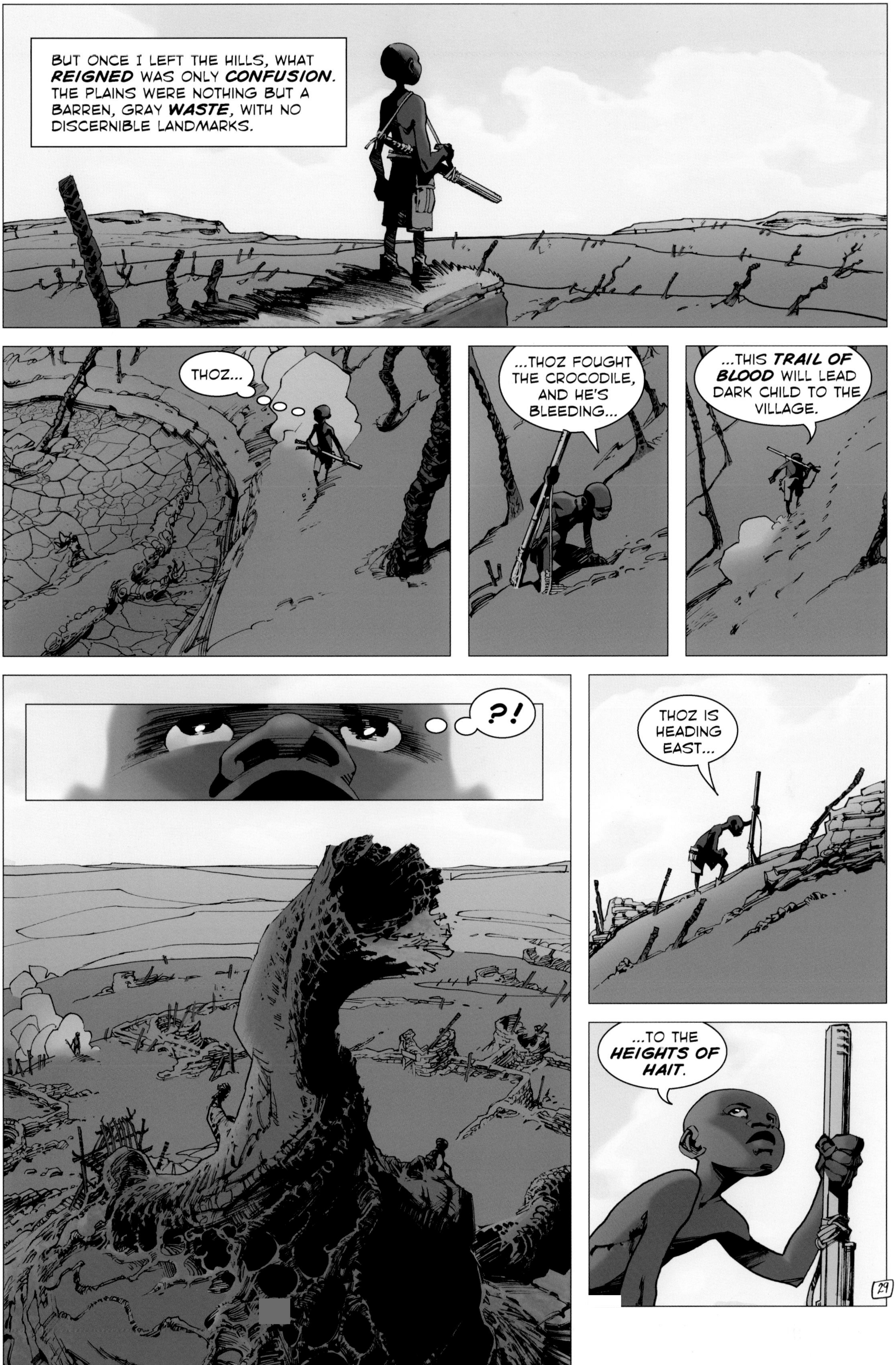
BUT ONCE I LEFT THE HILLS, WHAT **REIGNED** WAS ONLY **CONFUSION**. THE PLAINS WERE NOTHING BUT A BARREN, GRAY **WASTE**, WITH NO DISCERNIBLE LANDMARKS.
THOZ...
...THOZ FOUGHT THE CROCODILE, AND HE'S BLEEDING...
...THIS **TRAIL OF BLOOD** WILL LEAD DARK CHILD TO THE VILLAGE.
?!
THOZ IS HEADING EAST...
...TO THE **HEIGHTS OF HAIT**.

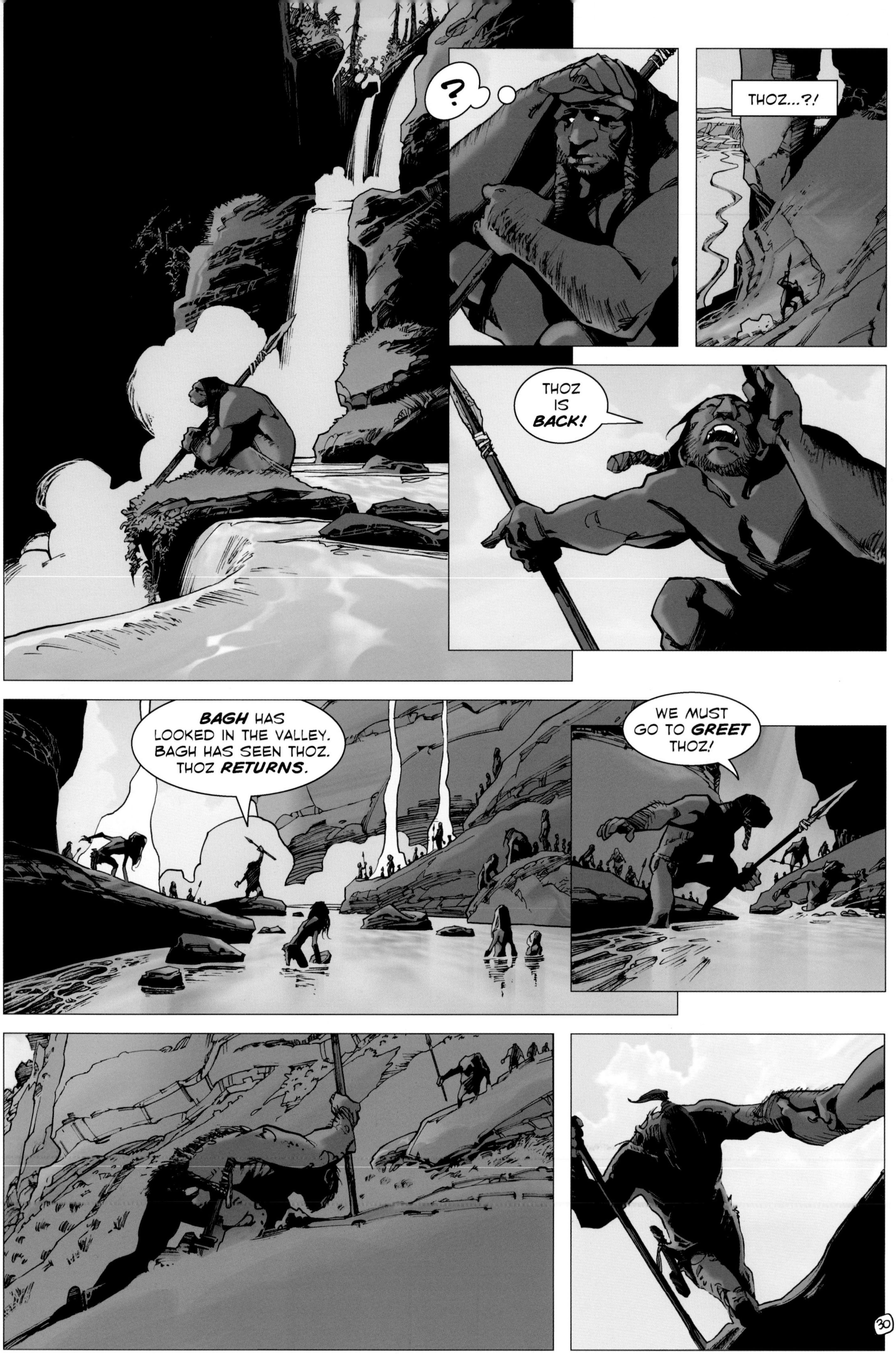
?
THOZ...?!
THOZ IS BACK!
BAGH HAS LOOKED IN THE VALLEY. BAGH HAS SEEN THOZ. THOZ RETURNS.
WE MUST GO TO GREET THOZ!

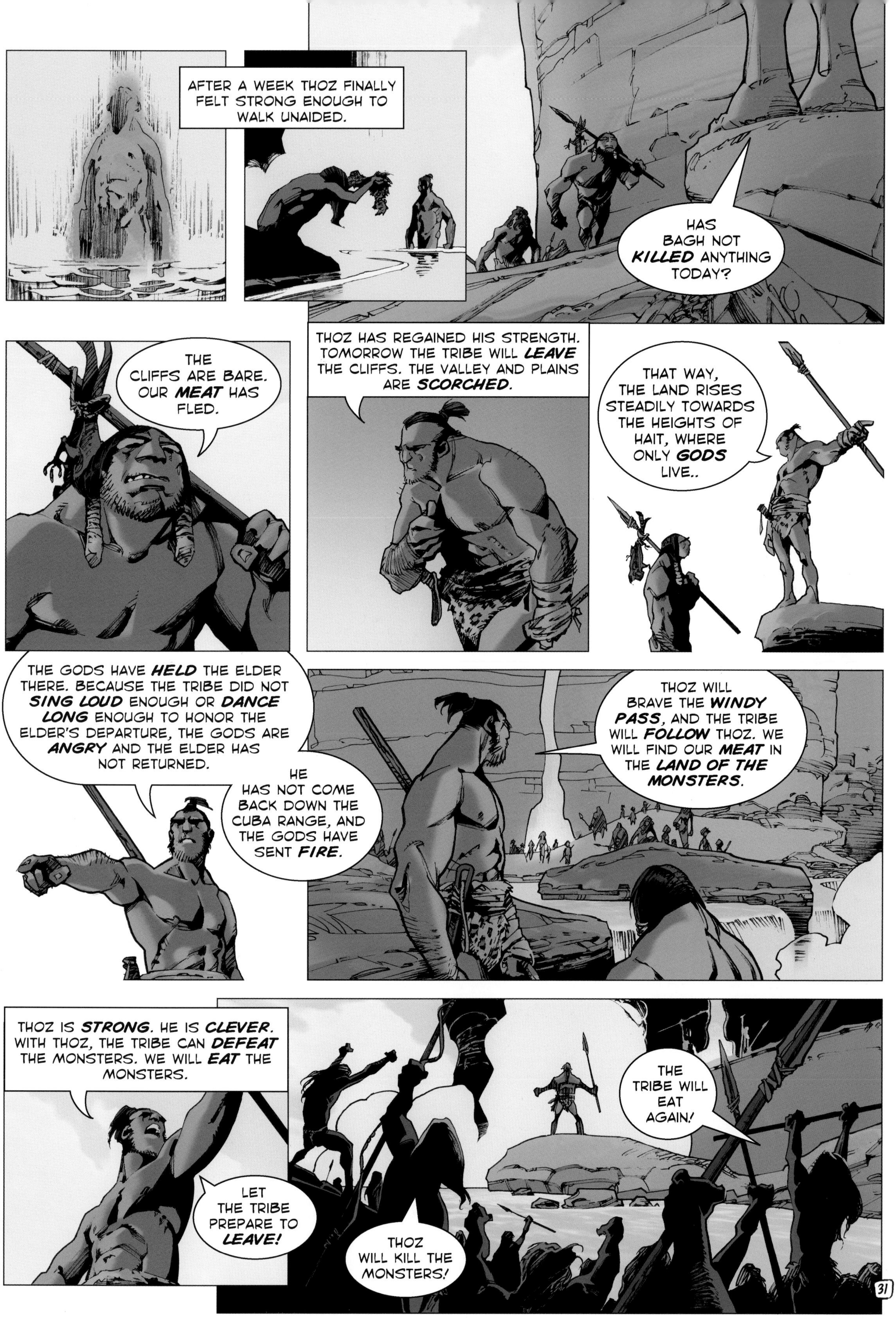
AFTER A WEEK THOZ FINALLY FELT STRONG ENOUGH TO WALK UNAIDED.
HAS BAGH NOT KILLED ANYTHING TODAY?
THE CLIFFS ARE BARE. OUR MEAT HAS FLED.
THOZ HAS REGAINED HIS STRENGTH. TOMORROW THE TRIBE WILL LEAVE THE CLIFFS. THE VALLEY AND PLAINS ARE SCORCHED.
THAT WAY, THE LAND RISES STEADILY TOWARDS THE HEIGHTS OF HAIT, WHERE ONLY GODS LIVE..
THE GODS HAVE HELD THE ELDER THERE. BECAUSE THE TRIBE DID NOT SING LOUD ENOUGH OR DANCE LONG ENOUGH TO HONOR THE ELDER'S DEPARTURE, THE GODS ARE ANGRY AND THE ELDER HAS NOT RETURNED.
HE HAS NOT COME BACK DOWN THE CUBA RANGE, AND THE GODS HAVE SENT FIRE.
THOZ WILL BRAVE THE WINDY PASS, AND THE TRIBE WILL FOLLOW THOZ. WE WILL FIND OUR MEAT IN THE LAND OF THE MONSTERS.
THOZ IS STRONG. HE IS CLEVER. WITH THOZ, THE TRIBE CAN DEFEAT THE MONSTERS. WE WILL EAT THE MONSTERS.
LET THE TRIBE PREPARE TO LEAVE!
THOZ WILL KILL THE MONSTERS!
THE TRIBE WILL EAT AGAIN!

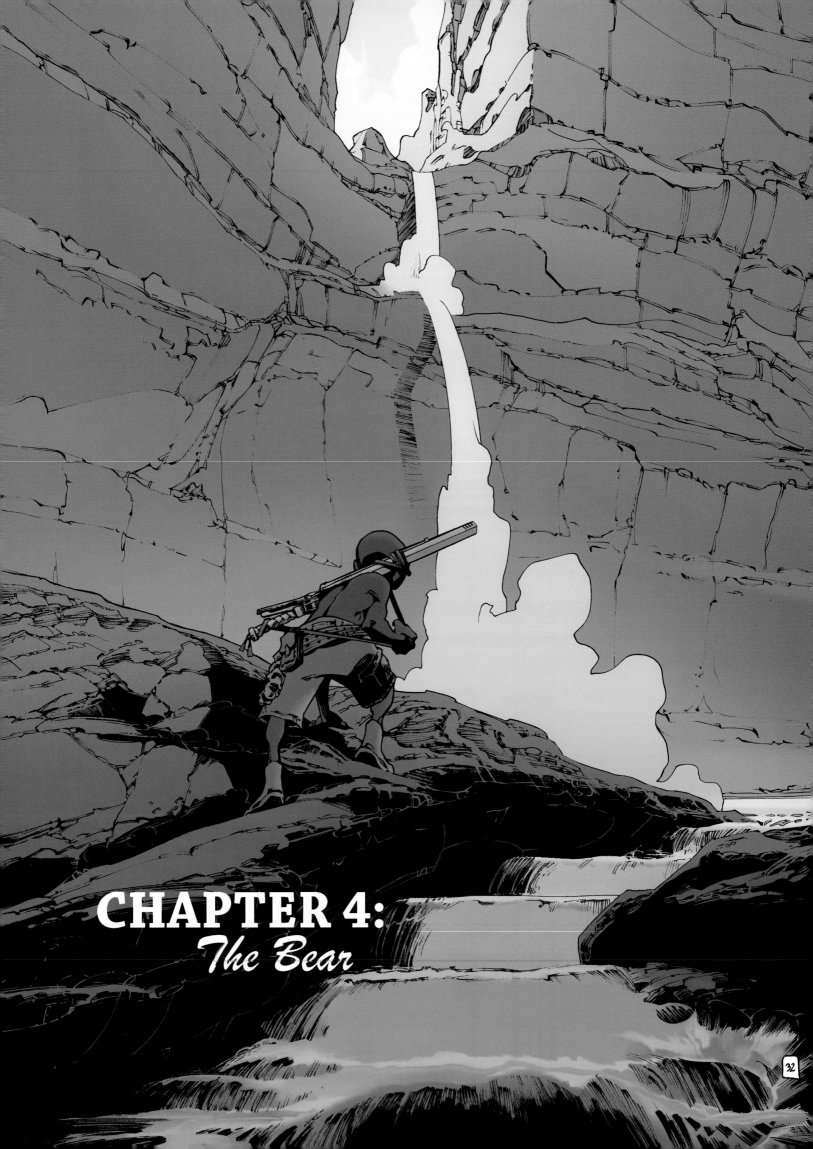

CHAPTER 4:
The Bear

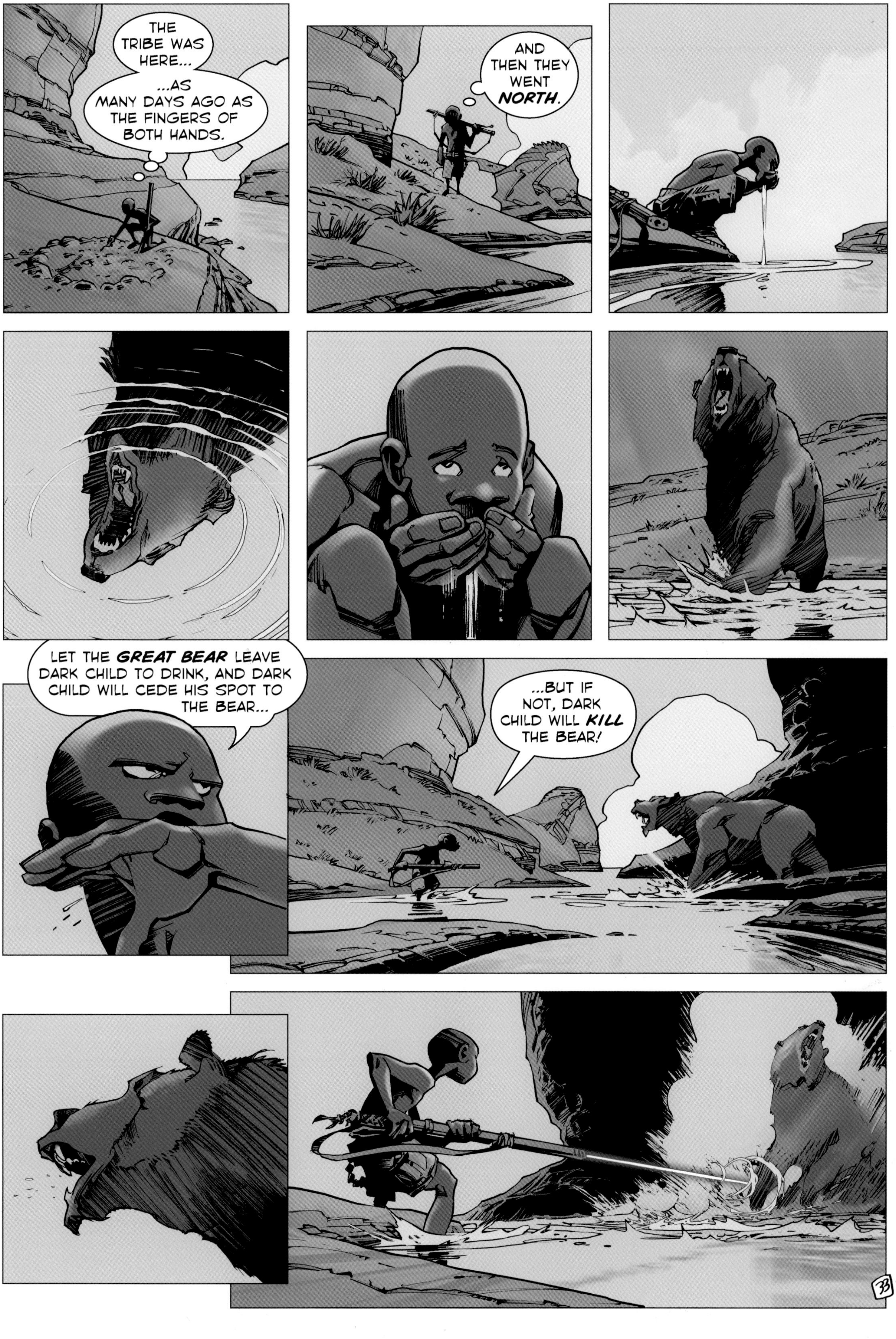

THE TRIBE WAS HERE...
...AS MANY DAYS AGO AS THE FINGERS OF BOTH HANDS.
AND THEN THEY WENT NORTH.
LET THE GREAT BEAR LEAVE DARK CHILD TO DRINK, AND DARK CHILD WILL CEDE HIS SPOT TO THE BEAR...
...BUT IF NOT, DARK CHILD WILL KILL THE BEAR!

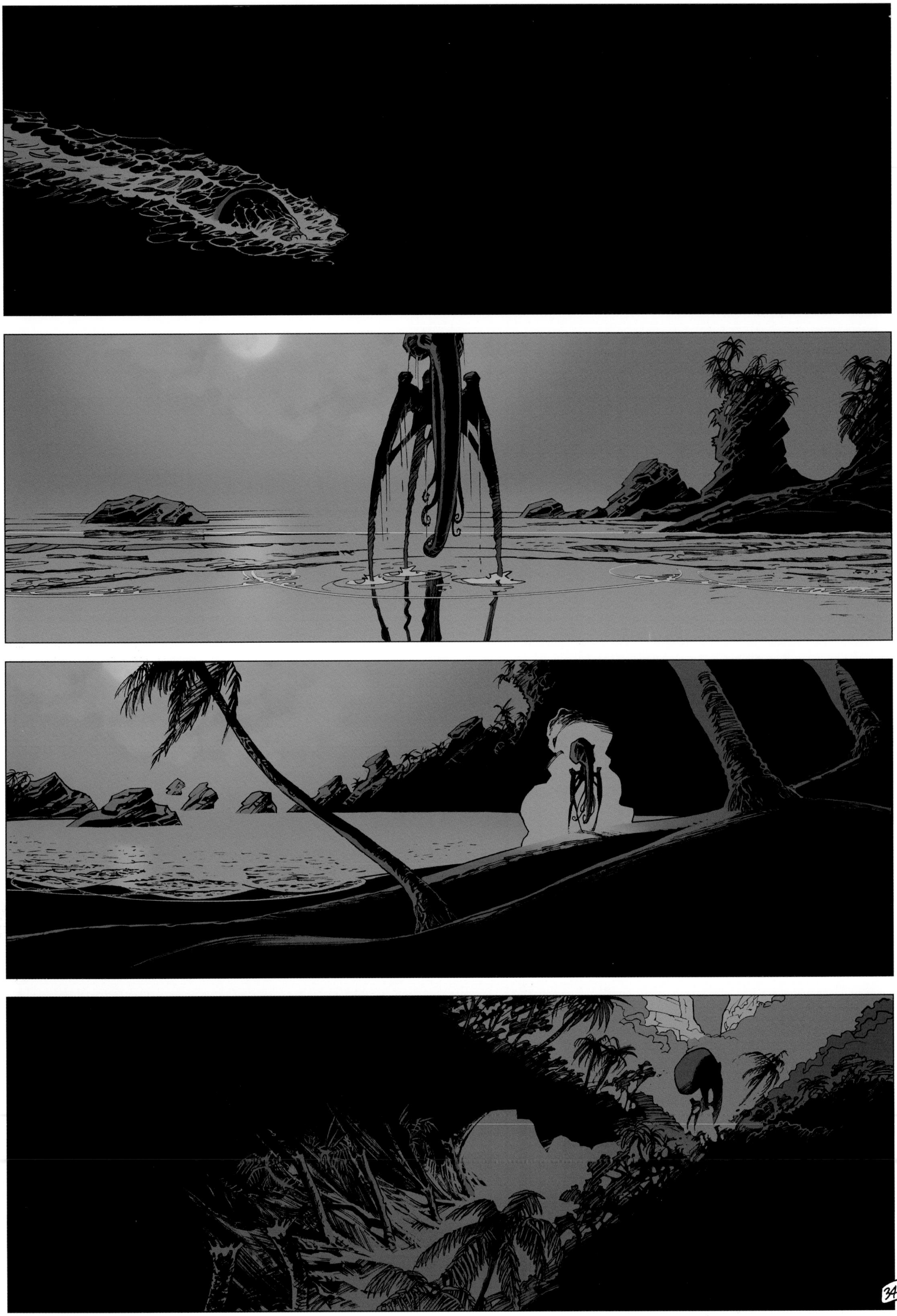

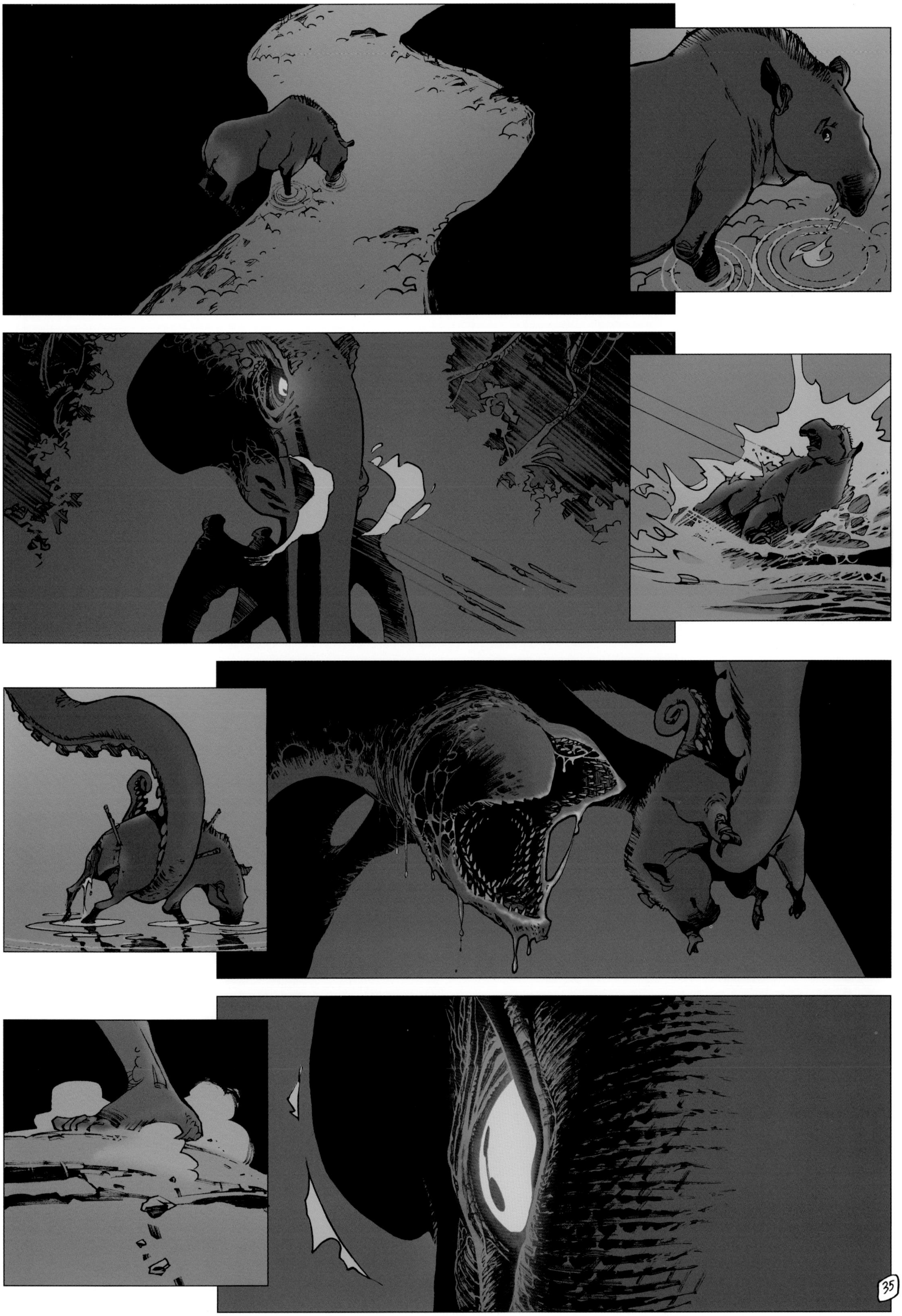

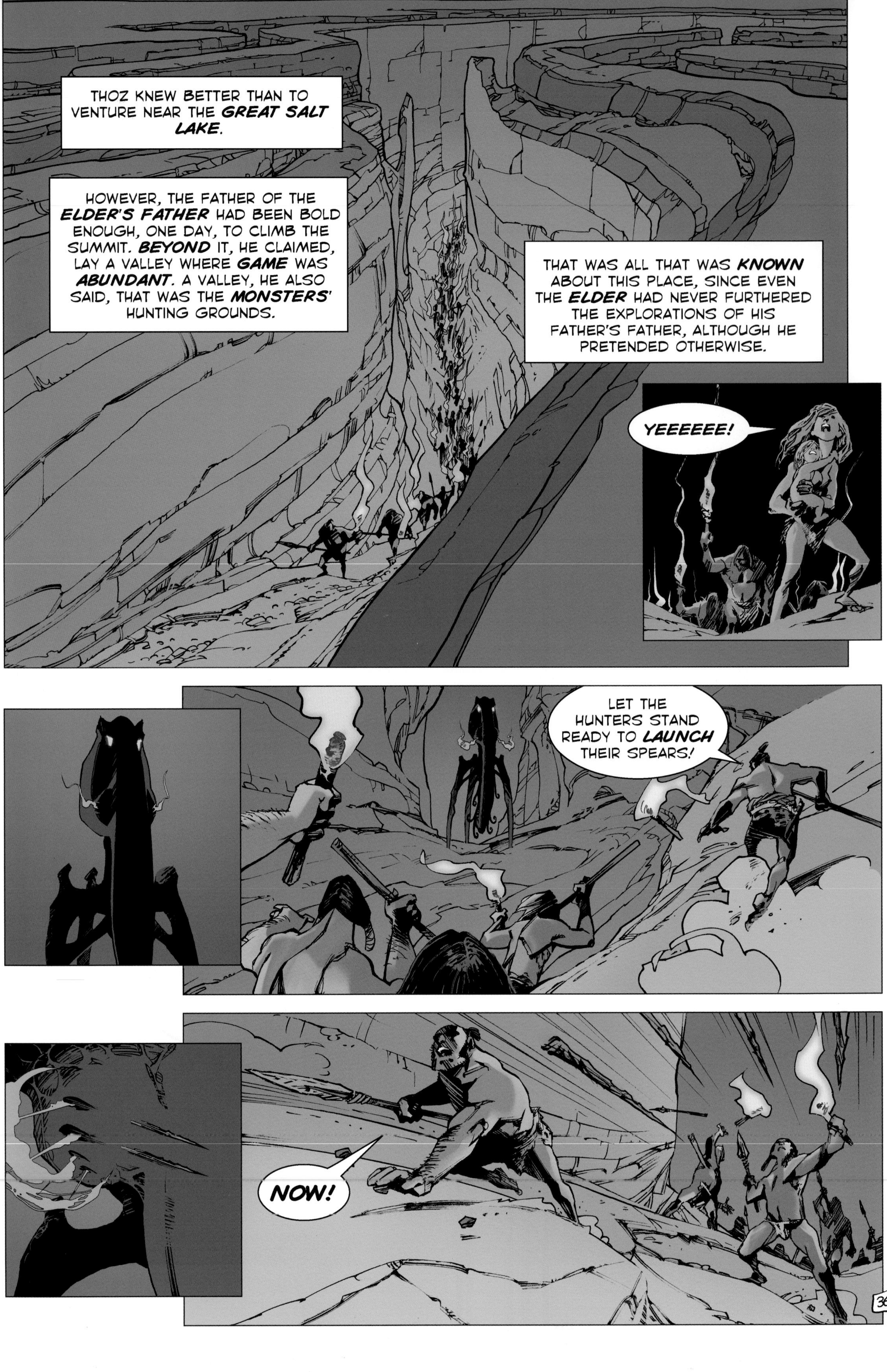
THOZ KNEW BETTER THAN TO VENTURE NEAR THE GREAT SALT LAKE.
HOWEVER, THE FATHER OF THE ELDER'S FATHER HAD BEEN BOLD ENOUGH, ONE DAY, TO CLIMB THE SUMMIT. BEYOND IT, HE CLAIMED, LAY A VALLEY WHERE GAME WAS ABUNDANT. A VALLEY, HE ALSO SAID, THAT WAS THE MONSTERS' HUNTING GROUNDS.
THAT WAS ALL THAT WAS KNOWN ABOUT THIS PLACE, SINCE EVEN THE ELDER HAD NEVER FURTHERED THE EXPLORATIONS OF HIS FATHER'S FATHER, ALTHOUGH HE PRETENDED OTHERWISE.
YEEEEEE!
LET THE HUNTERS STAND READY TO LAUNCH THEIR SPEARS!
NOW!

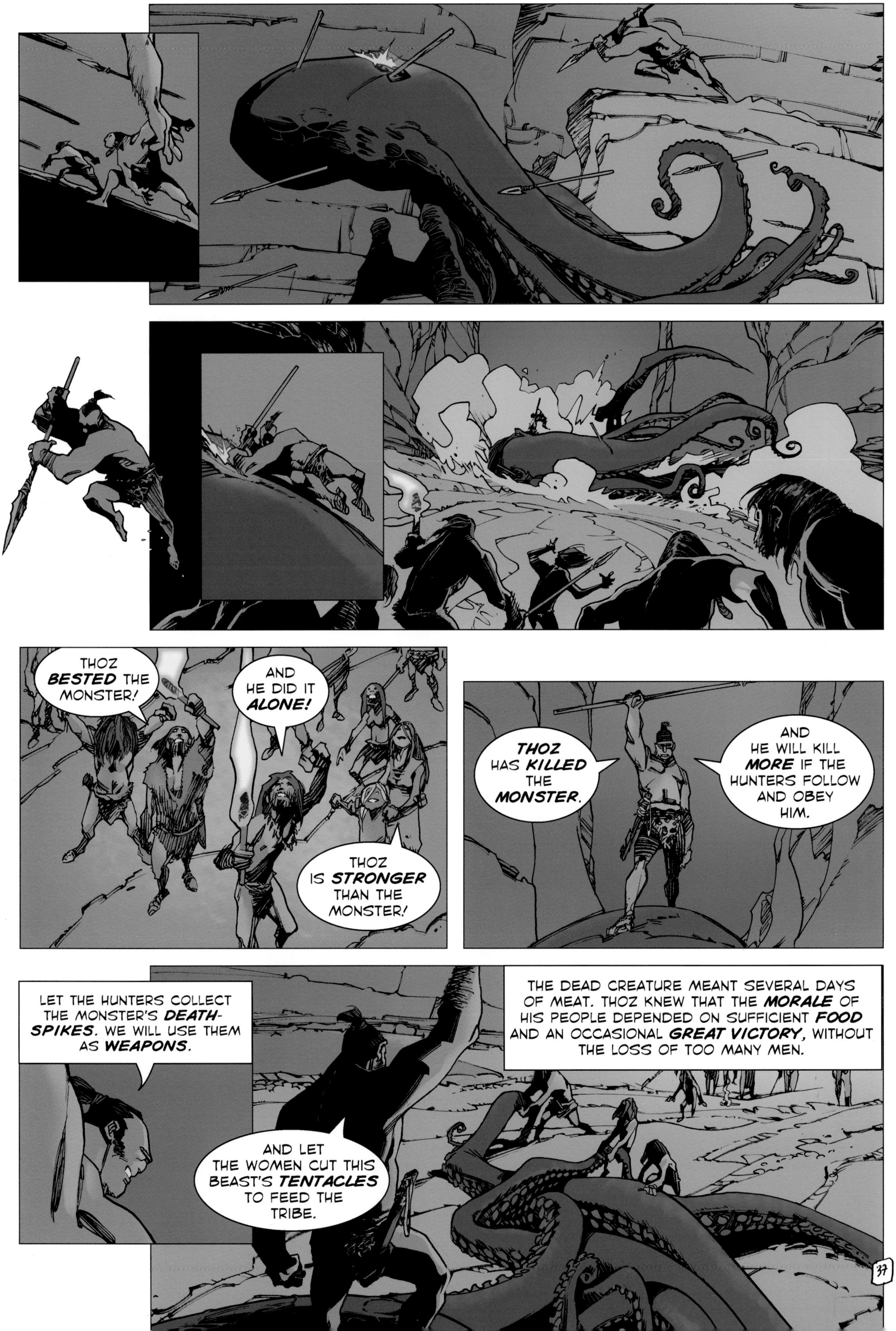

THOZ BESTED THE MONSTER!
AND HE DID IT ALONE!
THOZ IS STRONGER THAN THE MONSTER!
THOZ HAS KILLED THE MONSTER.
AND HE WILL KILL MORE IF THE HUNTERS FOLLOW AND OBEY HIM.
LET THE HUNTERS COLLECT THE MONSTER'S DEATH-SPIKES. WE WILL USE THEM AS WEAPONS.
AND LET THE WOMEN CUT THIS BEAST'S TENTACLES TO FEED THE TRIBE.
THE DEAD CREATURE MEANT SEVERAL DAYS OF MEAT. THOZ KNEW THAT THE MORALE OF HIS PEOPLE DEPENDED ON SUFFICIENT FOOD AND AN OCCASIONAL GREAT VICTORY, WITHOUT THE LOSS OF TOO MANY MEN.

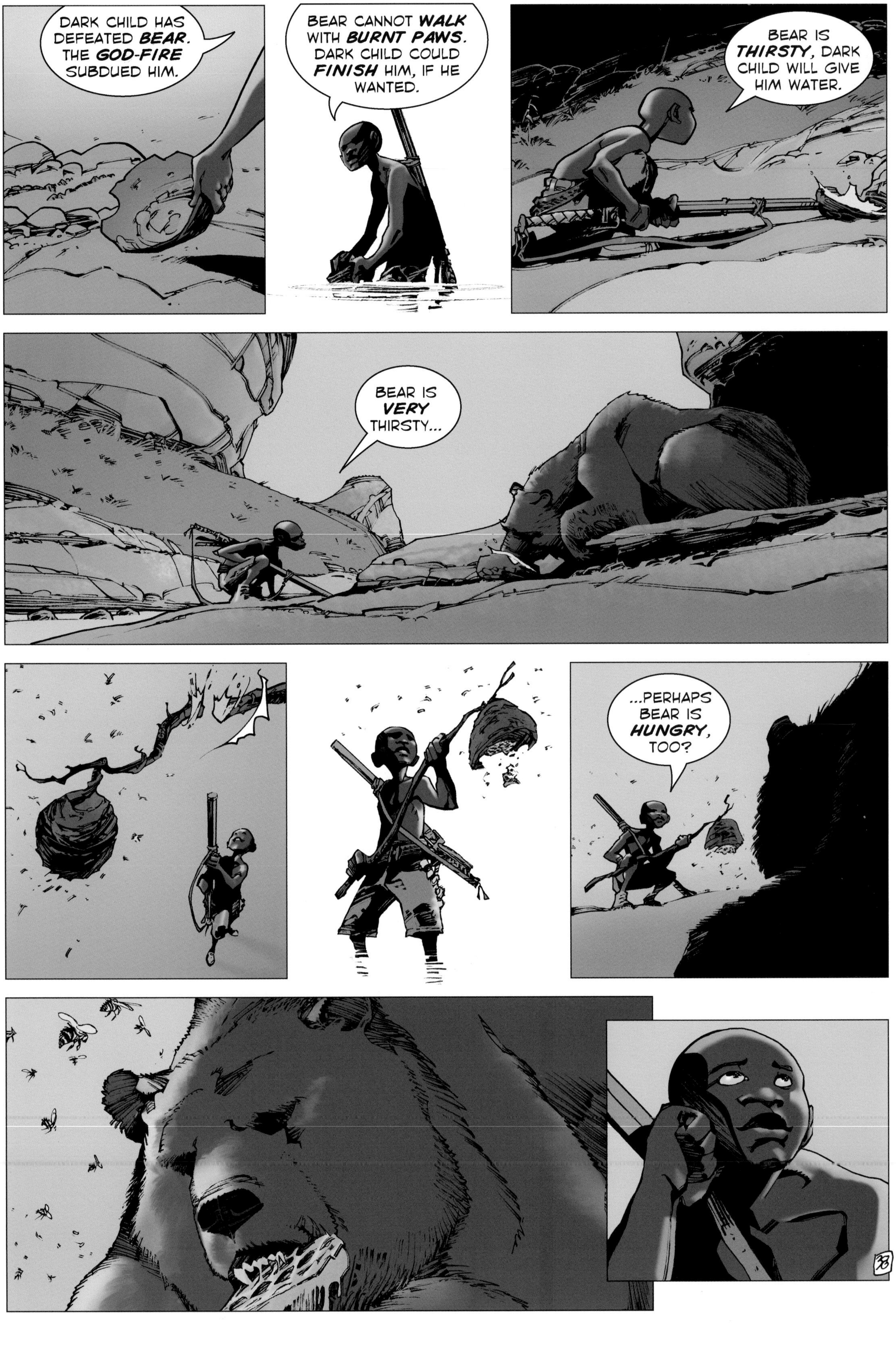
DARK CHILD HAS DEFEATED BEAR. THE GOD-FIRE SUBDUED HIM.
BEAR CANNOT WALK WITH BURNT PAWS. DARK CHILD COULD FINISH HIM, IF HE WANTED.
BEAR IS THIRSTY, DARK CHILD WILL GIVE HIM WATER.
BEAR IS VERY THIRSTY...
...PERHAPS BEAR IS HUNGRY, TOO?
33

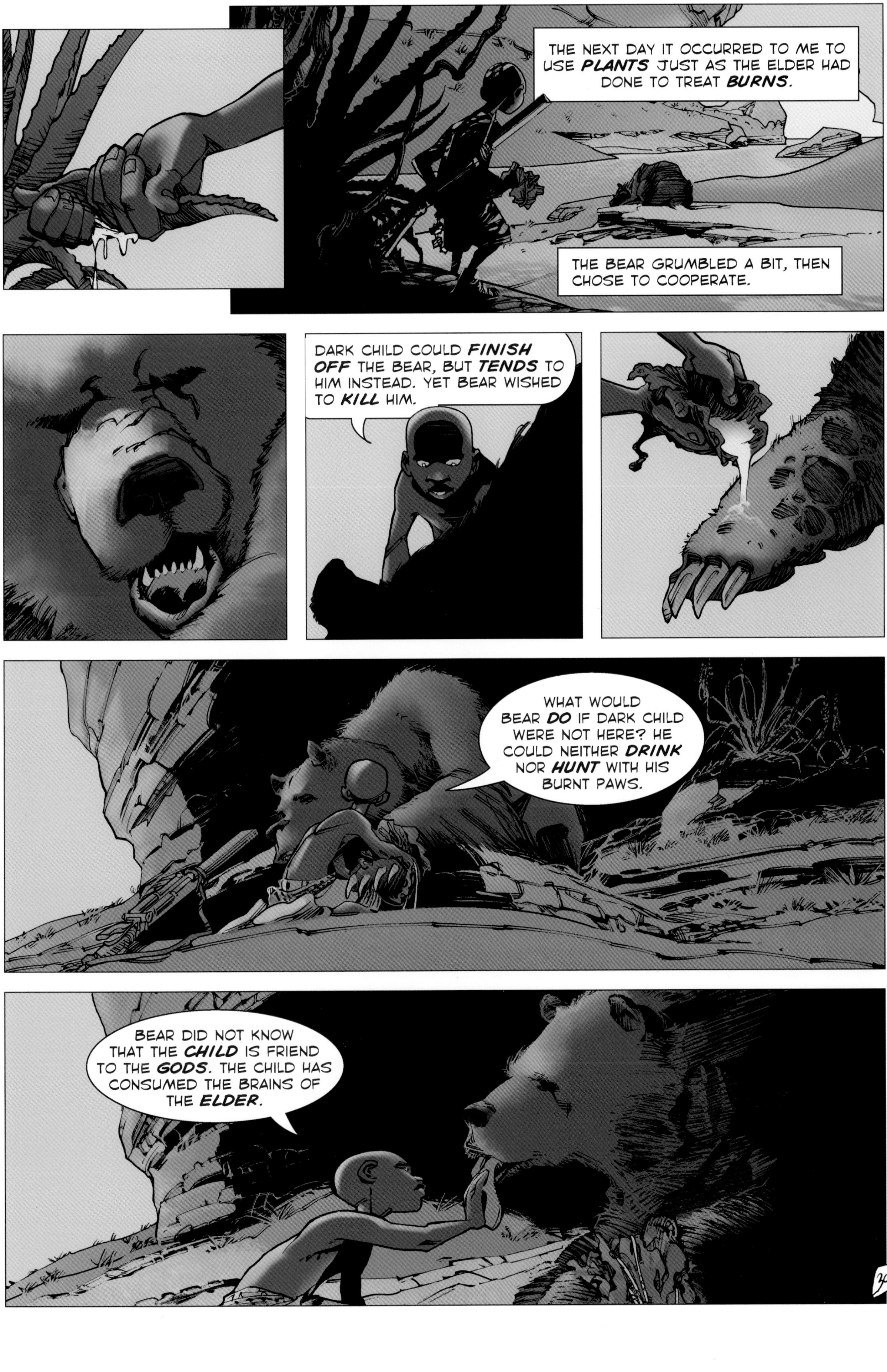
THE NEXT DAY IT OCCURRED TO ME TO USE PLANTS JUST AS THE ELDER HAD DONE TO TREAT BURNS.
THE BEAR GRUMBLED A BIT, THEN CHOSE TO COOPERATE.
DARK CHILD COULD FINISH OFF THE BEAR, BUT TENDS TO HIM INSTEAD. YET BEAR WISHED TO KILL HIM.
WHAT WOULD BEAR DO IF DARK CHILD WERE NOT HERE? HE COULD NEITHER DRINK NOR HUNT WITH HIS BURNT PAWS.
BEAR DID NOT KNOW THAT THE CHILD IS FRIEND TO THE GODS. THE CHILD HAS CONSUMED THE BRAINS OF THE ELDER.
39

CHAPTER 5: *Monsters*

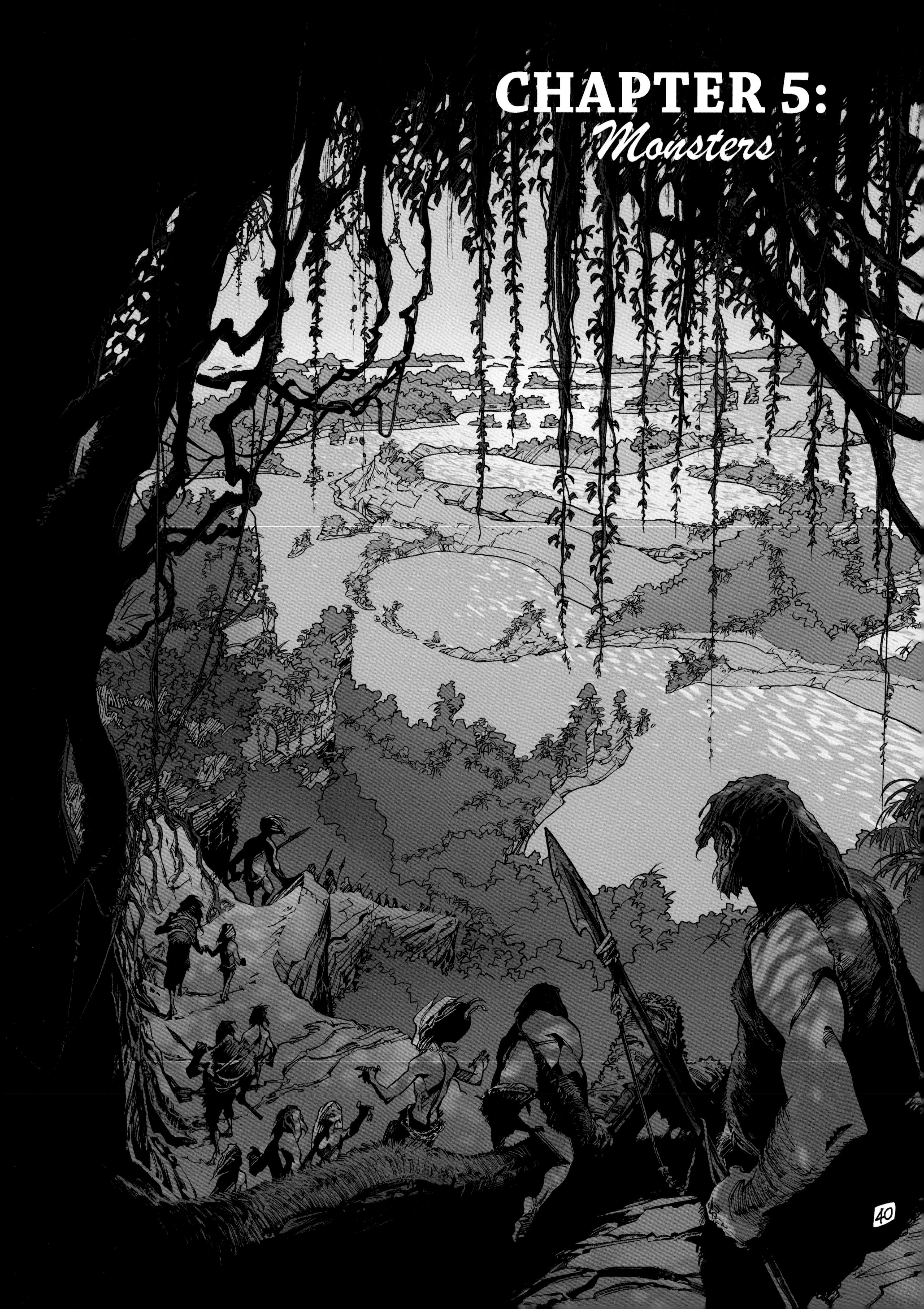

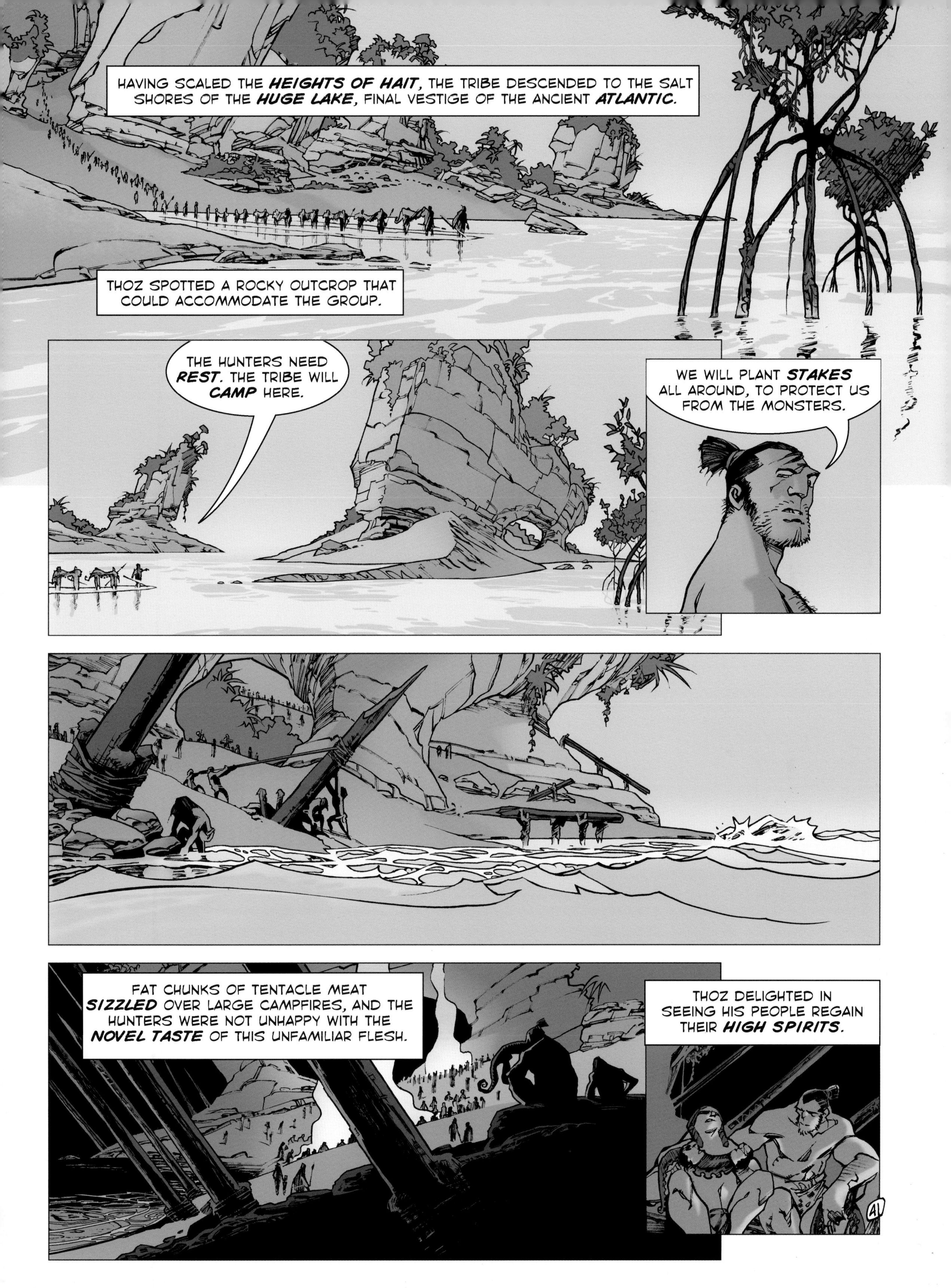
HAVING SCALED THE HEIGHTS OF HAIT, THE TRIBE DESCENDED TO THE SALT SHORES OF THE HUGE LAKE, FINAL VESTIGE OF THE ANCIENT ATLANTIC.
THOZ SPOTTED A ROCKY OUTCROP THAT COULD ACCOMMODATE THE GROUP.
THE HUNTERS NEED REST. THE TRIBE WILL CAMP HERE.
WE WILL PLANT STAKES ALL AROUND, TO PROTECT US FROM THE MONSTERS.
FAT CHUNKS OF TENTACLE MEAT SIZZLED OVER LARGE CAMPFIRES, AND THE HUNTERS WERE NOT UNHAPPY WITH THE NOVEL TASTE OF THIS UNFAMILIAR FLESH.
THOZ DELIGHTED IN SEEING HIS PEOPLE REGAIN THEIR HIGH SPIRITS.
41

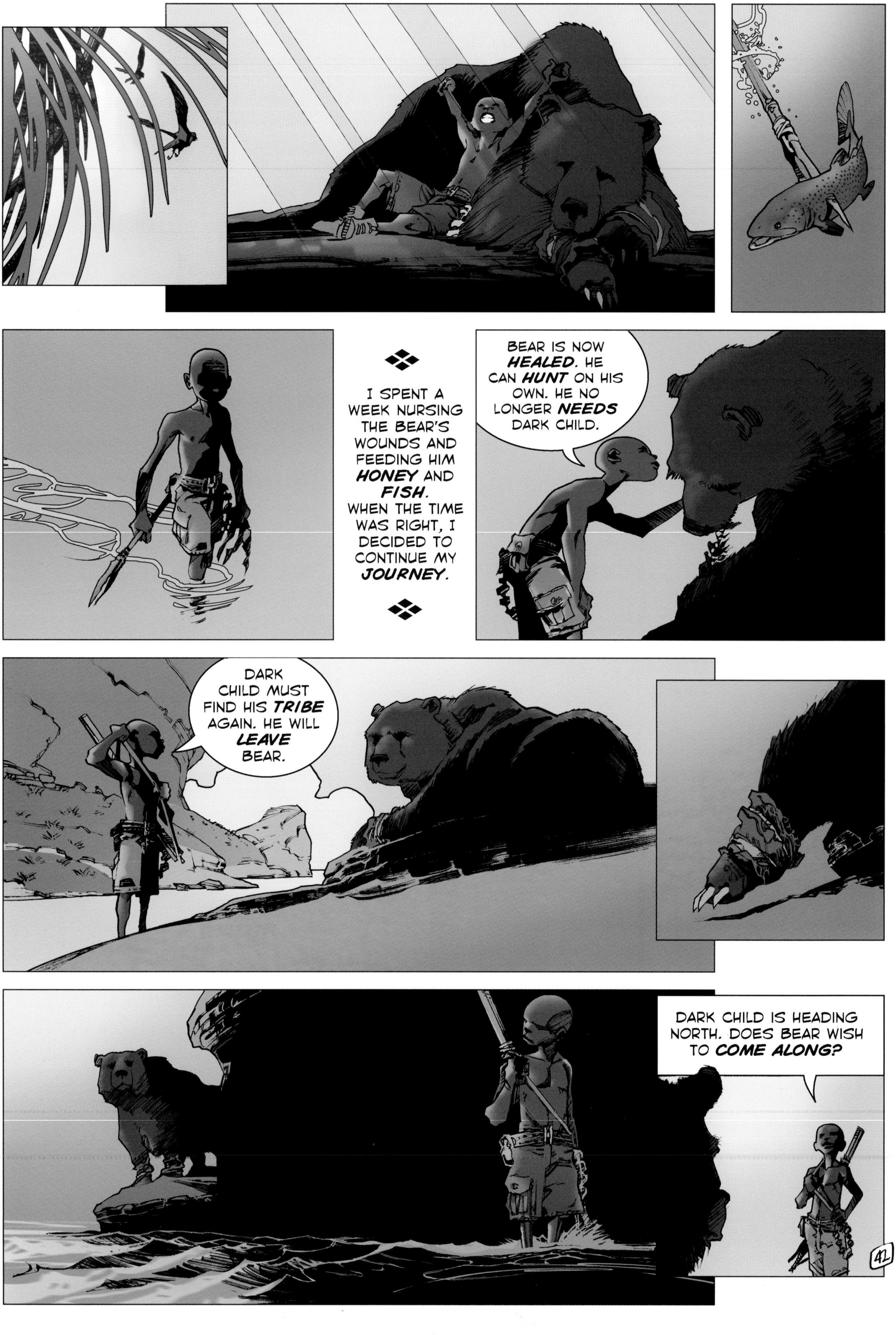
I SPENT A WEEK NURSING THE BEAR'S WOUNDS AND FEEDING HIM HONEY AND FISH. WHEN THE TIME WAS RIGHT, I DECIDED TO CONTINUE MY JOURNEY.
BEAR IS NOW HEALED. HE CAN HUNT ON HIS OWN. HE NO LONGER NEEDS DARK CHILD.
DARK CHILD MUST FIND HIS TRIBE AGAIN. HE WILL LEAVE BEAR.
DARK CHILD IS HEADING NORTH. DOES BEAR WISH TO COME ALONG?
41

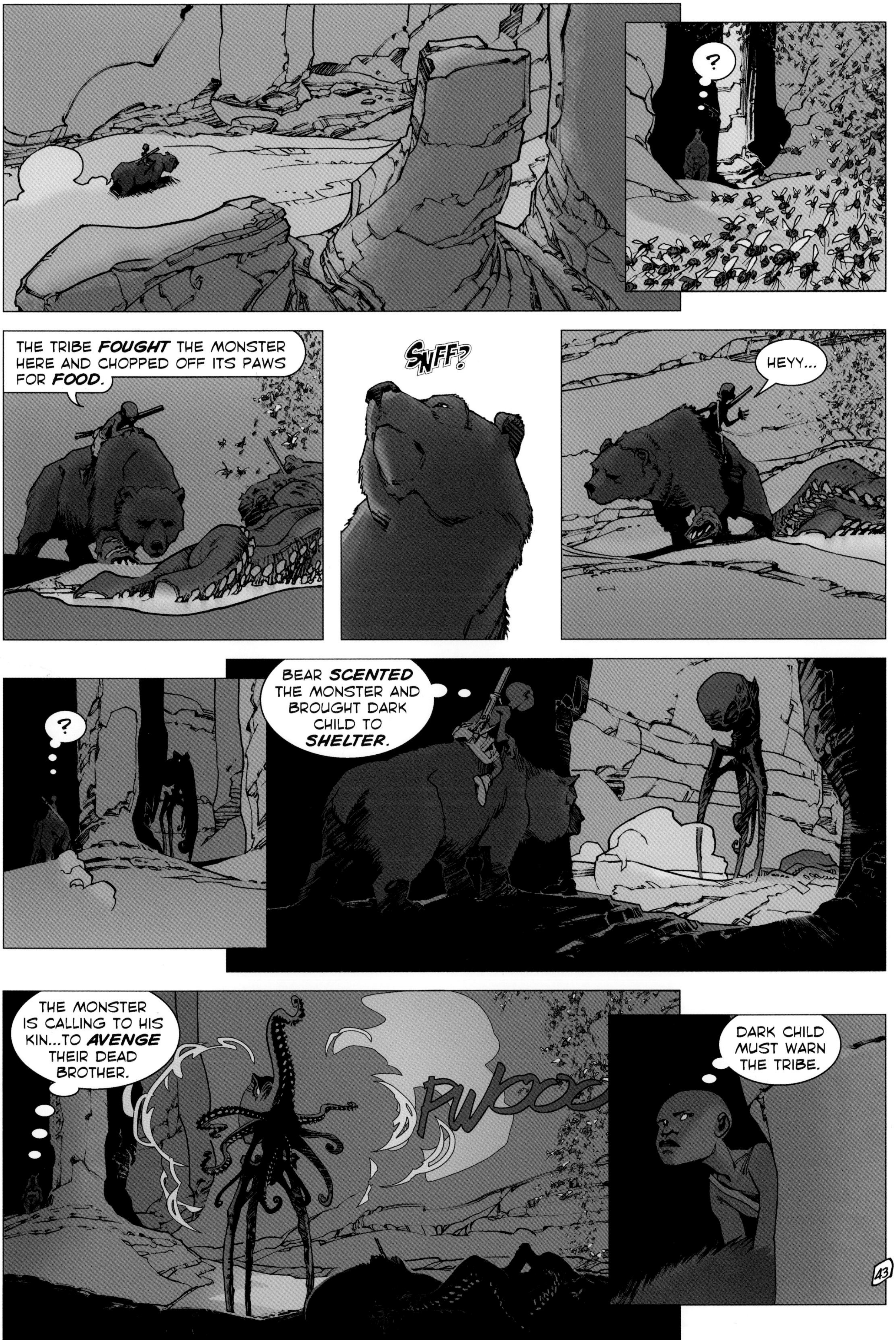
?
THE TRIBE FOUGHT THE MONSTER HERE AND CHOPPED OFF ITS PAWS FOR FOOD.
SNFF?
HEYY...
?
BEAR SCENTED THE MONSTER AND BROUGHT DARK CHILD TO SHELTER.
THE MONSTER IS CALLING TO HIS KIN...TO AVENGE THEIR DEAD BROTHER.
PWOOO
DARK CHILD MUST WARN THE TRIBE.

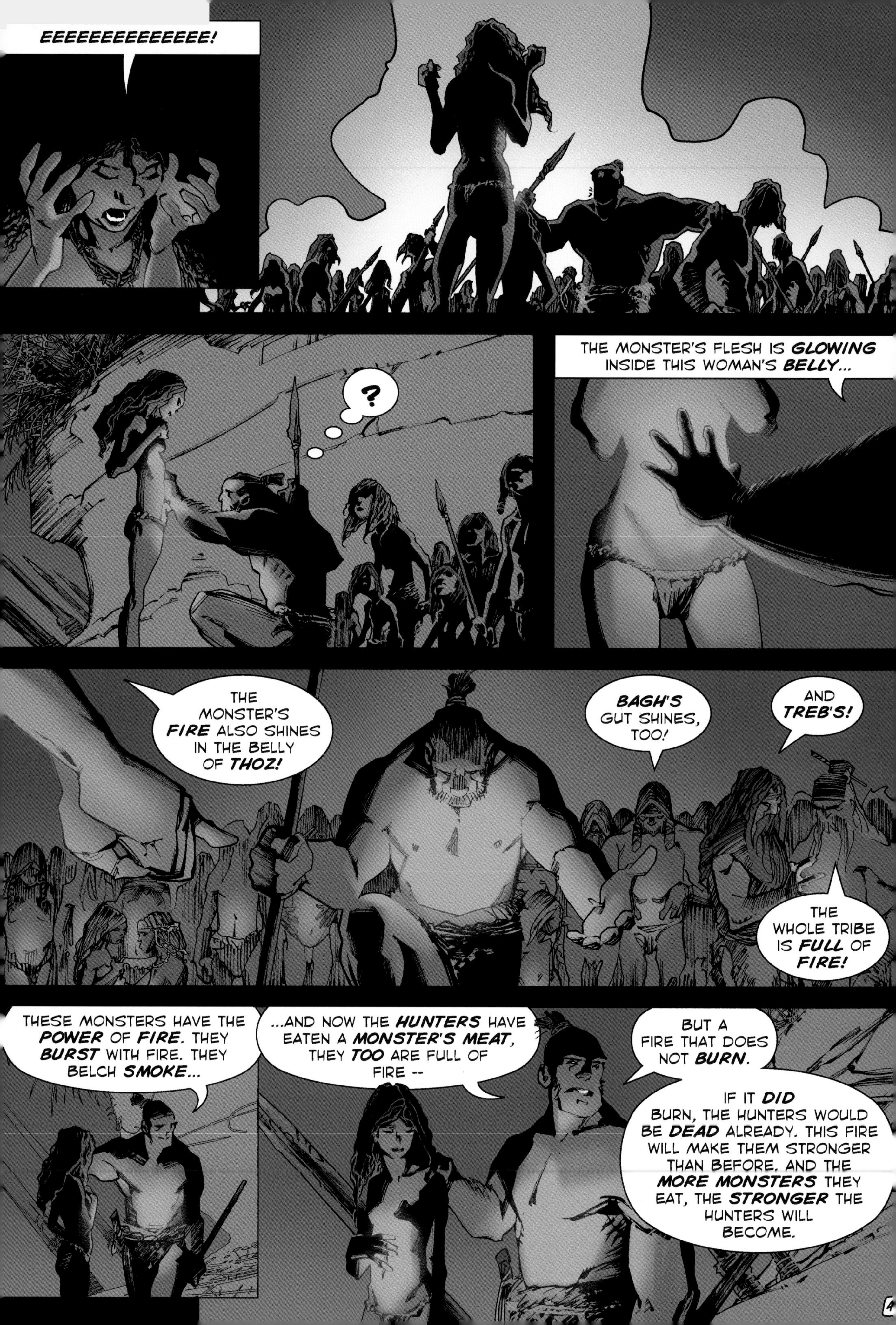

EEEEEEEEEEEEEE!
?
THE MONSTER'S FLESH IS GLOWING INSIDE THIS WOMAN'S BELLY...
THE MONSTER'S FIRE ALSO SHINES IN THE BELLY OF THOZ!
BAGH'S GUT SHINES, TOO!
AND TREB'S!
THE WHOLE TRIBE IS FULL OF FIRE!
THESE MONSTERS HAVE THE POWER OF FIRE. THEY BURST WITH FIRE. THEY BELCH SMOKE...
...AND NOW THE HUNTERS HAVE EATEN A MONSTER'S MEAT, THEY TOO ARE FULL OF FIRE --
BUT A FIRE THAT DOES NOT BURN.
IF IT DID BURN, THE HUNTERS WOULD BE DEAD ALREADY. THIS FIRE WILL MAKE THEM STRONGER THAN BEFORE. AND THE MORE MONSTERS THEY EAT, THE STRONGER THE HUNTERS WILL BECOME.

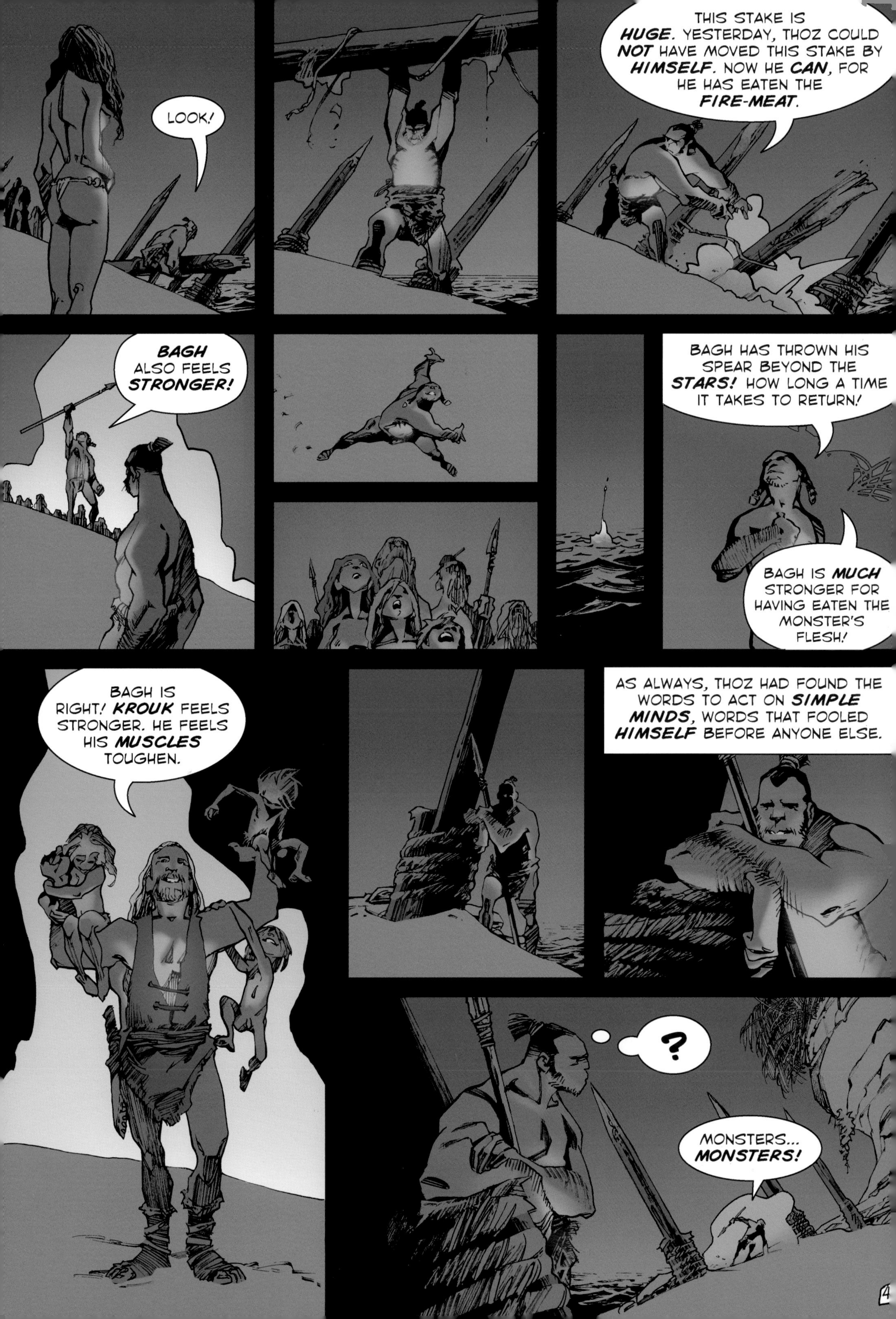
LOOK!
THIS STAKE IS HUGE. YESTERDAY, THOZ COULD NOT HAVE MOVED THIS STAKE BY HIMSELF. NOW HE CAN, FOR HE HAS EATEN THE FIRE-MEAT.
BAGH ALSO FEELS STRONGER!
BAGH HAS THROWN HIS SPEAR BEYOND THE STARS! HOW LONG A TIME IT TAKES TO RETURN!
BAGH IS MUCH STRONGER FOR HAVING EATEN THE MONSTER'S FLESH!
BAGH IS RIGHT! KROUK FEELS STRONGER. HE FEELS HIS MUSCLES TOUGHEN.
AS ALWAYS, THOZ HAD FOUND THE WORDS TO ACT ON SIMPLE MINDS, WORDS THAT FOOLED HIMSELF BEFORE ANYONE ELSE.
?
MONSTERS... MONSTERS!
49

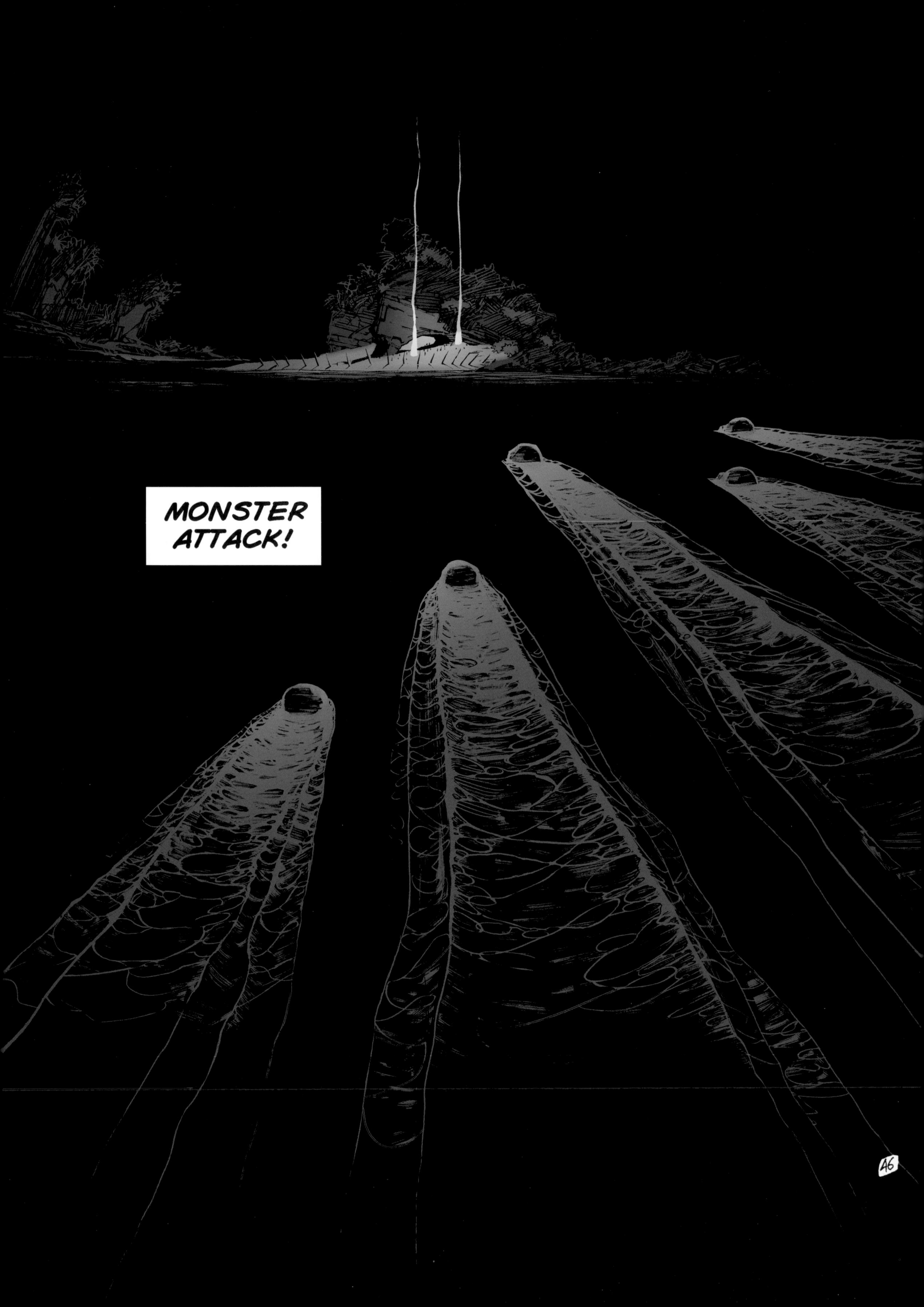
MONSTER
ATTACK!

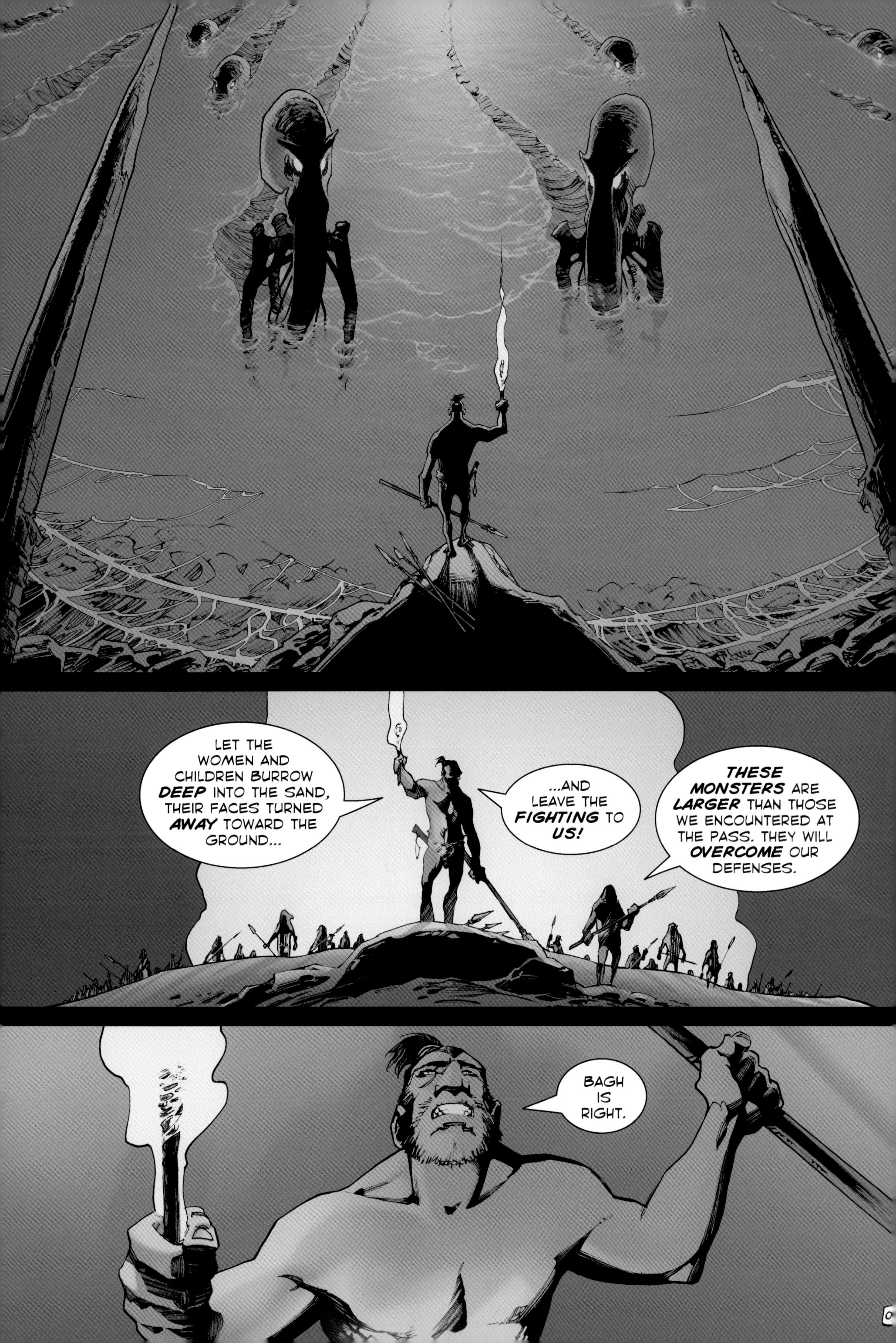
LET THE WOMEN AND CHILDREN BURROW DEEP INTO THE SAND, THEIR FACES TURNED AWAY TOWARD THE GROUND...
...AND LEAVE THE FIGHTING TO US!
THESE MONSTERS ARE LARGER THAN THOSE WE ENCOUNTERED AT THE PASS. THEY WILL OVERCOME OUR DEFENSES.
BAGH IS RIGHT.

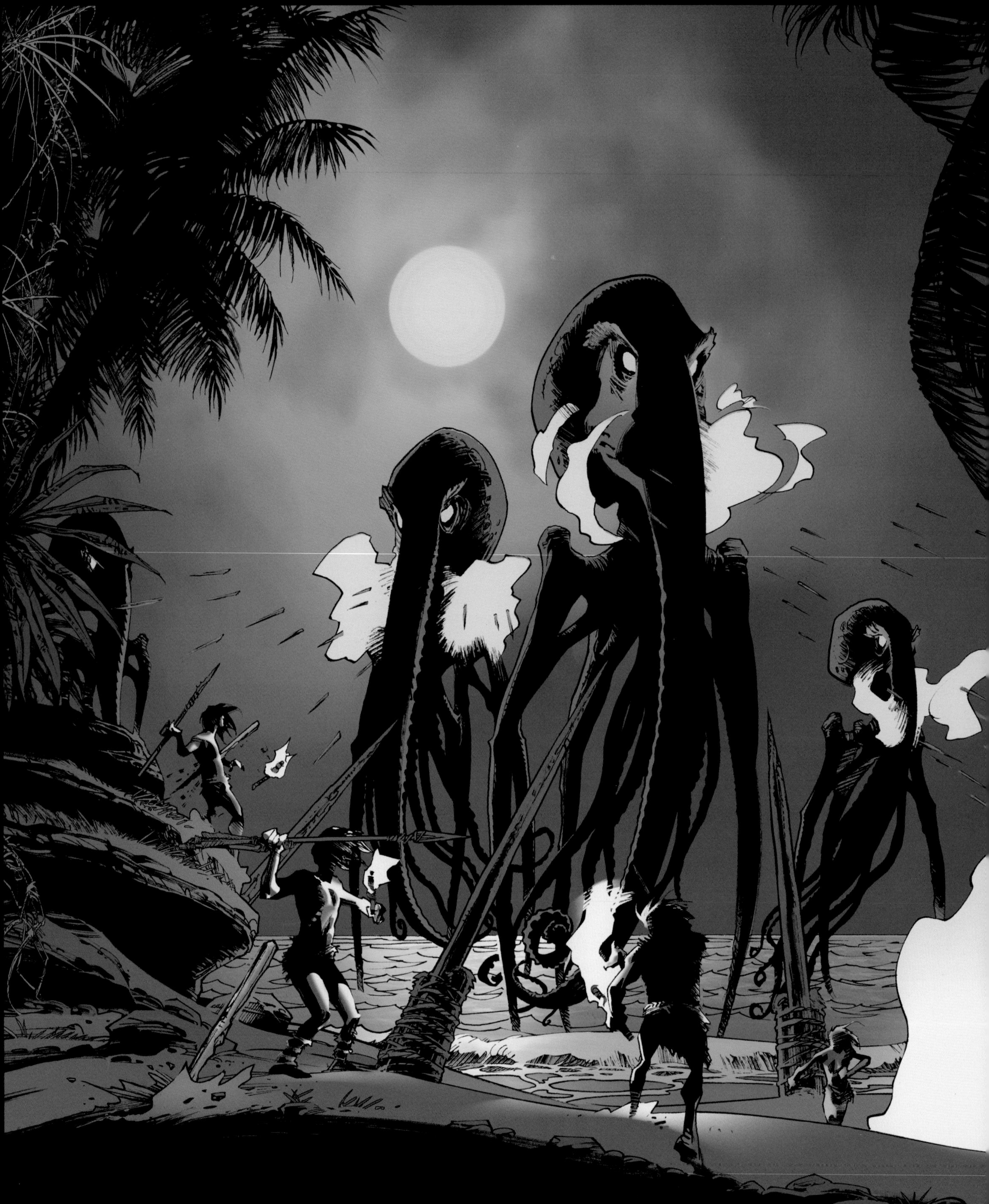

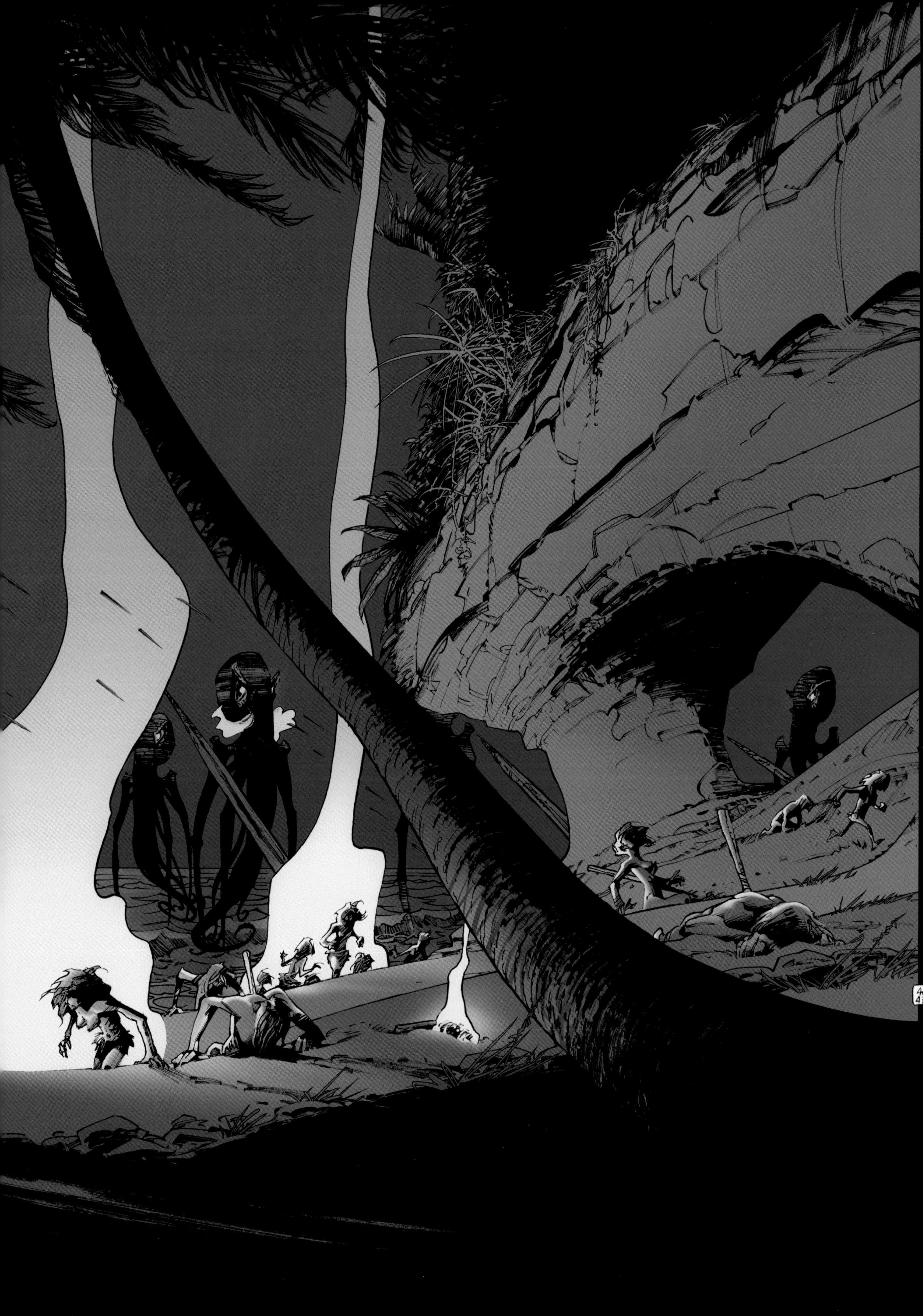
46
47

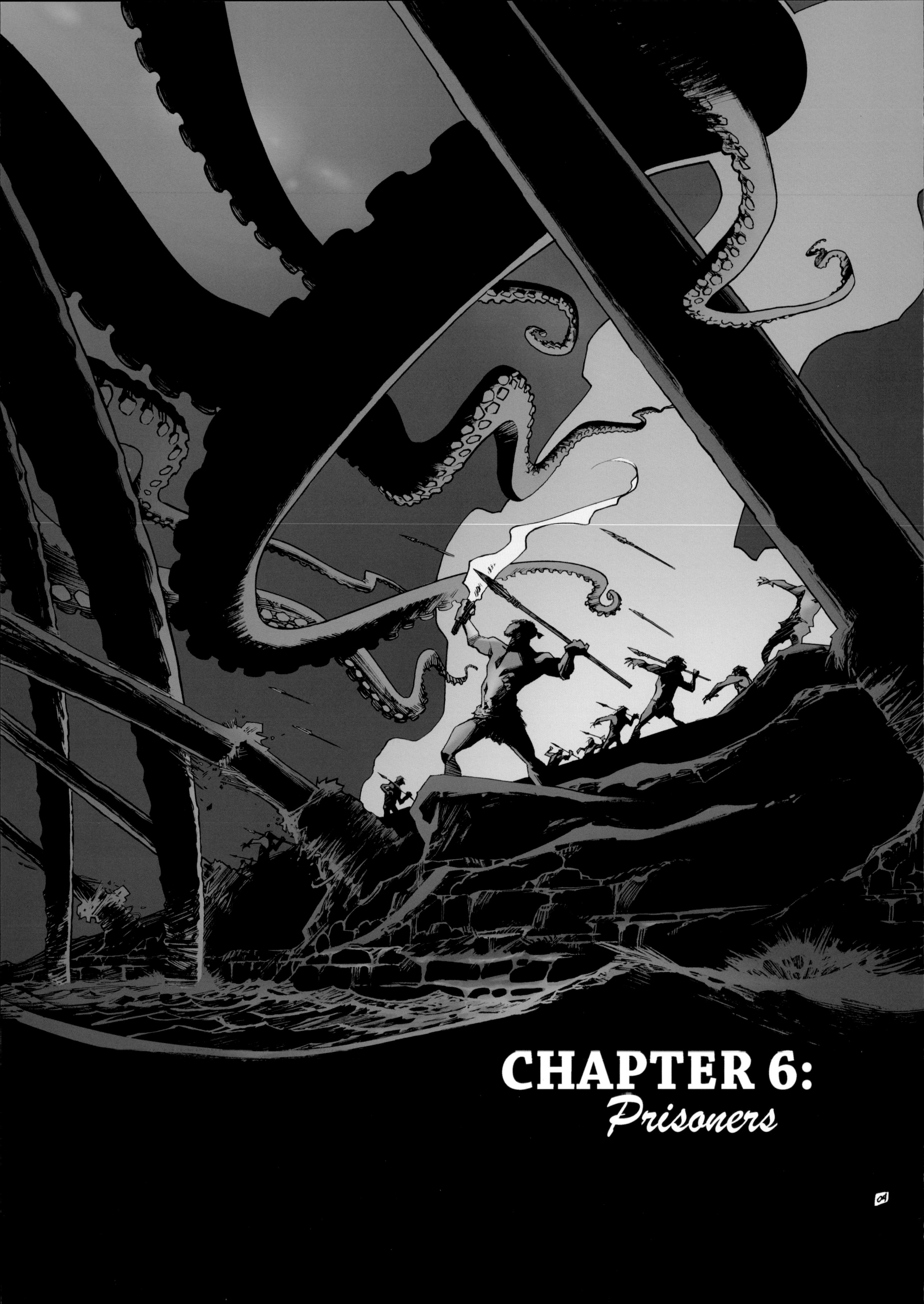

CHAPTER 6: *Prisoners*

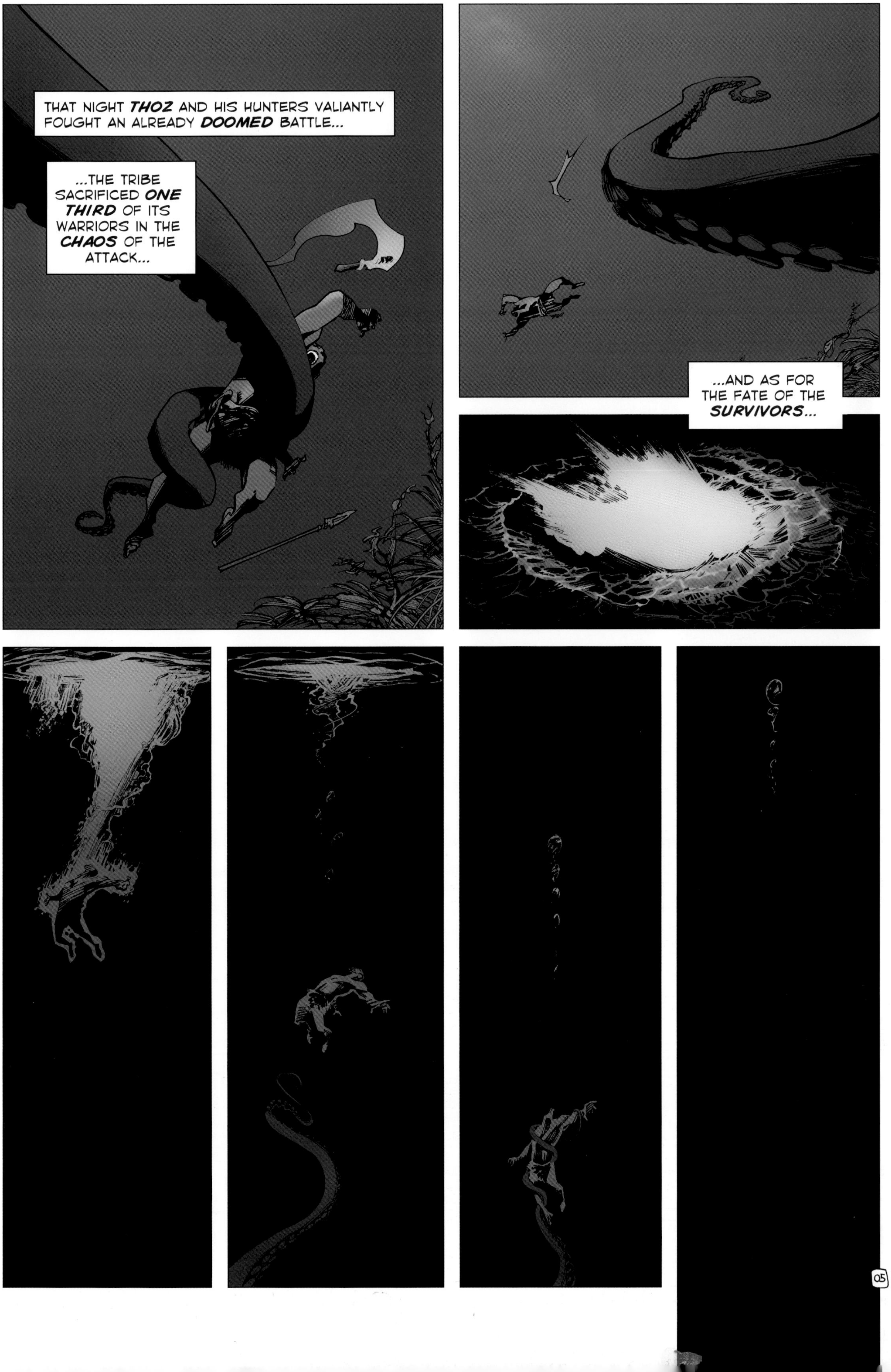
THAT NIGHT THOZ AND HIS HUNTERS VALIANTLY FOUGHT AN ALREADY DOOMED BATTLE...
...THE TRIBE SACRIFICED ONE THIRD OF ITS WARRIORS IN THE CHAOS OF THE ATTACK...
...AND AS FOR THE FATE OF THE SURVIVORS...

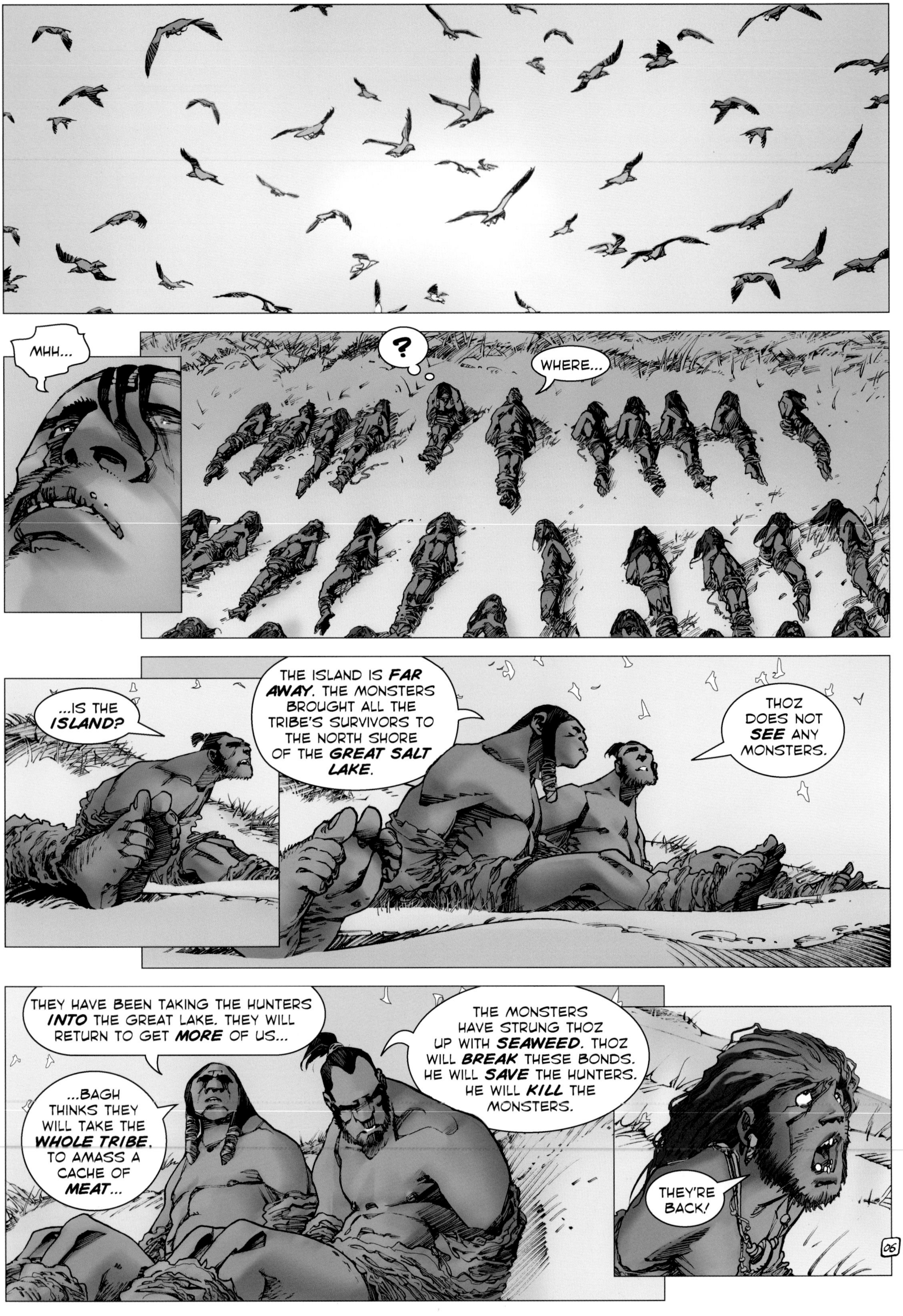
MHH...
?
WHERE...
...IS THE ISLAND?
THE ISLAND IS FAR AWAY. THE MONSTERS BROUGHT ALL THE TRIBE'S SURVIVORS TO THE NORTH SHORE OF THE GREAT SALT LAKE.
THOZ DOES NOT SEE ANY MONSTERS.
THEY HAVE BEEN TAKING THE HUNTERS INTO THE GREAT LAKE. THEY WILL RETURN TO GET MORE OF US...
...BAGH THINKS THEY WILL TAKE THE WHOLE TRIBE, TO AMASS A CACHE OF MEAT...
THE MONSTERS HAVE STRUNG THOZ UP WITH SEAWEED. THOZ WILL BREAK THESE BONDS. HE WILL SAVE THE HUNTERS. HE WILL KILL THE MONSTERS.
THEY'RE BACK!

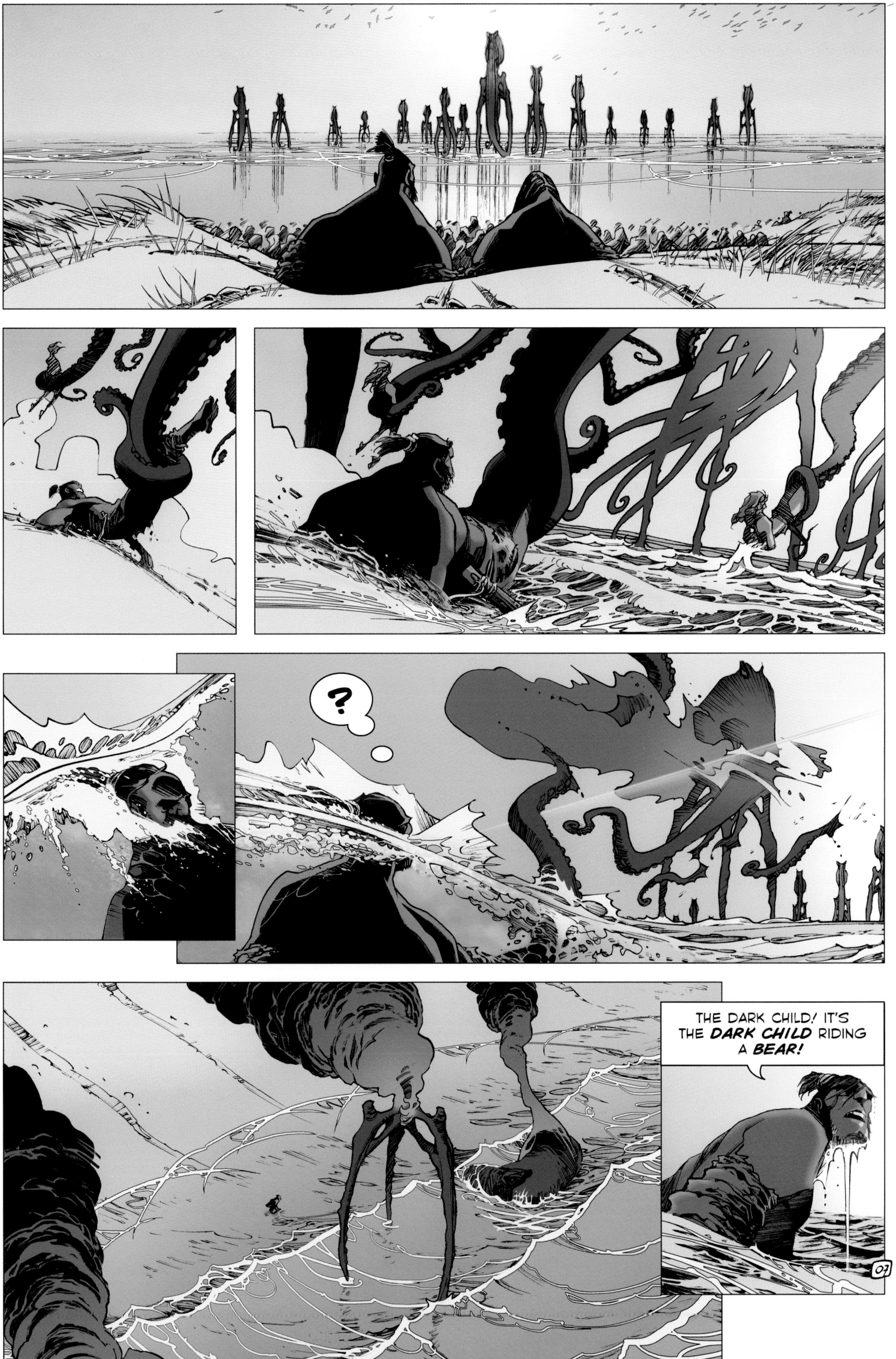
?
THE DARK CHILD! IT'S THE DARK CHILD RIDING A BEAR!
07

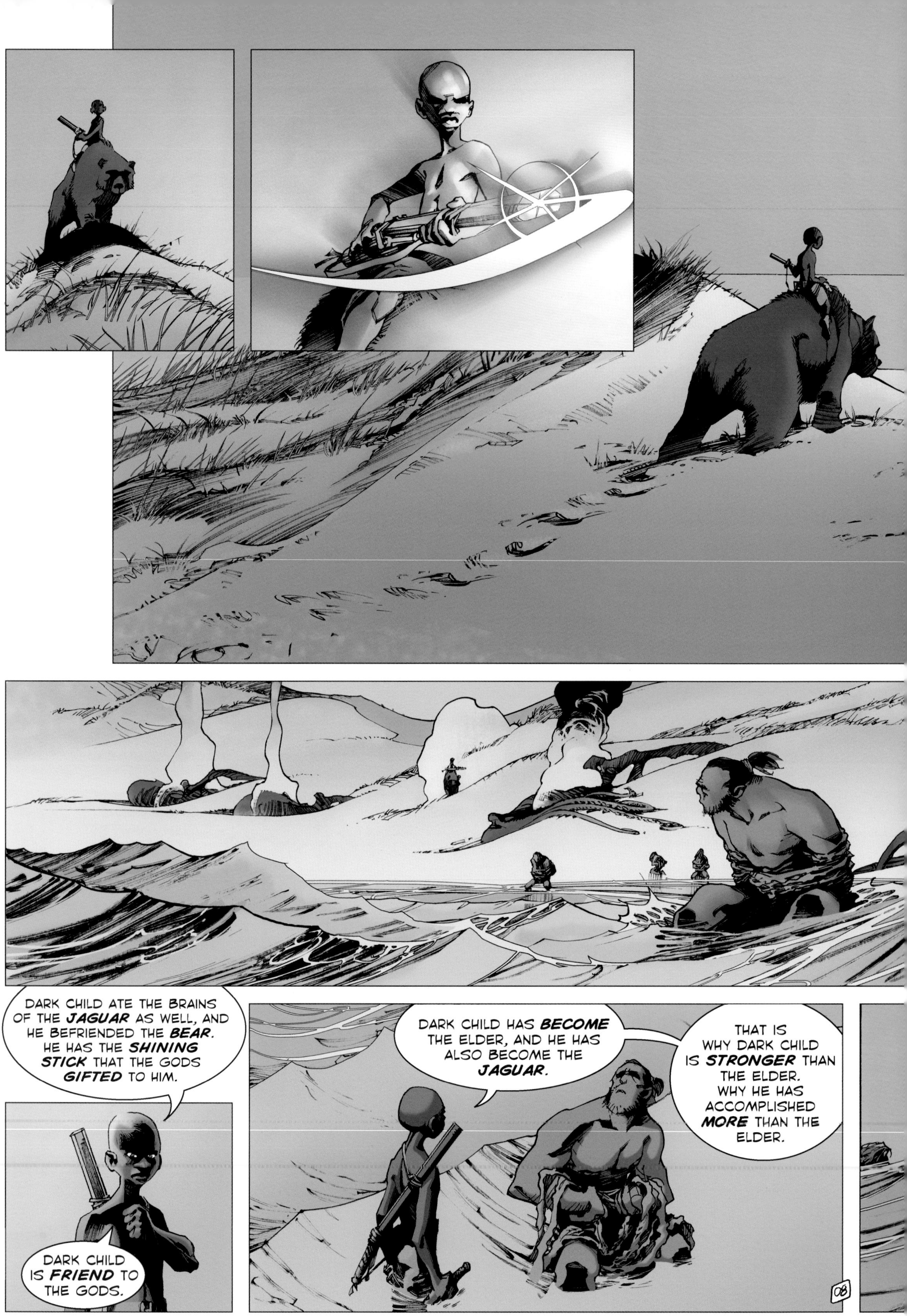

DARK CHILD ATE THE BRAINS OF THE **JAGUAR** AS WELL, AND HE BEFRIENDED THE **BEAR**. HE HAS THE **SHINING STICK** THAT THE GODS **GIFTED** TO HIM.
DARK CHILD IS **FRIEND** TO THE GODS.
DARK CHILD HAS **BECOME** THE ELDER, AND HE HAS ALSO BECOME THE **JAGUAR**.
THAT IS WHY DARK CHILD IS **STRONGER** THAN THE ELDER. WHY HE HAS ACCOMPLISHED **MORE** THAN THE ELDER.
08

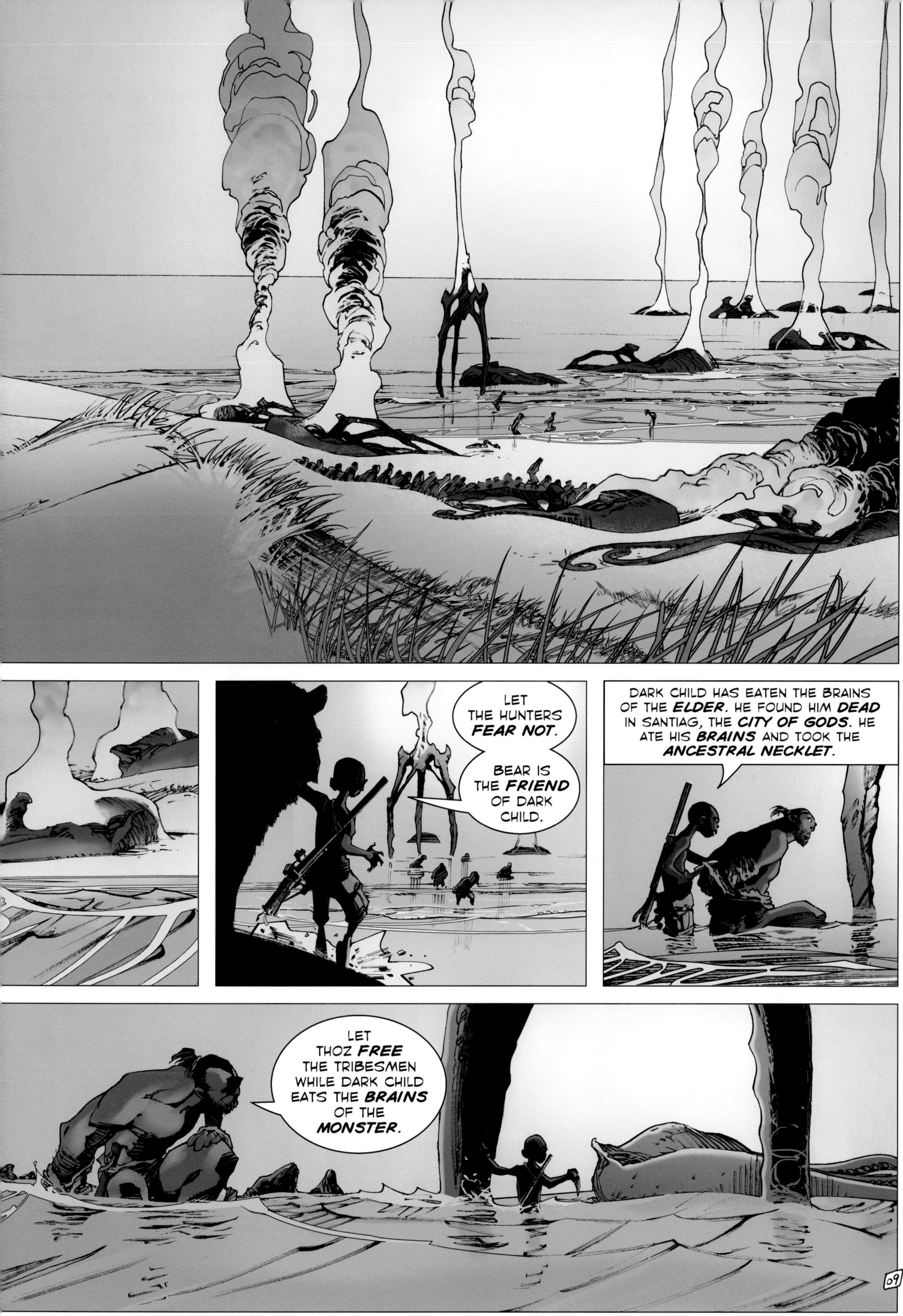
LET THE HUNTERS FEAR NOT.
BEAR IS THE FRIEND OF DARK CHILD.
DARK CHILD HAS EATEN THE BRAINS OF THE ELDER. HE FOUND HIM DEAD IN SANTIAG, THE CITY OF GODS. HE ATE HIS BRAINS AND TOOK THE ANCESTRAL NECKLET.
LET THOZ FREE THE TRIBESMEN WHILE DARK CHILD EATS THE BRAINS OF THE MONSTER.

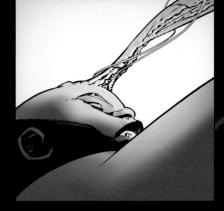

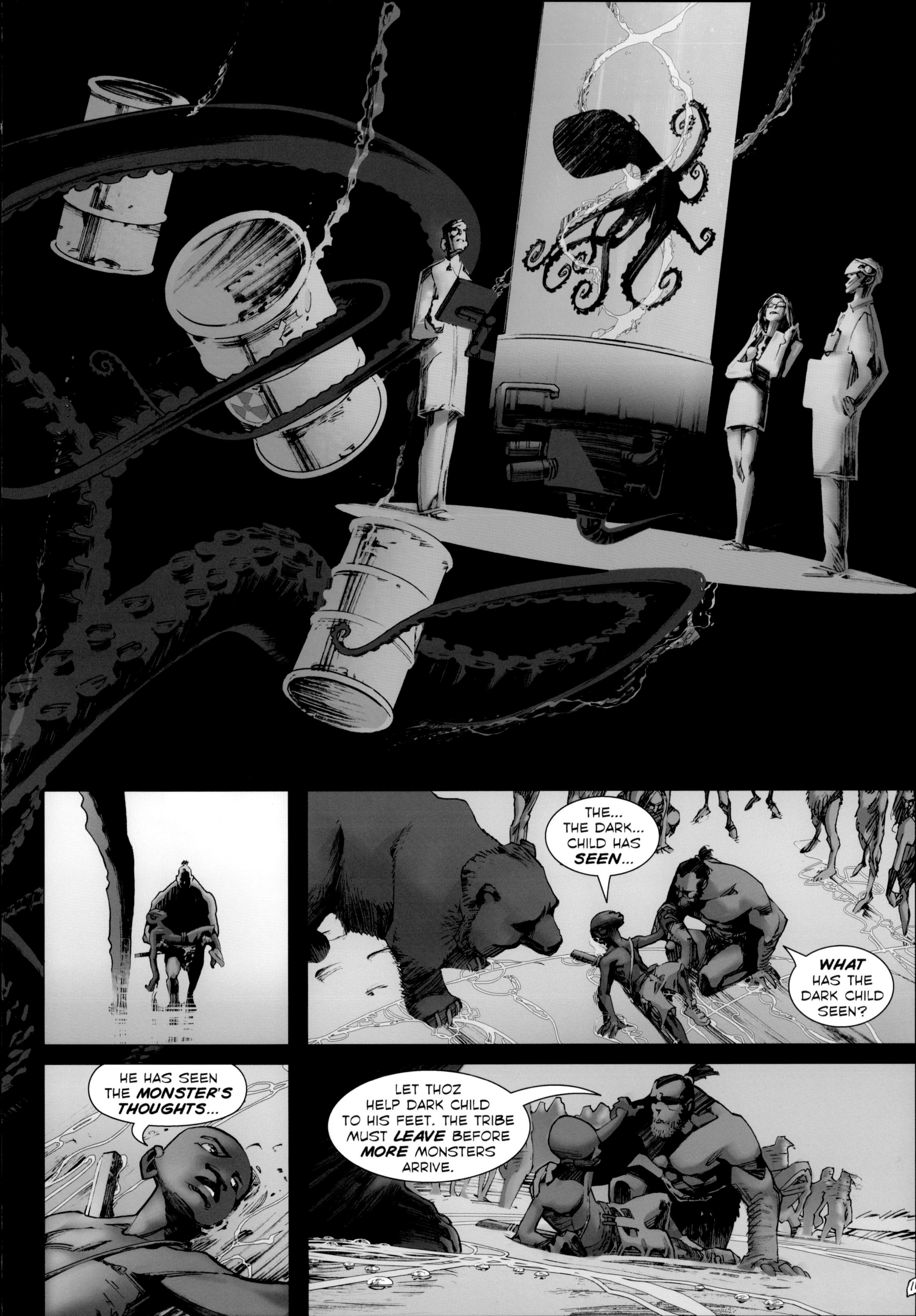
THE... THE DARK... CHILD HAS SEEN...
WHAT HAS THE DARK CHILD SEEN?
HE HAS SEEN THE MONSTER'S THOUGHTS...
LET THOZ HELP DARK CHILD TO HIS FEET. THE TRIBE MUST LEAVE BEFORE MORE MONSTERS ARRIVE.

CHAPTER 7: *The Flying God*

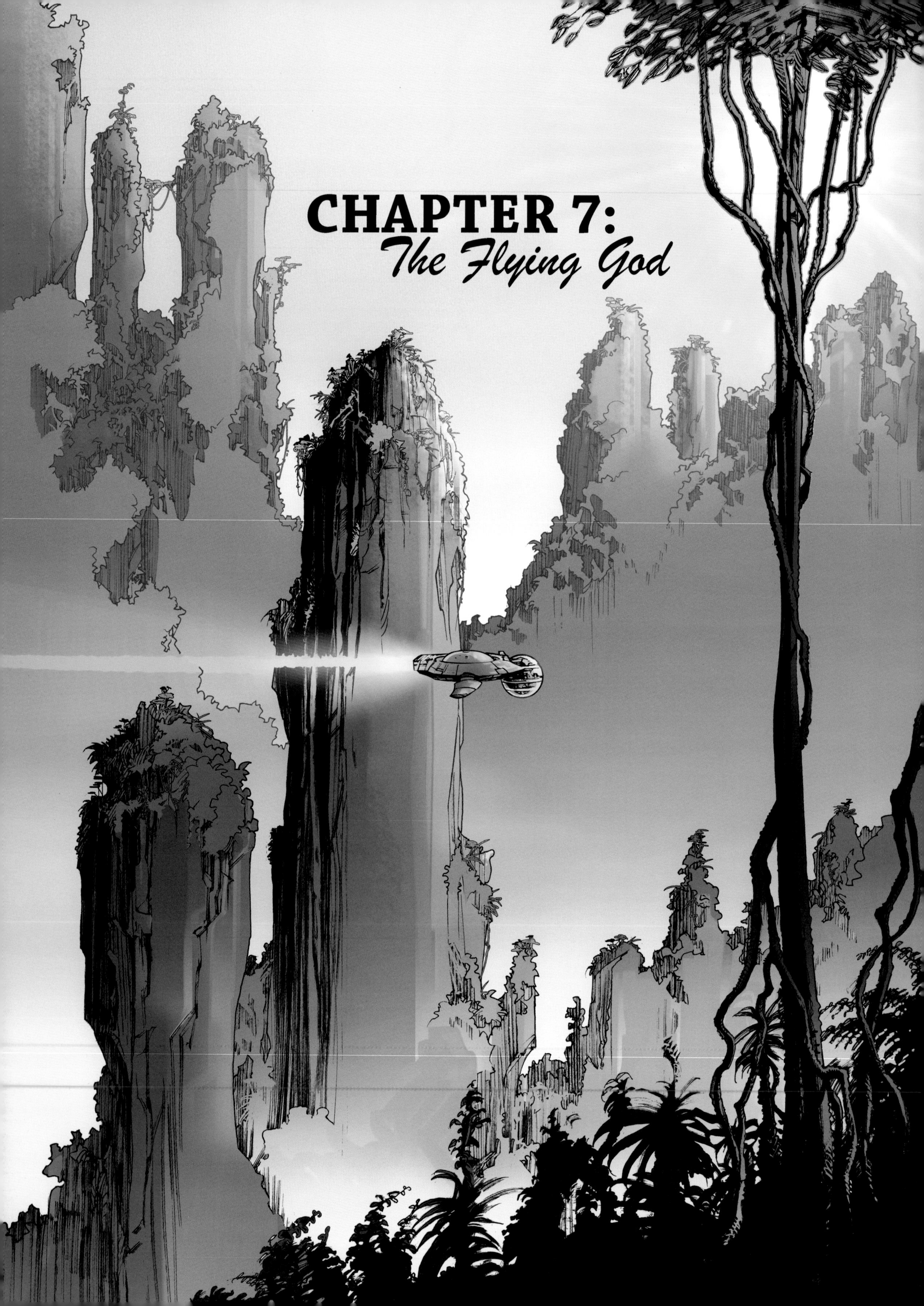

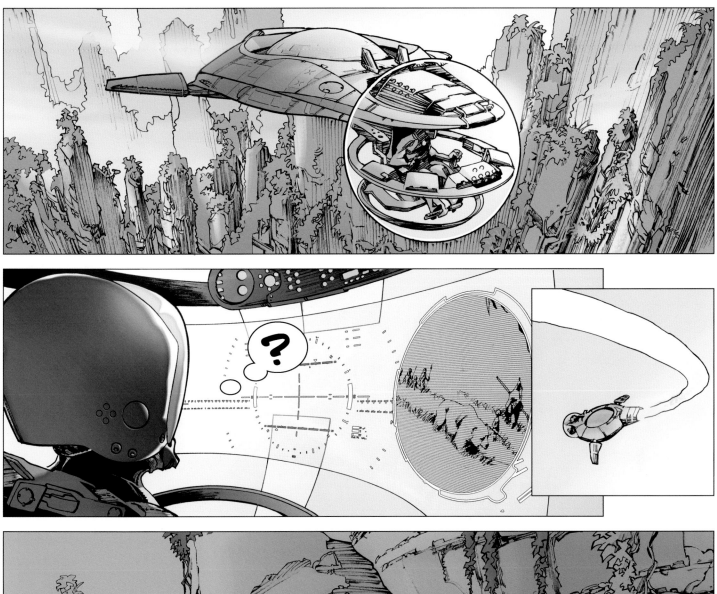

HELLO!

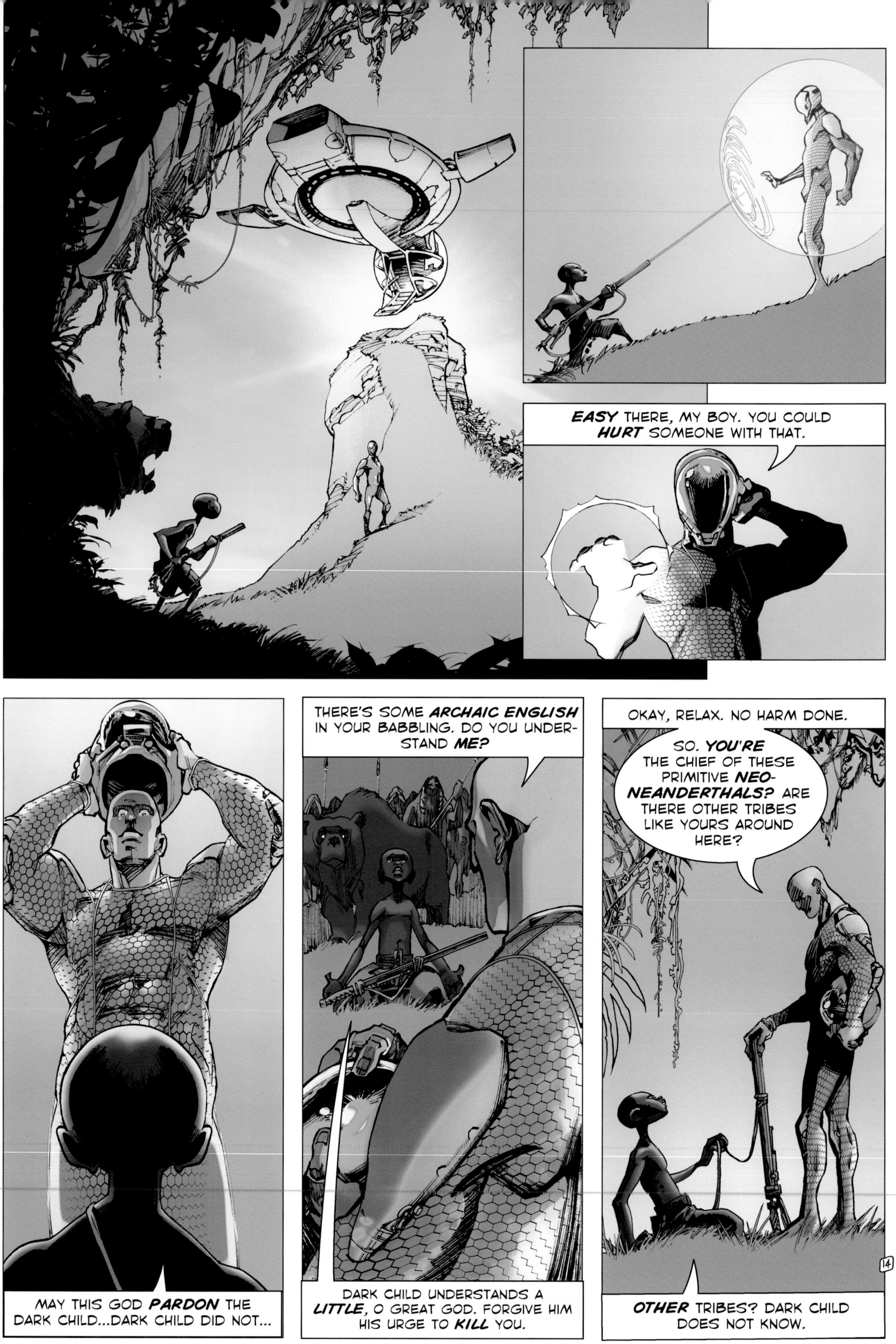

EASY THERE, MY BOY. YOU COULD HURT SOMEONE WITH THAT.
MAY THIS GOD PARDON THE DARK CHILD...DARK CHILD DID NOT...
THERE'S SOME ARCHAIC ENGLISH IN YOUR BABBLING. DO YOU UNDERSTAND ME?
DARK CHILD UNDERSTANDS A LITTLE, O GREAT GOD. FORGIVE HIM HIS URGE TO KILL YOU.
OKAY, RELAX. NO HARM DONE.
SO. YOU'RE THE CHIEF OF THESE PRIMITIVE NEO-NEANDERTHALS? ARE THERE OTHER TRIBES LIKE YOURS AROUND HERE?
OTHER TRIBES? DARK CHILD DOES NOT KNOW.

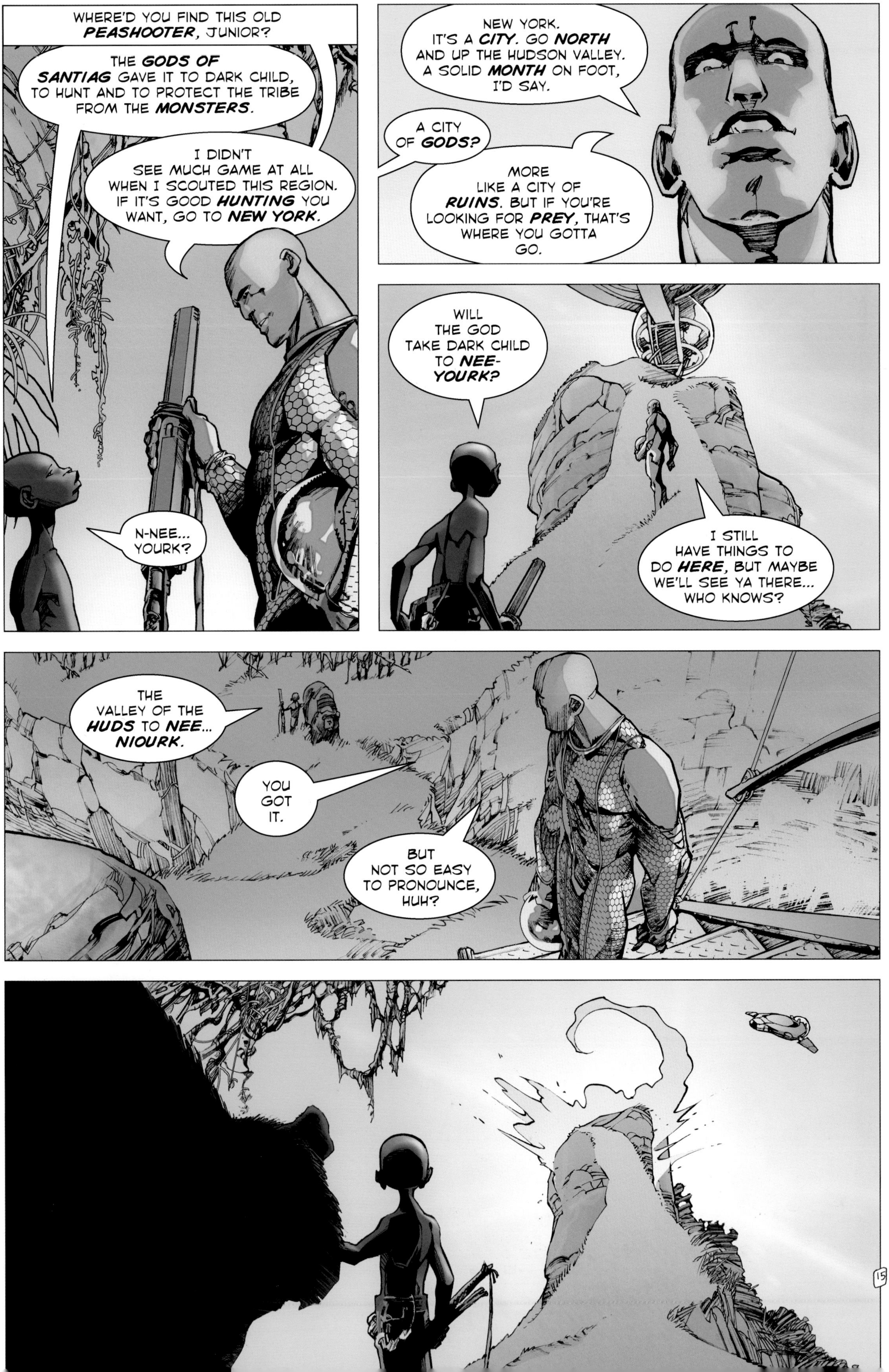

WHERE'D YOU FIND THIS OLD PEASHOOTER, JUNIOR?
THE GODS OF SANTIAG GAVE IT TO DARK CHILD, TO HUNT AND TO PROTECT THE TRIBE FROM THE MONSTERS.
I DIDN'T SEE MUCH GAME AT ALL WHEN I SCOUTED THIS REGION. IF IT'S GOOD HUNTING YOU WANT, GO TO NEW YORK.
N-NEE... YOURK?
NEW YORK. IT'S A CITY. GO NORTH AND UP THE HUDSON VALLEY. A SOLID MONTH ON FOOT, I'D SAY.
A CITY OF GODS?
MORE LIKE A CITY OF RUINS. BUT IF YOU'RE LOOKING FOR PREY, THAT'S WHERE YOU GOTTA GO.
WILL THE GOD TAKE DARK CHILD TO NEE-YOURK?
I STILL HAVE THINGS TO DO HERE, BUT MAYBE WE'LL SEE YA THERE... WHO KNOWS?
THE VALLEY OF THE HUDS TO NEE... NIOURK.
YOU GOT IT.
BUT NOT SO EASY TO PRONOUNCE, HUH?

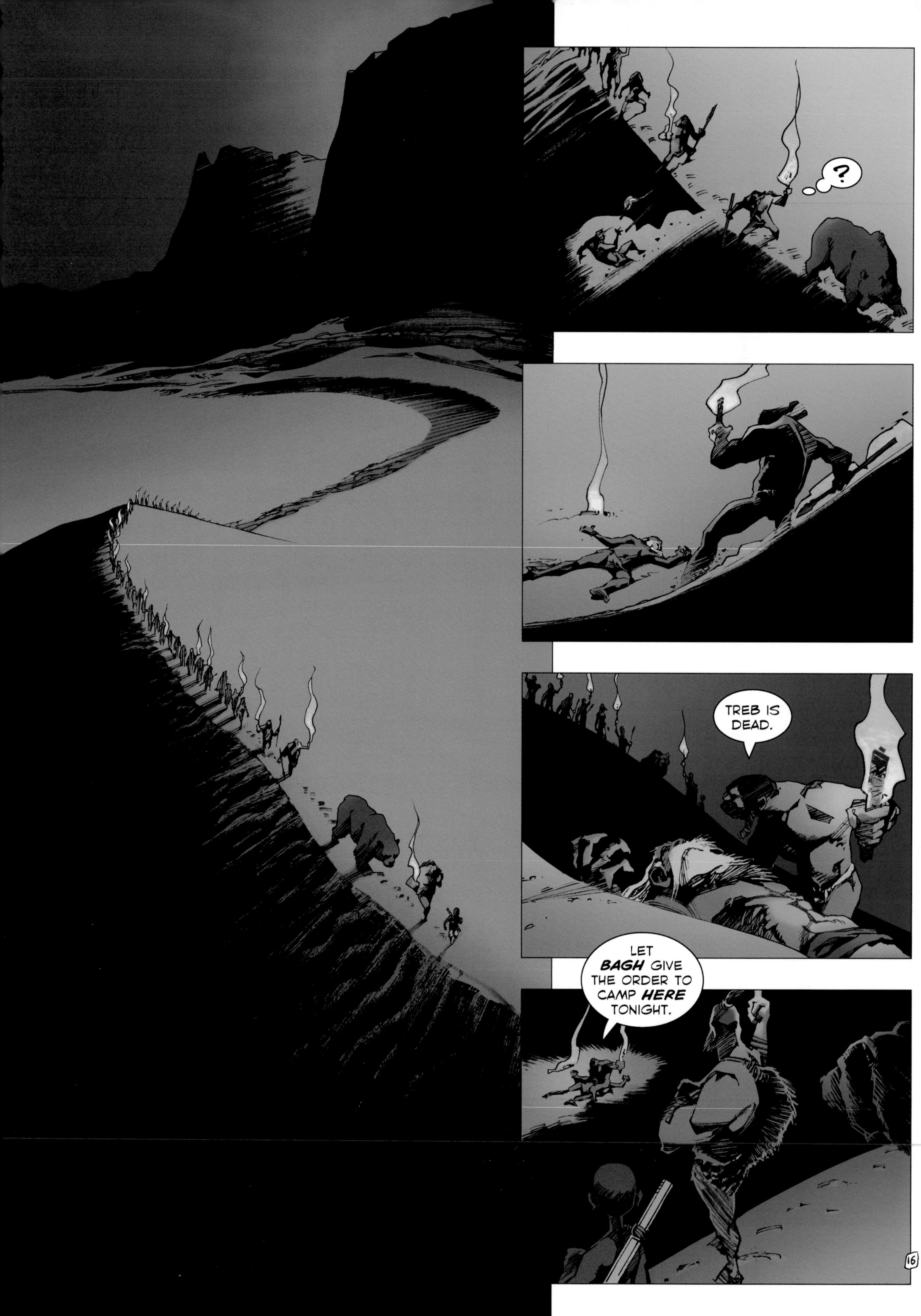
?
TREB IS DEAD.
LET BAGH GIVE THE ORDER TO CAMP HERE TONIGHT.
16

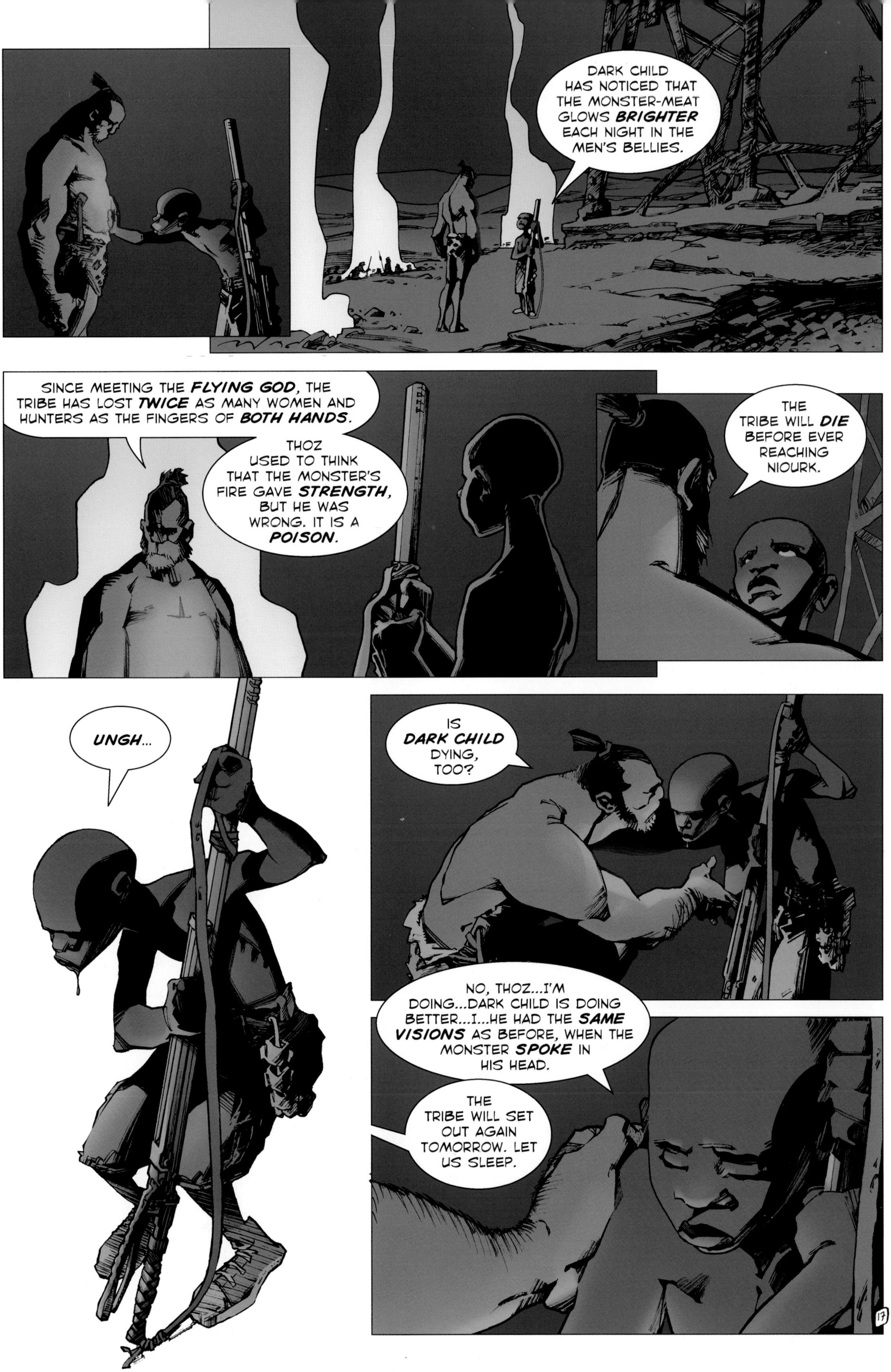
DARK CHILD HAS NOTICED THAT THE MONSTER-MEAT GLOWS BRIGHTER EACH NIGHT IN THE MEN'S BELLIES.
SINCE MEETING THE FLYING GOD, THE TRIBE HAS LOST TWICE AS MANY WOMEN AND HUNTERS AS THE FINGERS OF BOTH HANDS.
THOZ USED TO THINK THAT THE MONSTER'S FIRE GAVE STRENGTH, BUT HE WAS WRONG. IT IS A POISON.
THE TRIBE WILL DIE BEFORE EVER REACHING NIOURK.
UNGH...
IS DARK CHILD DYING, TOO?
NO, THOZ...I'M DOING...DARK CHILD IS DOING BETTER...I...HE HAD THE SAME VISIONS AS BEFORE, WHEN THE MONSTER SPOKE IN HIS HEAD.
THE TRIBE WILL SET OUT AGAIN TOMORROW. LET US SLEEP.

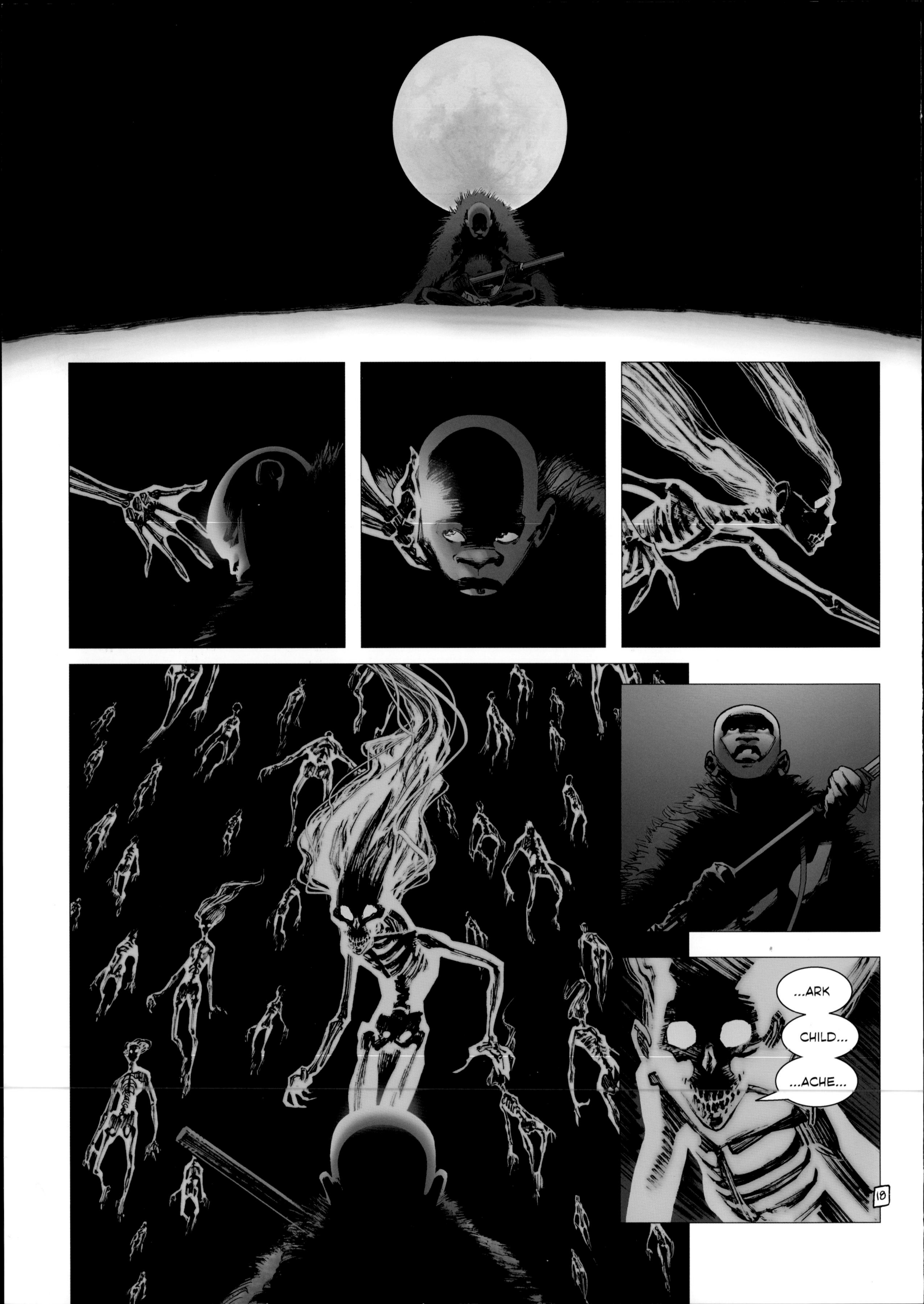
...ARK
CHILD...
...ACHE...

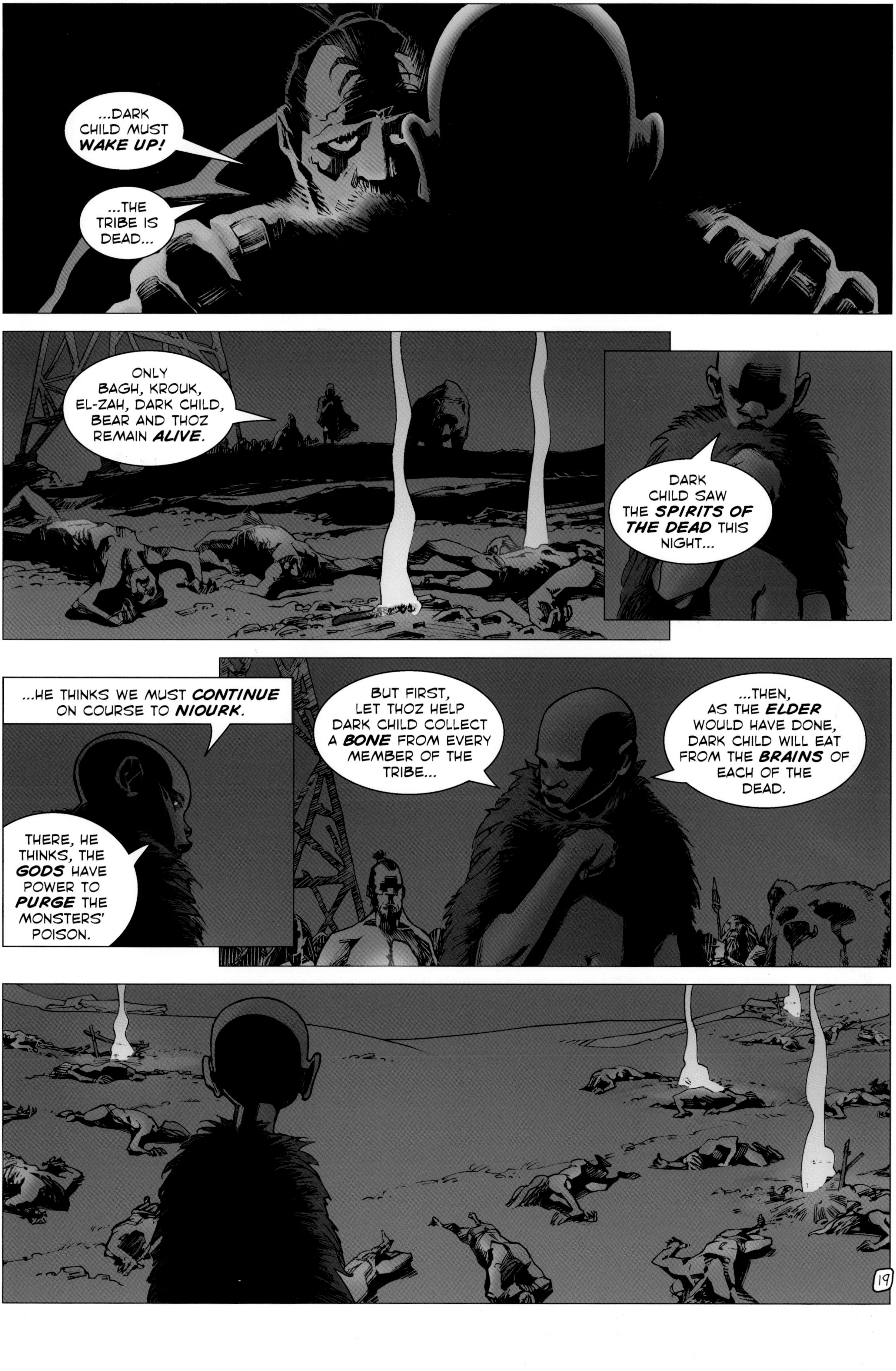
...DARK CHILD MUST WAKE UP!
...THE TRIBE IS DEAD...
ONLY BAGH, KROUK, EL-ZAH, DARK CHILD, BEAR AND THOZ REMAIN ALIVE.
DARK CHILD SAW THE SPIRITS OF THE DEAD THIS NIGHT...
...HE THINKS WE MUST CONTINUE ON COURSE TO NIOURK.
THERE, HE THINKS, THE GODS HAVE POWER TO PURGE THE MONSTERS' POISON.
BUT FIRST, LET THOZ HELP DARK CHILD COLLECT A BONE FROM EVERY MEMBER OF THE TRIBE...
...THEN, AS THE ELDER WOULD HAVE DONE, DARK CHILD WILL EAT FROM THE BRAINS OF EACH OF THE DEAD.

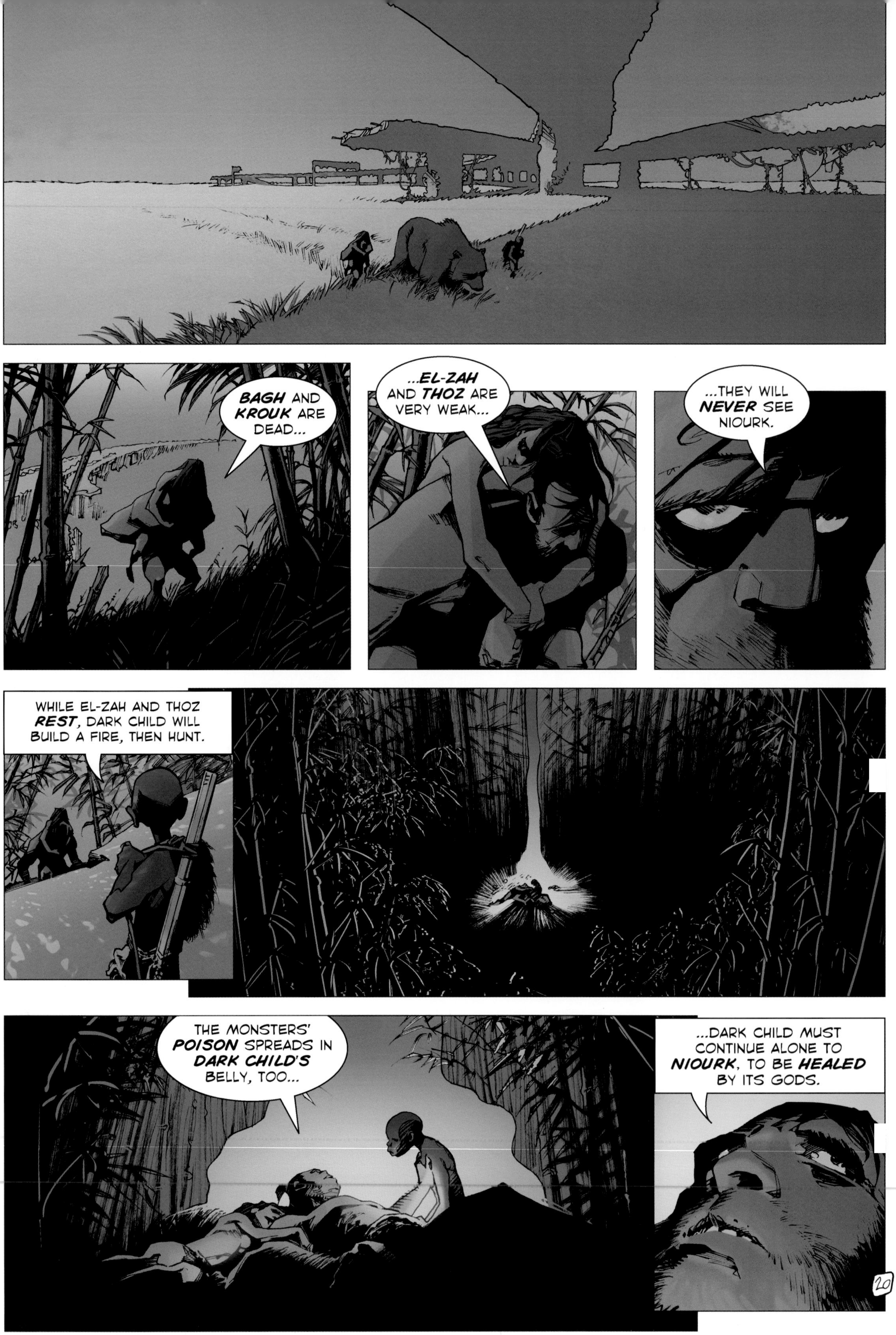
BAGH AND KROUK ARE DEAD...
...EL-ZAH AND THOZ ARE VERY WEAK...
...THEY WILL NEVER SEE NIOURK.
WHILE EL-ZAH AND THOZ REST, DARK CHILD WILL BUILD A FIRE, THEN HUNT.
THE MONSTERS' POISON SPREADS IN DARK CHILD'S BELLY, TOO...
...DARK CHILD MUST CONTINUE ALONE TO NIOURK, TO BE HEALED BY ITS GODS.
20

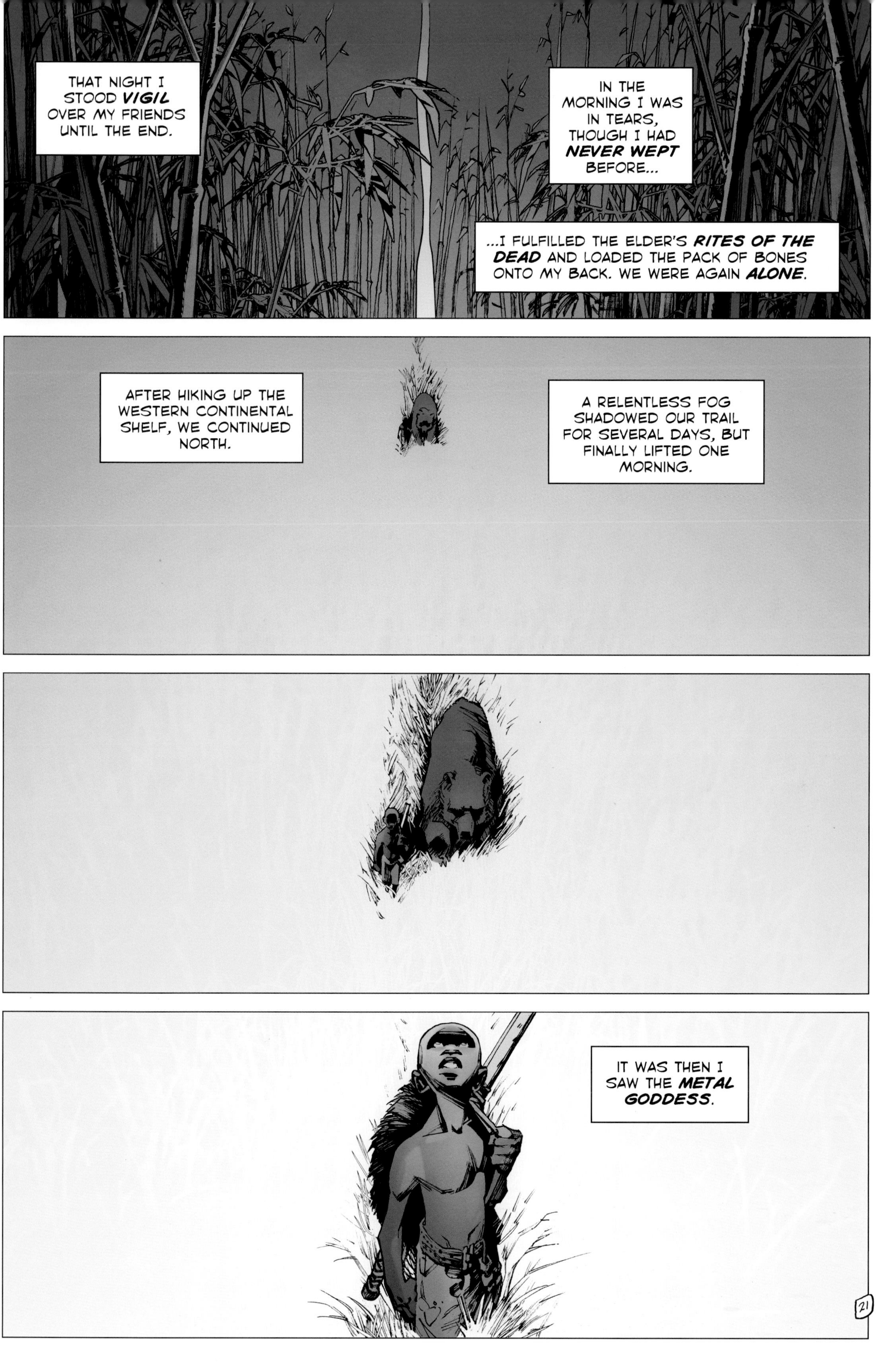
THAT NIGHT I STOOD VIGIL OVER MY FRIENDS UNTIL THE END.
IN THE MORNING I WAS IN TEARS, THOUGH I HAD NEVER WEPT BEFORE...
...I FULFILLED THE ELDER'S RITES OF THE DEAD AND LOADED THE PACK OF BONES ONTO MY BACK. WE WERE AGAIN ALONE.
AFTER HIKING UP THE WESTERN CONTINENTAL SHELF, WE CONTINUED NORTH.
A RELENTLESS FOG SHADOWED OUR TRAIL FOR SEVERAL DAYS, BUT FINALLY LIFTED ONE MORNING.
IT WAS THEN I SAW THE METAL GODDESS.

CHAPTER 8:
Niourk

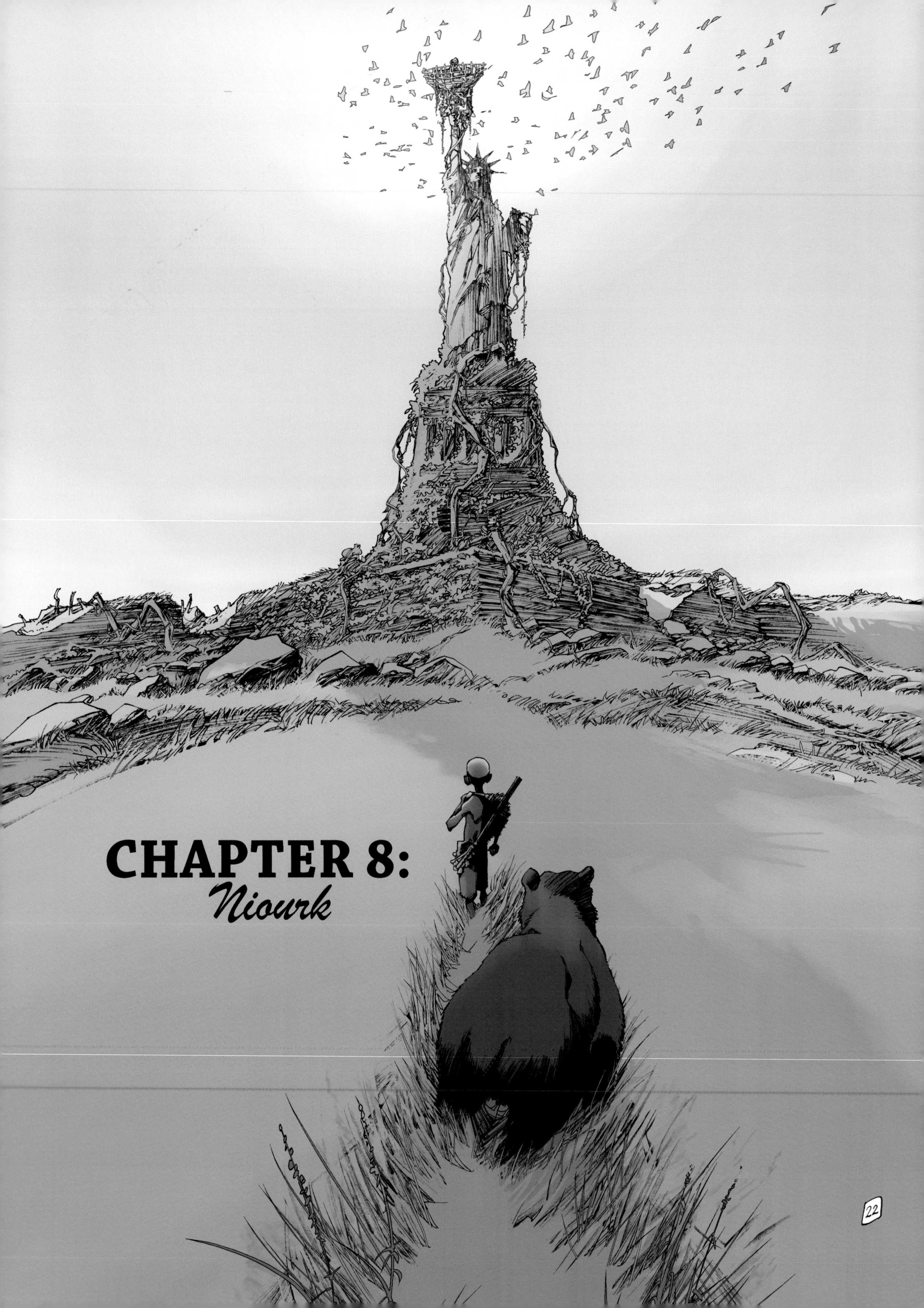

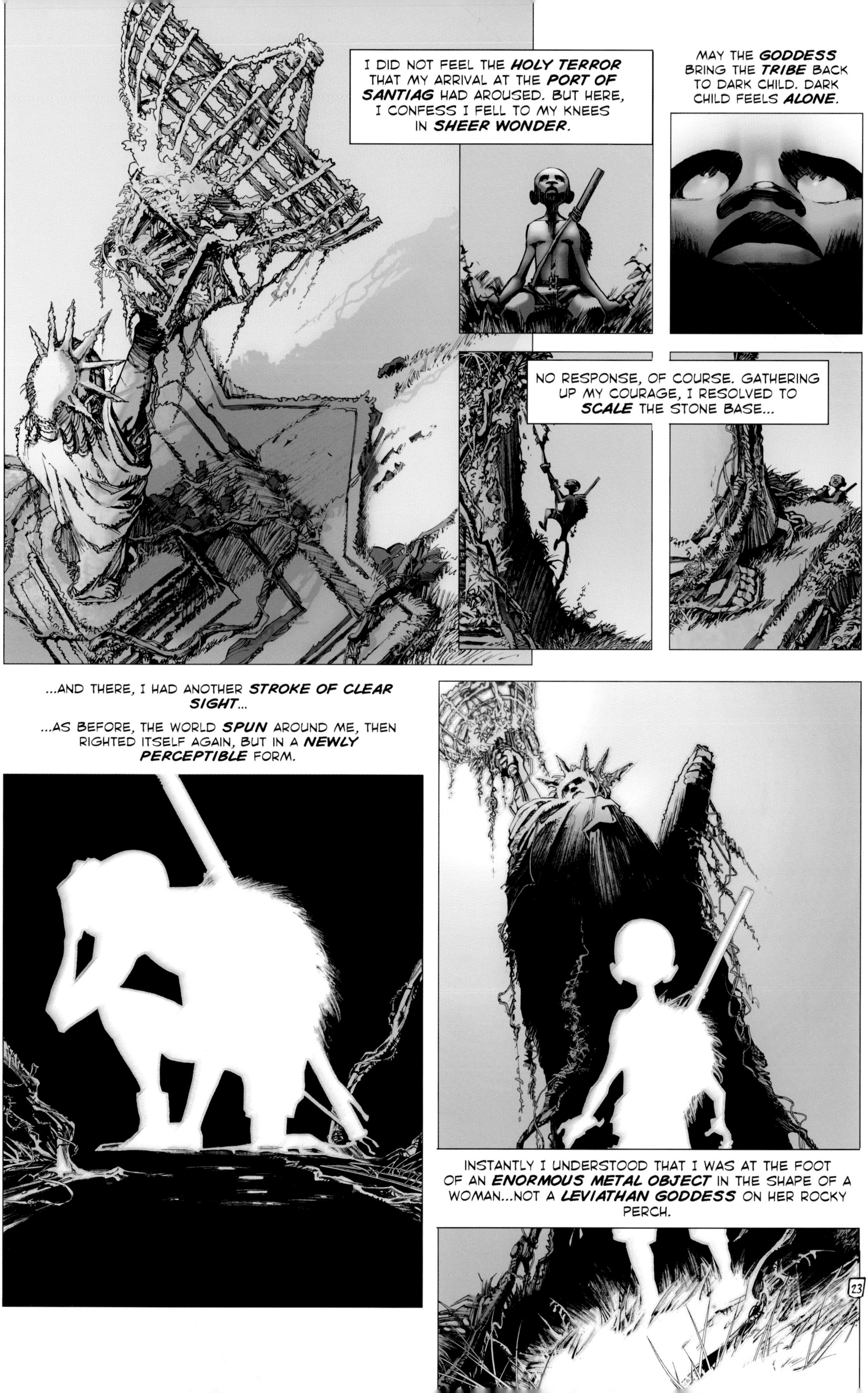
I DID NOT FEEL THE HOLY TERROR THAT MY ARRIVAL AT THE PORT OF SANTIAG HAD AROUSED. BUT HERE, I CONFESS I FELL TO MY KNEES IN SHEER WONDER.
MAY THE GODDESS BRING THE TRIBE BACK TO DARK CHILD. DARK CHILD FEELS ALONE.
NO RESPONSE, OF COURSE. GATHERING UP MY COURAGE, I RESOLVED TO SCALE THE STONE BASE...
...AND THERE, I HAD ANOTHER STROKE OF CLEAR SIGHT...
...AS BEFORE, THE WORLD SPUN AROUND ME, THEN RIGHTED ITSELF AGAIN, BUT IN A NEWLY PERCEPTIBLE FORM.
INSTANTLY I UNDERSTOOD THAT I WAS AT THE FOOT OF AN ENORMOUS METAL OBJECT IN THE SHAPE OF A WOMAN...NOT A LEVIATHAN GODDESS ON HER ROCKY PERCH.

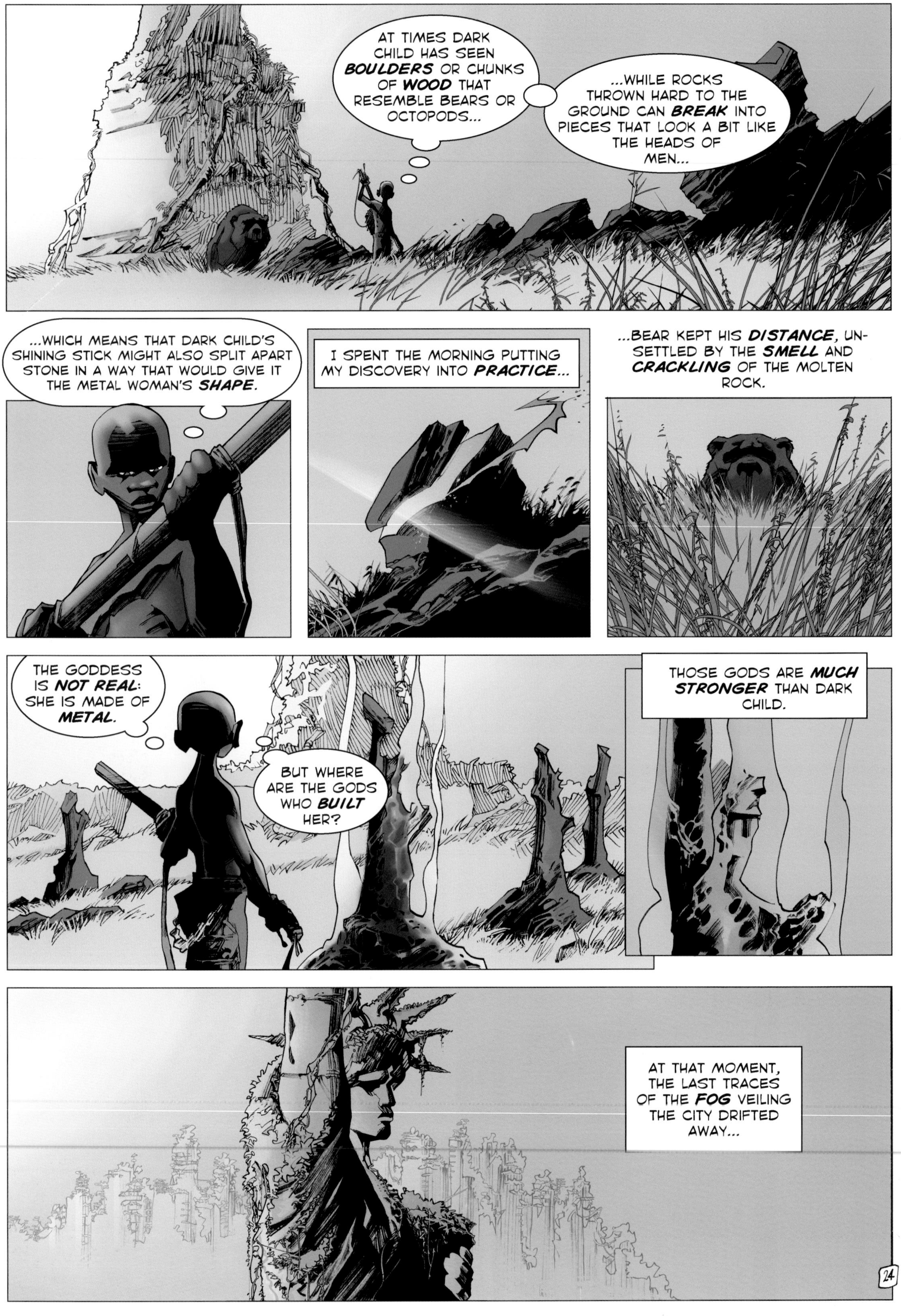
AT TIMES DARK CHILD HAS SEEN BOULDERS OR CHUNKS OF WOOD THAT RESEMBLE BEARS OR OCTOPODS...
...WHILE ROCKS THROWN HARD TO THE GROUND CAN BREAK INTO PIECES THAT LOOK A BIT LIKE THE HEADS OF MEN...
...WHICH MEANS THAT DARK CHILD'S SHINING STICK MIGHT ALSO SPLIT APART STONE IN A WAY THAT WOULD GIVE IT THE METAL WOMAN'S SHAPE.
I SPENT THE MORNING PUTTING MY DISCOVERY INTO PRACTICE...
...BEAR KEPT HIS DISTANCE, UN-SETTLED BY THE SMELL AND CRACKLING OF THE MOLTEN ROCK.
THE GODDESS IS NOT REAL: SHE IS MADE OF METAL.
BUT WHERE ARE THE GODS WHO BUILT HER?
THOSE GODS ARE MUCH STRONGER THAN DARK CHILD.
AT THAT MOMENT, THE LAST TRACES OF THE FOG VEILING THE CITY DRIFTED AWAY...

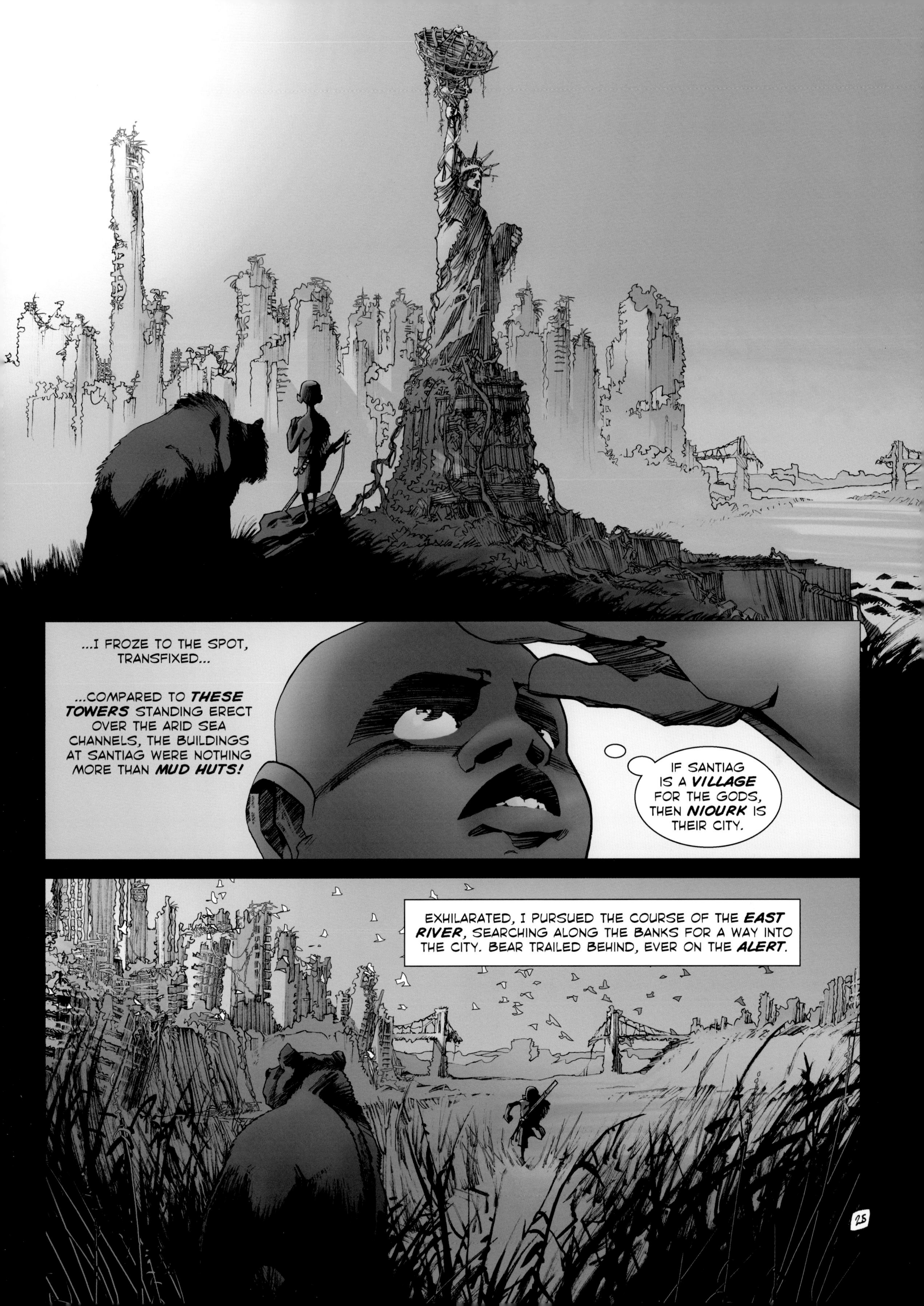
...I FROZE TO THE SPOT, TRANSFIXED...
...COMPARED TO THESE TOWERS STANDING ERECT OVER THE ARID SEA CHANNELS, THE BUILDINGS AT SANTIAG WERE NOTHING MORE THAN MUD HUTS!
IF SANTIAG IS A VILLAGE FOR THE GODS, THEN NIOURK IS THEIR CITY.
EXHILARATED, I PURSUED THE COURSE OF THE EAST RIVER, SEARCHING ALONG THE BANKS FOR A WAY INTO THE CITY. BEAR TRAILED BEHIND, EVER ON THE ALERT.

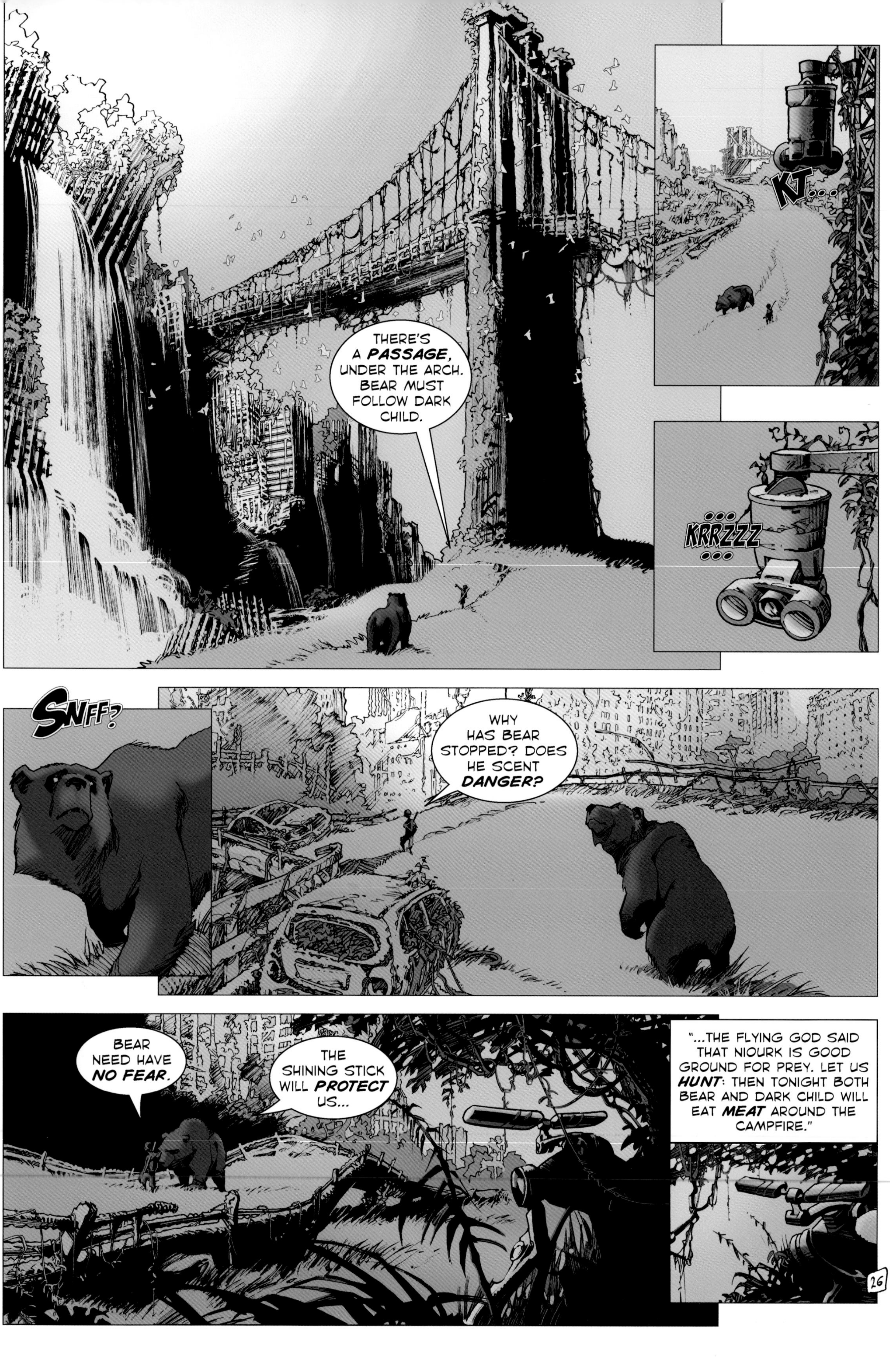
THERE'S A PASSAGE, UNDER THE ARCH. BEAR MUST FOLLOW DARK CHILD.
KT...
...KRRZZZ...
SNFF?
WHY HAS BEAR STOPPED? DOES HE SCENT DANGER?
BEAR NEED HAVE NO FEAR.
THE SHINING STICK WILL PROTECT US...
"...THE FLYING GOD SAID THAT NIOURK IS GOOD GROUND FOR PREY. LET US HUNT: THEN TONIGHT BOTH BEAR AND DARK CHILD WILL EAT MEAT AROUND THE CAMPFIRE."
26

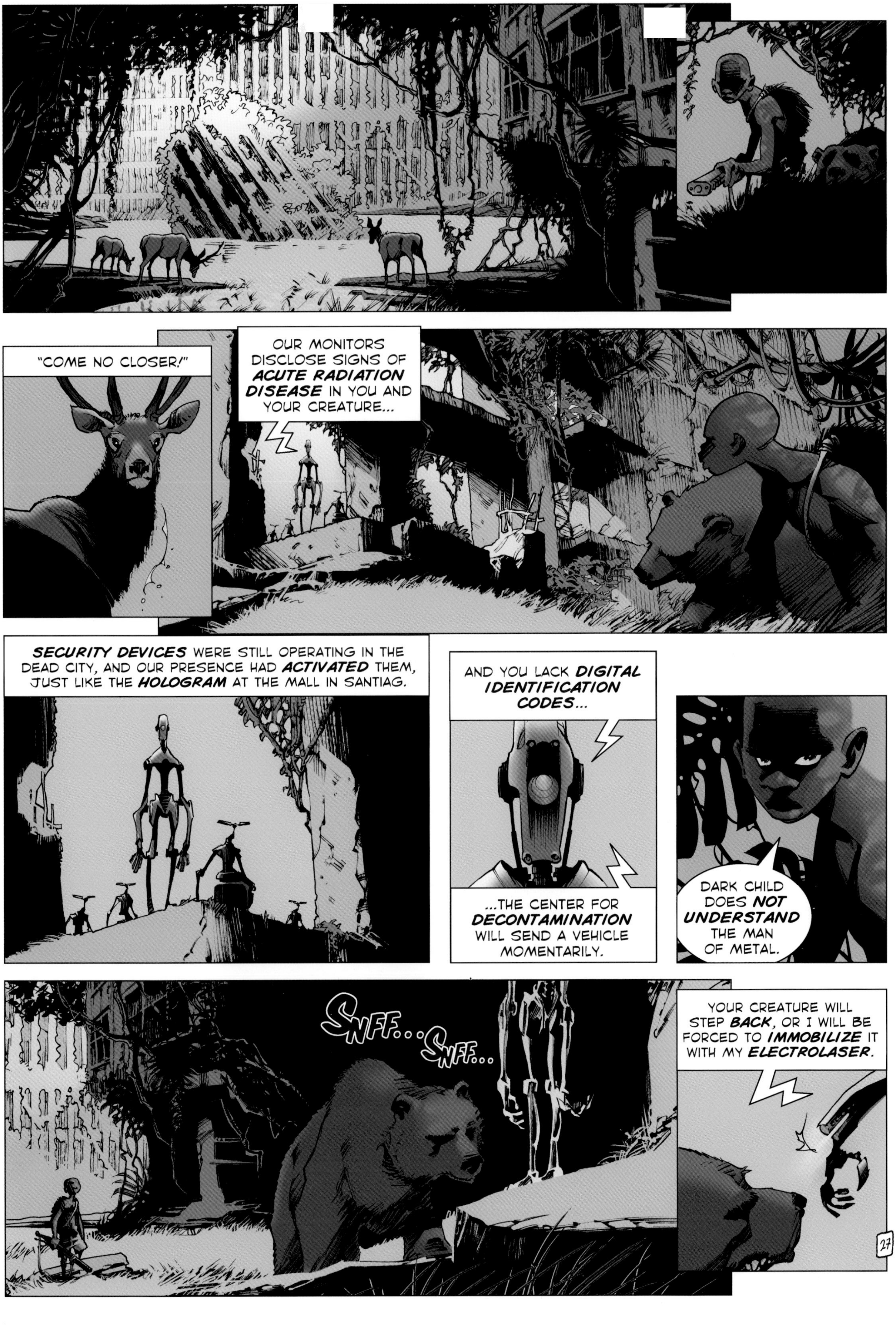
"COME NO CLOSER!"
OUR MONITORS DISCLOSE SIGNS OF ACUTE RADIATION DISEASE IN YOU AND YOUR CREATURE...
SECURITY DEVICES WERE STILL OPERATING IN THE DEAD CITY, AND OUR PRESENCE HAD ACTIVATED THEM, JUST LIKE THE HOLOGRAM AT THE MALL IN SANTIAG.
AND YOU LACK DIGITAL IDENTIFICATION CODES...
...THE CENTER FOR DECONTAMINATION WILL SEND A VEHICLE MOMENTARILY.
DARK CHILD DOES NOT UNDERSTAND THE MAN OF METAL.
SNFF... SNFF...
YOUR CREATURE WILL STEP BACK, OR I WILL BE FORCED TO IMMOBILIZE IT WITH MY ELECTROLASER.

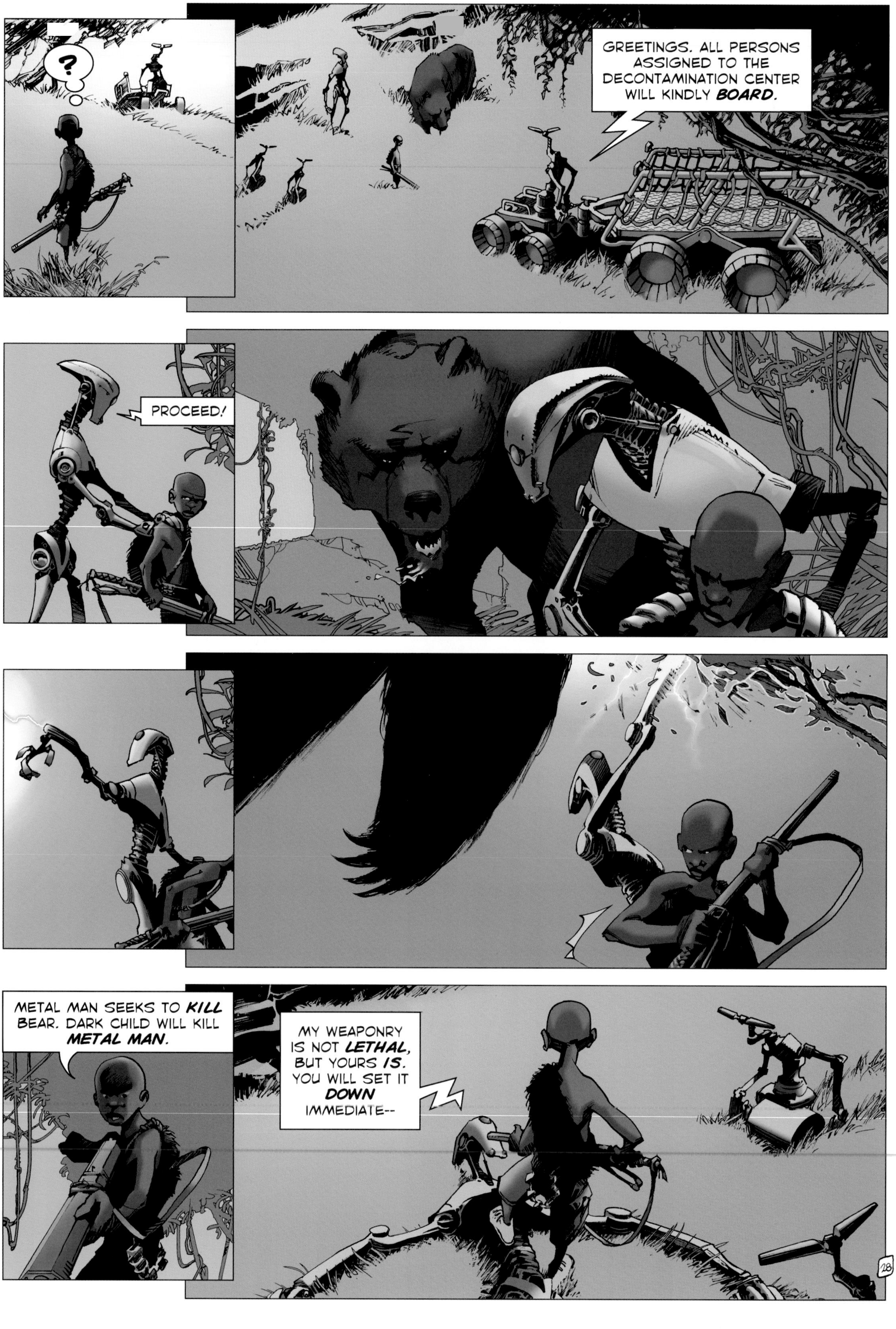

?
GREETINGS. ALL PERSONS ASSIGNED TO THE DECONTAMINATION CENTER WILL KINDLY **BOARD.**
PROCEED!
METAL MAN SEEKS TO **KILL** BEAR. DARK CHILD WILL KILL **METAL MAN.**
MY WEAPONRY IS NOT **LETHAL,** BUT YOURS **IS.** YOU WILL SET IT **DOWN** IMMEDIATE--

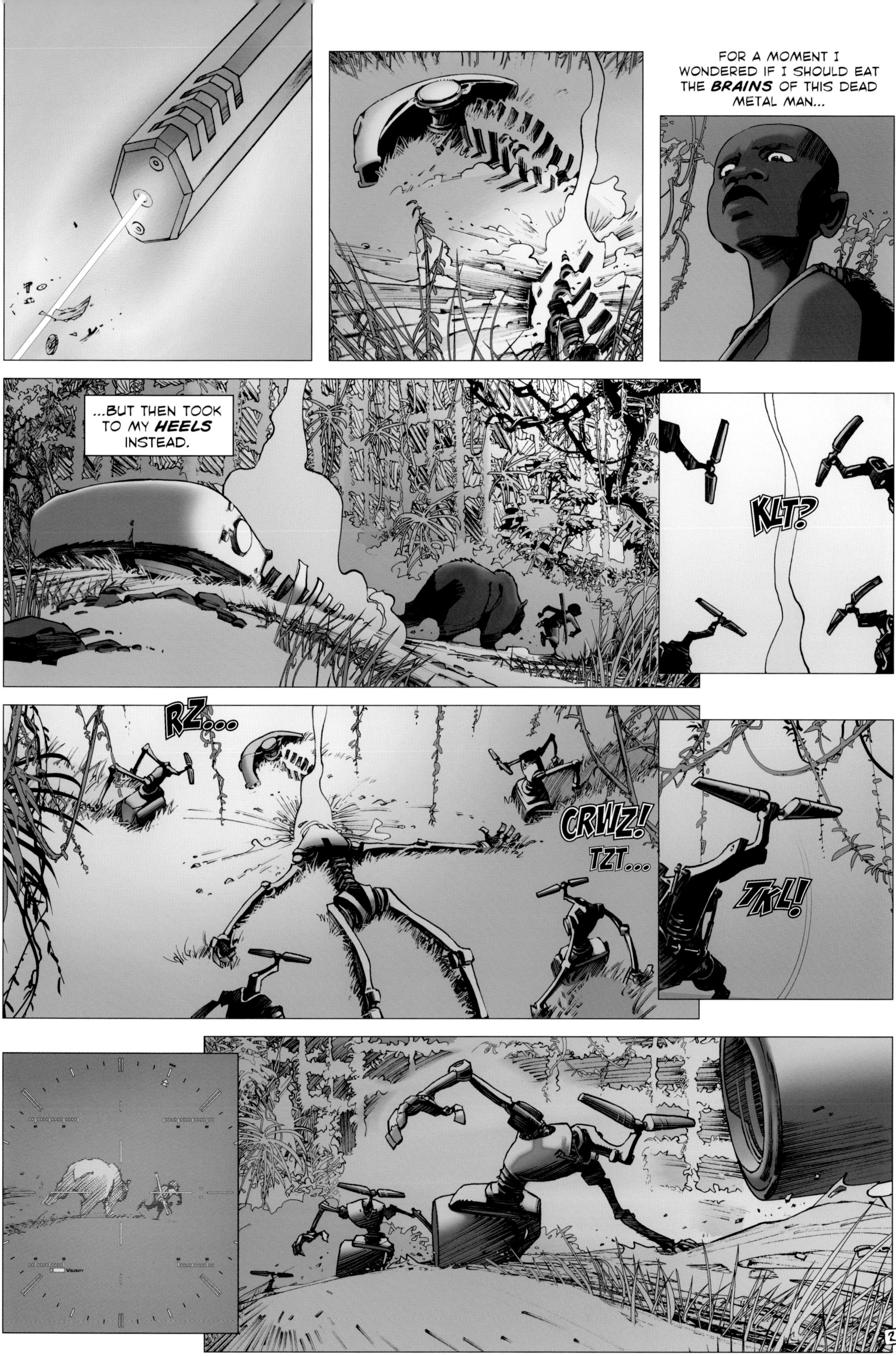
FOR A MOMENT I WONDERED IF I SHOULD EAT THE BRAINS OF THIS DEAD METAL MAN...
...BUT THEN TOOK TO MY HEELS INSTEAD.
KLT?
RZ...
CRWZ!
TZT...
TKL!

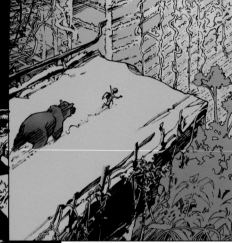

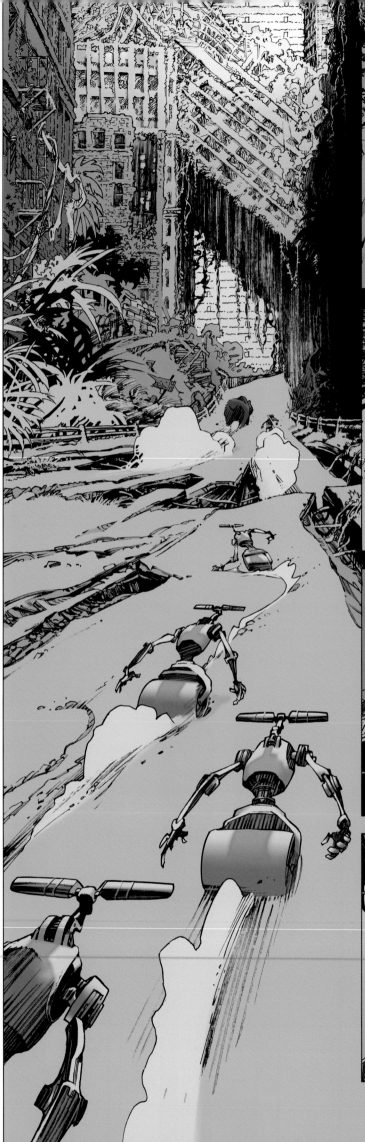

30

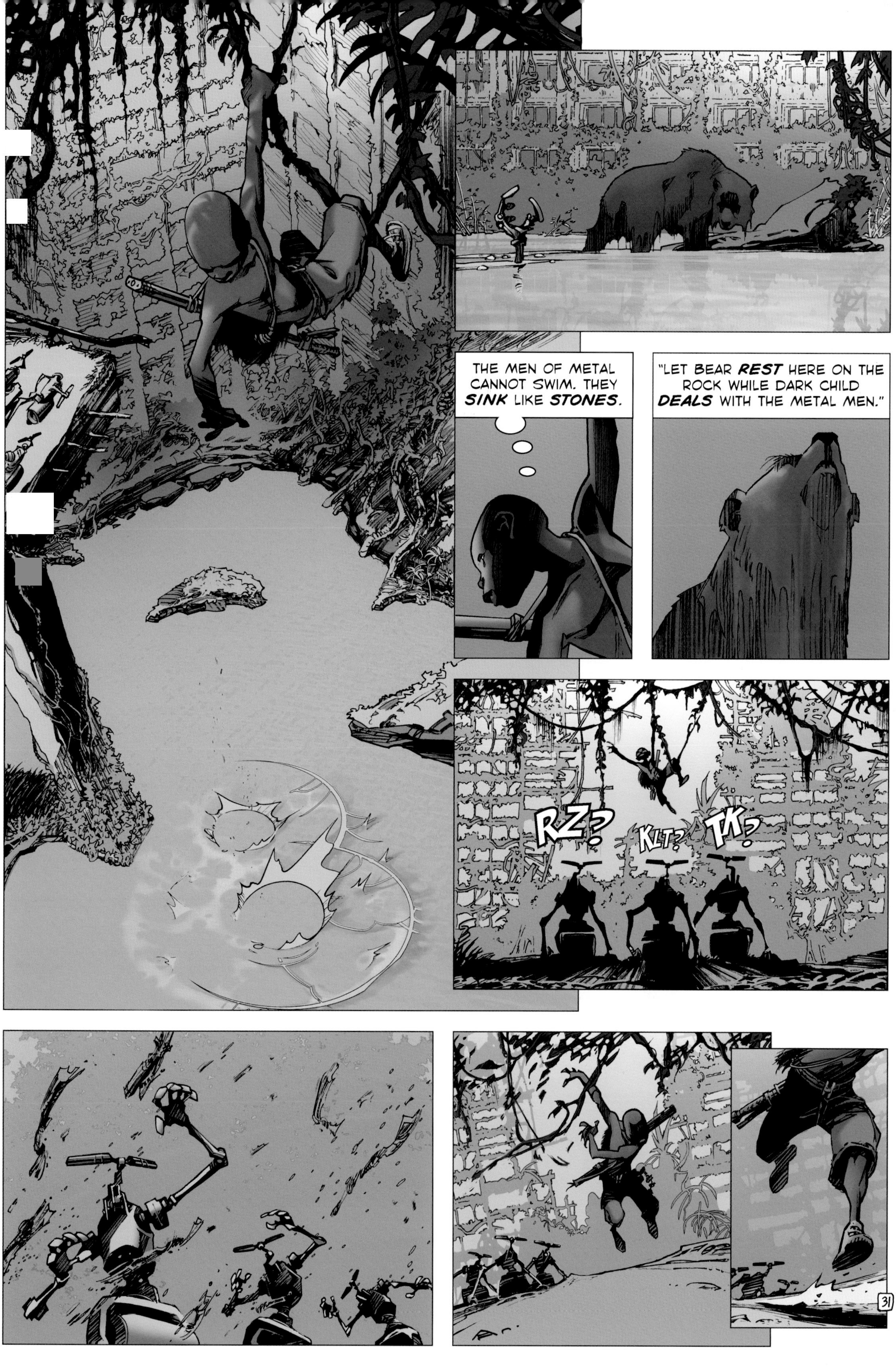
THE MEN OF METAL CANNOT SWIM. THEY SINK LIKE STONES.
"LET BEAR REST HERE ON THE ROCK WHILE DARK CHILD DEALS WITH THE METAL MEN."
RZ?
KLT?
TK?

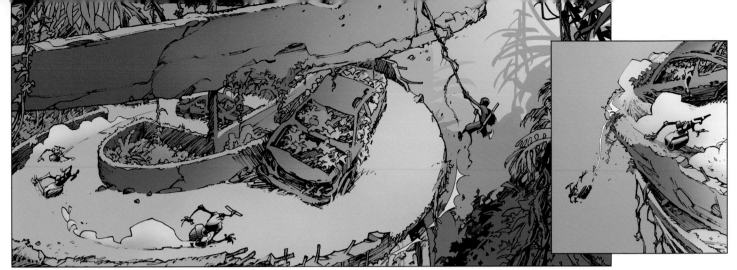

FORTUNATELY FOR ME, *THESE ROBOTS* HAD BEEN DESIGNED TO FUNCTION IN A *STERILE URBAN ENVIRONMENT*...

...AND DEFINITELY NOT IN THIS *RUBBLE* WHERE *NATURE* HAD RECLAIMED HER HOLD. HERE THE TERRAIN LEFT THEM AT SOME *DISADVANTAGE*.

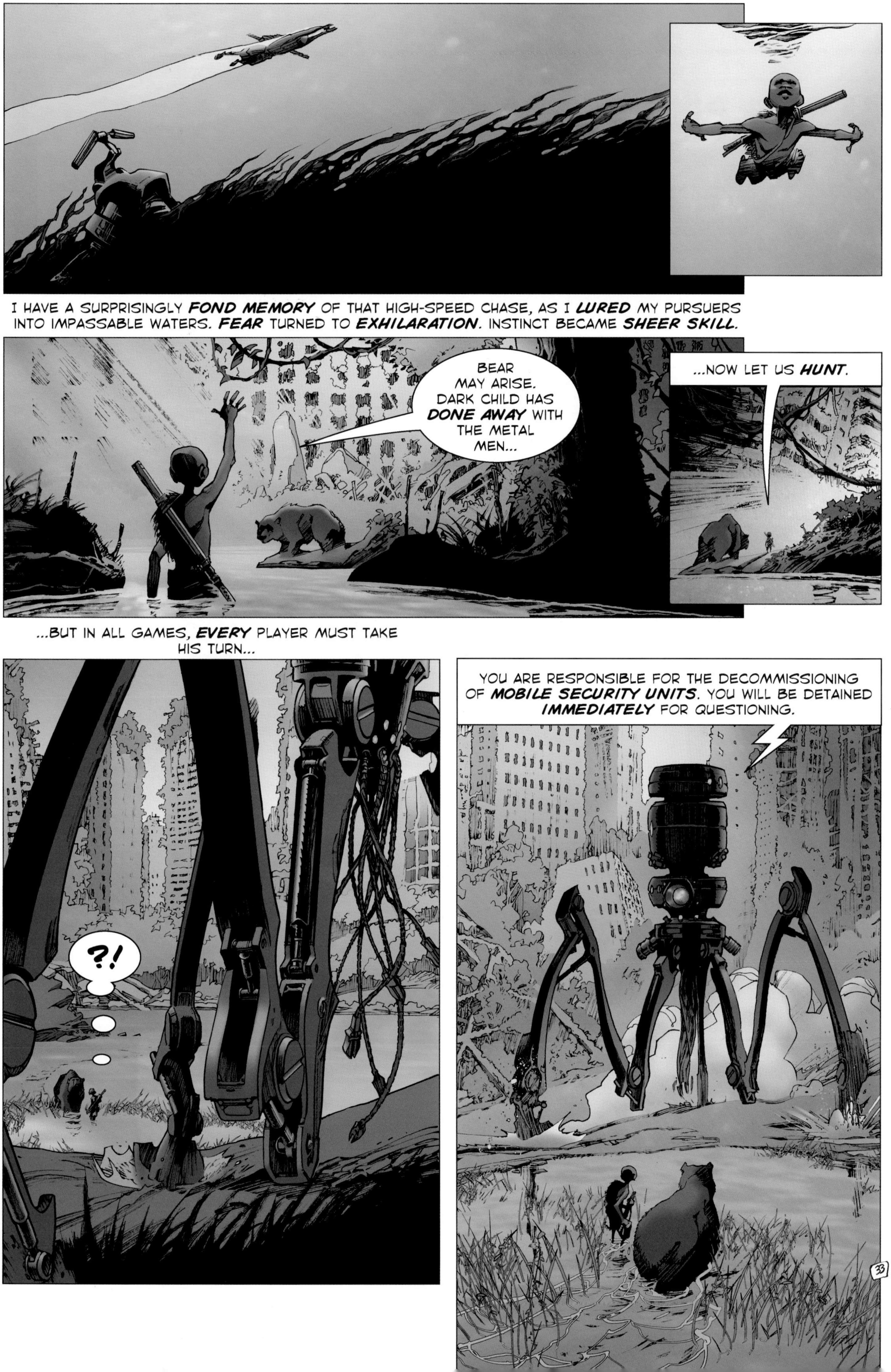

I HAVE A SURPRISINGLY FOND MEMORY OF THAT HIGH-SPEED CHASE, AS I LURED MY PURSUERS INTO IMPASSABLE WATERS. FEAR TURNED TO EXHILARATION. INSTINCT BECAME SHEER SKILL.
BEAR MAY ARISE. DARK CHILD HAS DONE AWAY WITH THE METAL MEN...
...NOW LET US HUNT.
...BUT IN ALL GAMES, EVERY PLAYER MUST TAKE HIS TURN...
?!
YOU ARE RESPONSIBLE FOR THE DECOMMISSIONING OF MOBILE SECURITY UNITS. YOU WILL BE DETAINED IMMEDIATELY FOR QUESTIONING.

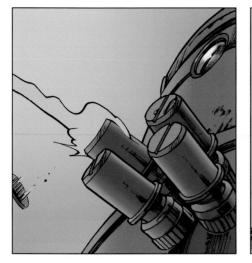

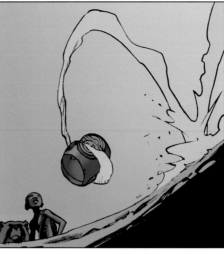

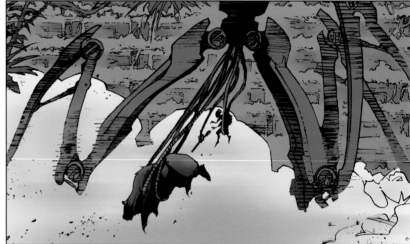

BEAR AND I WERE **FORCIBLY DRAGGED** TO THE DECONTAMINATION CENTER...

...WHERE, AFTER A BATTERY OF **TESTS**, WE WERE HANDED OVER TO A TEAM OF ROBOTS DIRECTING **HEALTHCARE PROTOCOLS**...

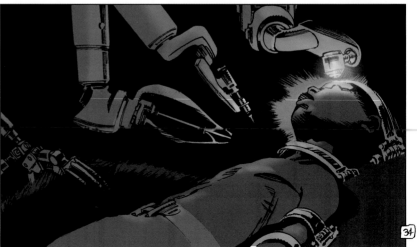

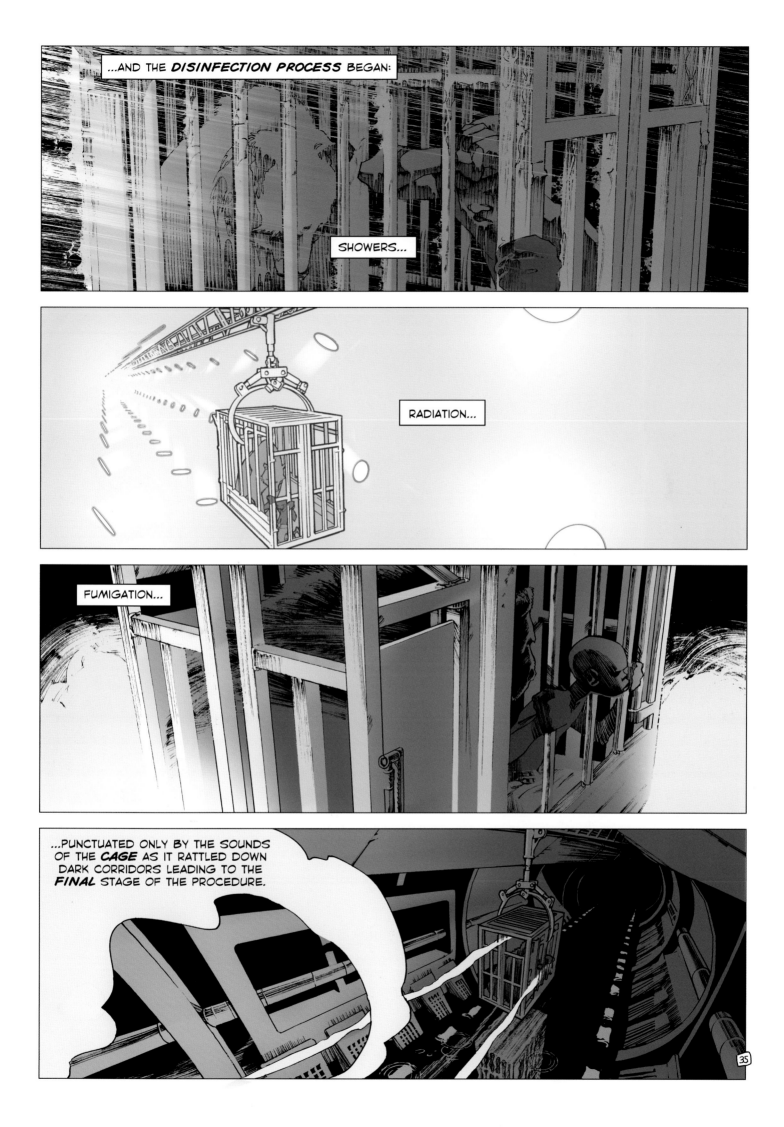

...AND THE *DISINFECTION PROCESS* BEGAN:

SHOWERS...

RADIATION...

FUMIGATION...

...PUNCTUATED ONLY BY THE SOUNDS OF THE *CAGE* AS IT RATTLED DOWN DARK CORRIDORS LEADING TO THE *FINAL* STAGE OF THE PROCEDURE.

35

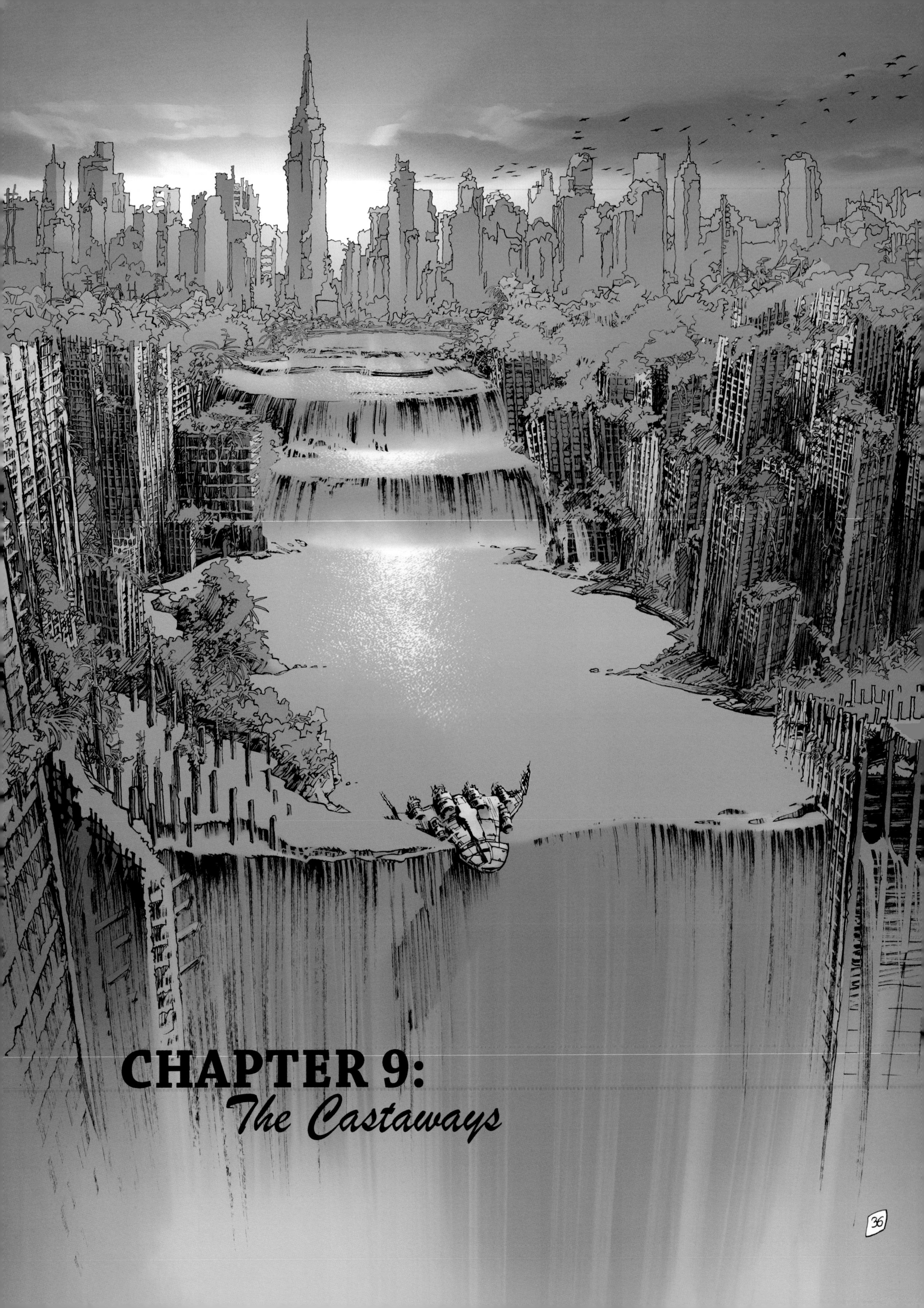

CHAPTER 9:
The Castaways

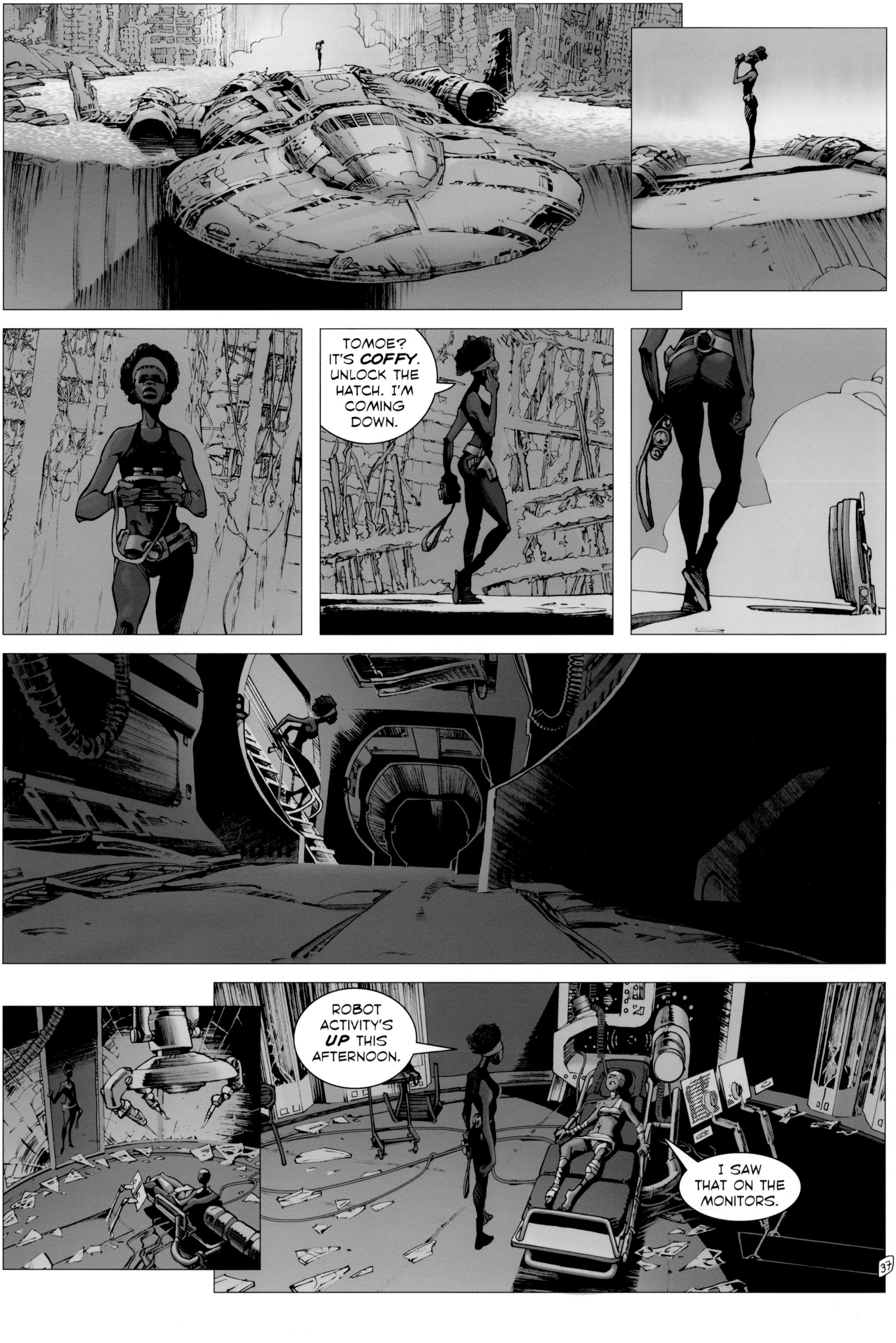
TOMOE? IT'S COFFY. UNLOCK THE HATCH. I'M COMING DOWN.
ROBOT ACTIVITY'S UP THIS AFTERNOON.
I SAW THAT ON THE MONITORS.
37

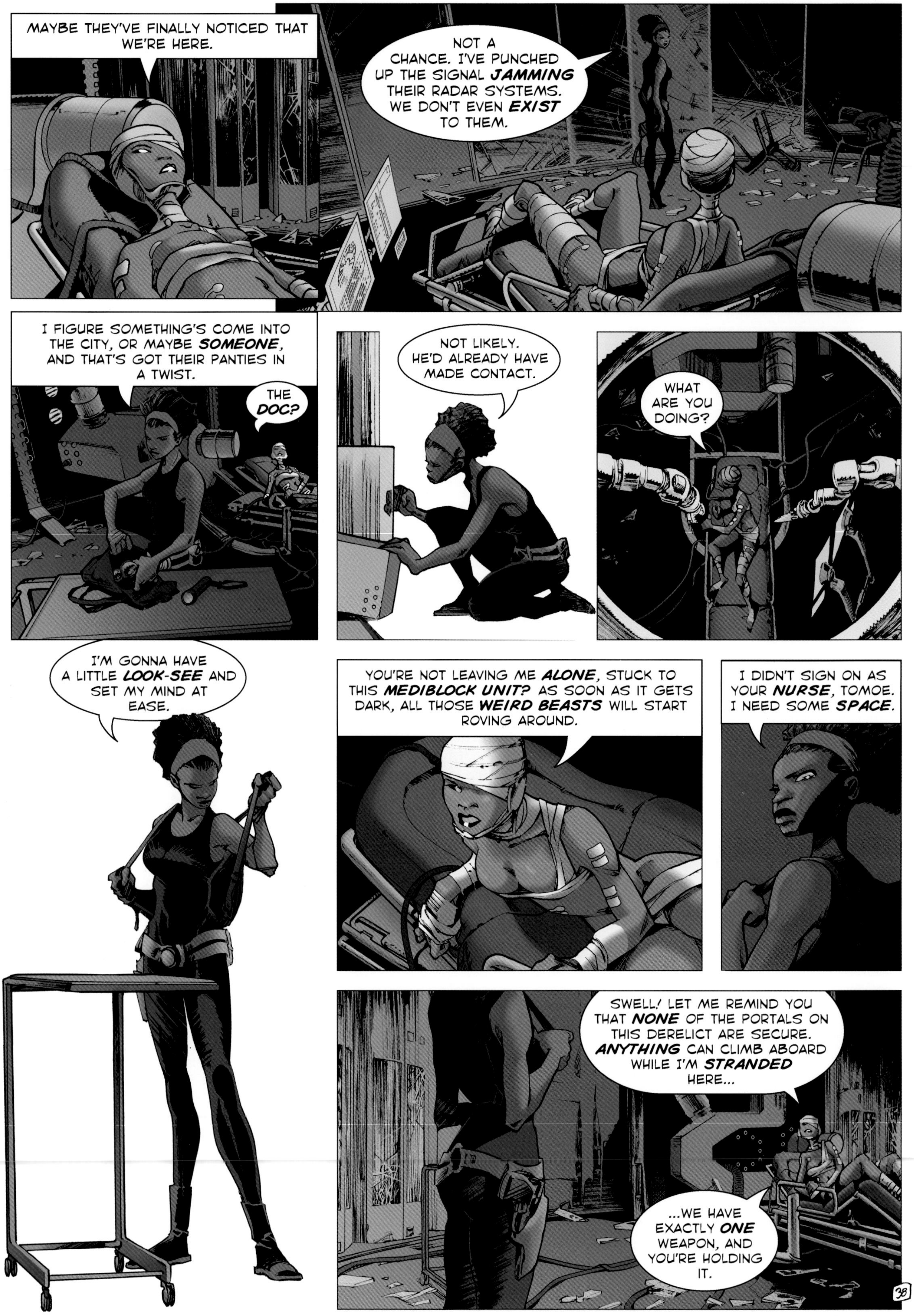
MAYBE THEY'VE FINALLY NOTICED THAT WE'RE HERE.
NOT A CHANCE. I'VE PUNCHED UP THE SIGNAL JAMMING THEIR RADAR SYSTEMS. WE DON'T EVEN EXIST TO THEM.
I FIGURE SOMETHING'S COME INTO THE CITY, OR MAYBE SOMEONE, AND THAT'S GOT THEIR PANTIES IN A TWIST.
THE DOC?
NOT LIKELY. HE'D ALREADY HAVE MADE CONTACT.
WHAT ARE YOU DOING?
I'M GONNA HAVE A LITTLE LOOK-SEE AND SET MY MIND AT EASE.
YOU'RE NOT LEAVING ME ALONE, STUCK TO THIS MEDIBLOCK UNIT? AS SOON AS IT GETS DARK, ALL THOSE WEIRD BEASTS WILL START ROVING AROUND.
I DIDN'T SIGN ON AS YOUR NURSE, TOMOE. I NEED SOME SPACE.
SWELL! LET ME REMIND YOU THAT NONE OF THE PORTALS ON THIS DERELICT ARE SECURE. ANYTHING CAN CLIMB ABOARD WHILE I'M STRANDED HERE...
...WE HAVE EXACTLY ONE WEAPON, AND YOU'RE HOLDING IT.

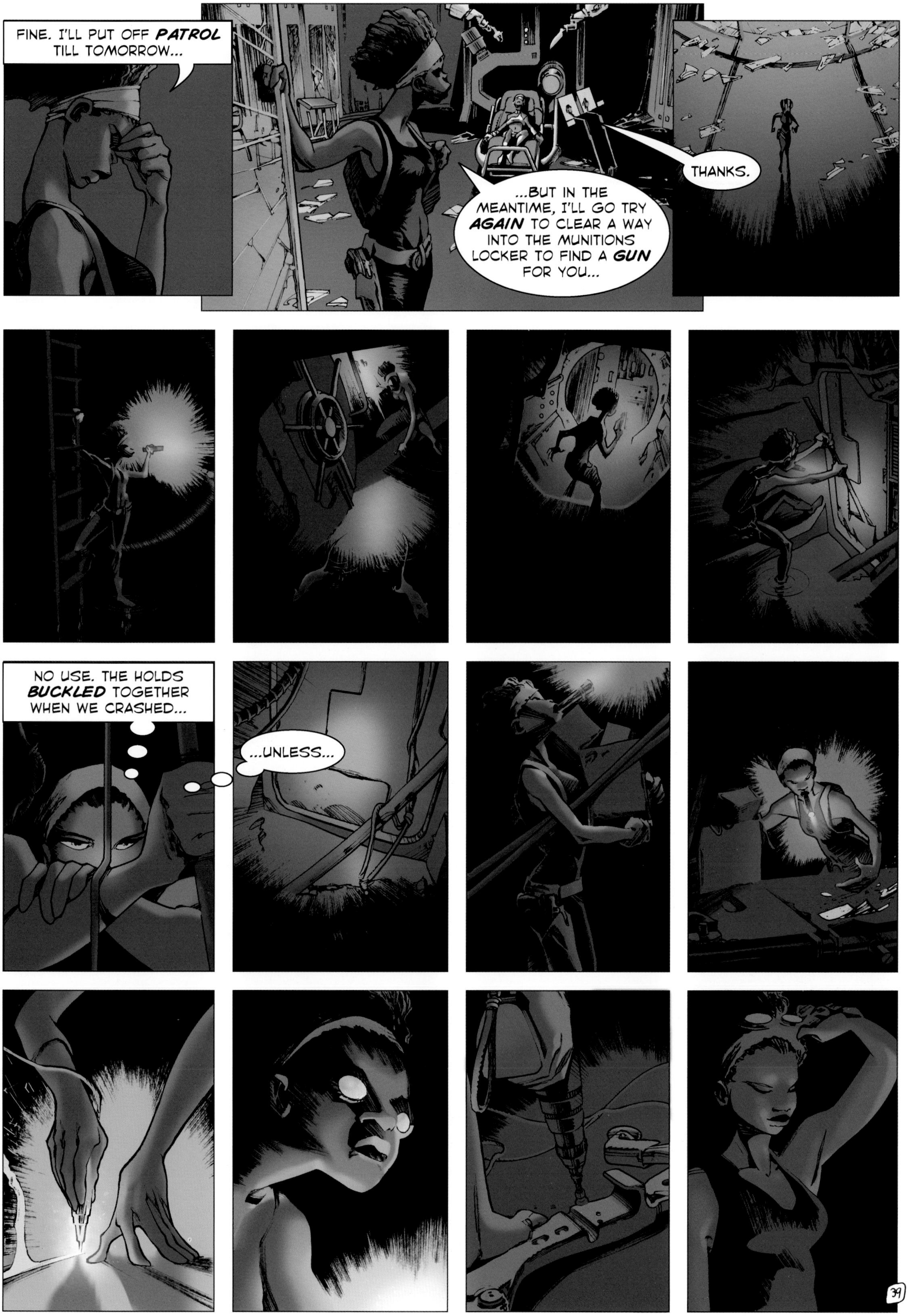
FINE. I'LL PUT OFF PATROL TILL TOMORROW...
...BUT IN THE MEANTIME, I'LL GO TRY AGAIN TO CLEAR A WAY INTO THE MUNITIONS LOCKER TO FIND A GUN FOR YOU...
THANKS.
NO USE. THE HOLDS BUCKLED TOGETHER WHEN WE CRASHED...
...UNLESS...

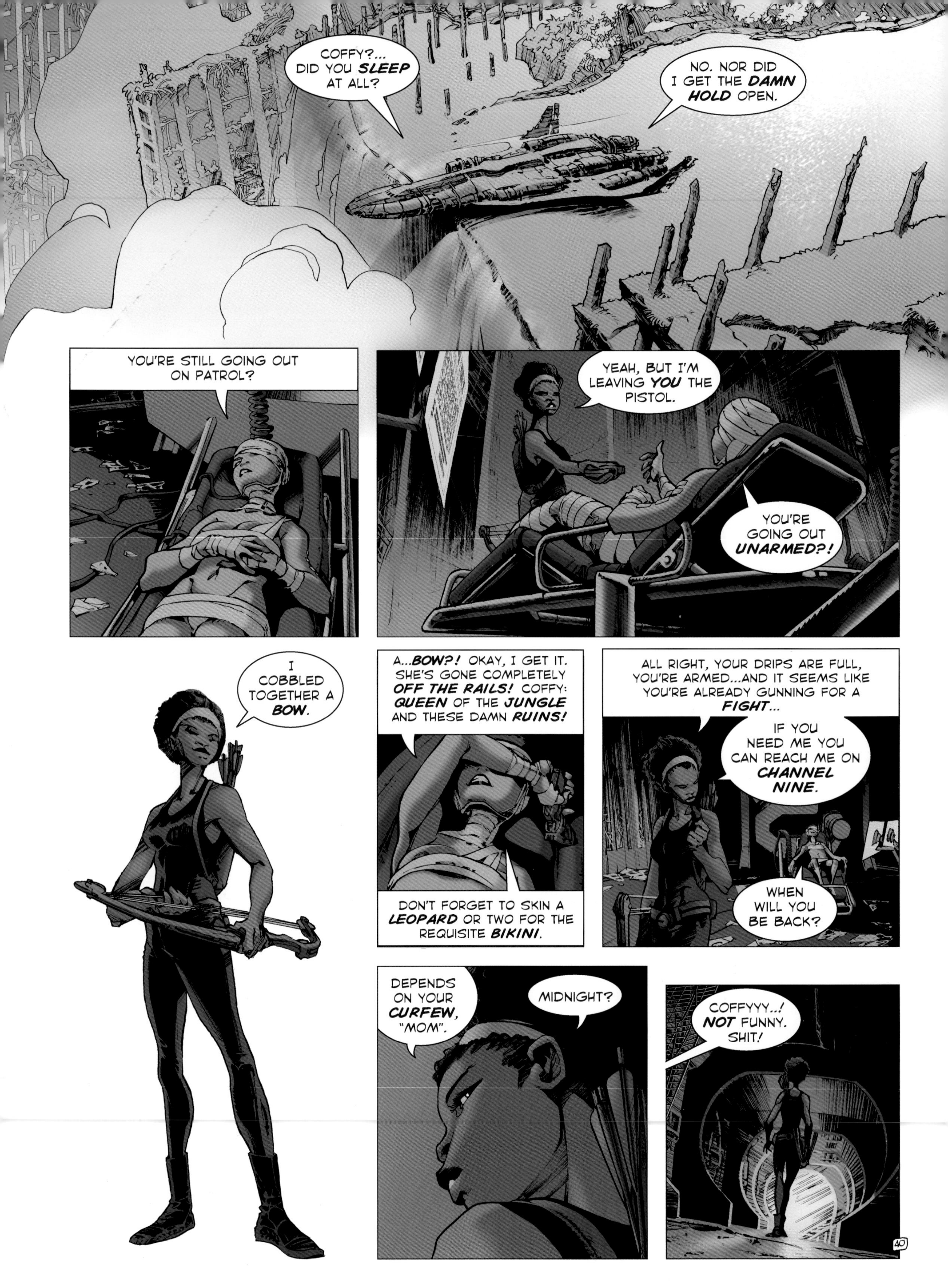

COFFY?... DID YOU SLEEP AT ALL?
NO. NOR DID I GET THE DAMN HOLD OPEN.
YOU'RE STILL GOING OUT ON PATROL?
YEAH, BUT I'M LEAVING YOU THE PISTOL.
YOU'RE GOING OUT UNARMED?!
I COBBLED TOGETHER A BOW.
A...BOW?! OKAY, I GET IT. SHE'S GONE COMPLETELY OFF THE RAILS! COFFY: QUEEN OF THE JUNGLE AND THESE DAMN RUINS!
DON'T FORGET TO SKIN A LEOPARD OR TWO FOR THE REQUISITE BIKINI.
ALL RIGHT, YOUR DRIPS ARE FULL, YOU'RE ARMED...AND IT SEEMS LIKE YOU'RE ALREADY GUNNING FOR A FIGHT...
IF YOU NEED ME YOU CAN REACH ME ON CHANNEL NINE.
WHEN WILL YOU BE BACK?
DEPENDS ON YOUR CURFEW, "MOM".
MIDNIGHT?
COFFYYY...! NOT FUNNY. SHIT!

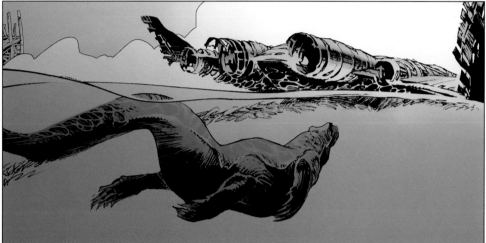

COFFY?
DO YOU READ
ME?

WHAT **NOW**,
TOMOE?

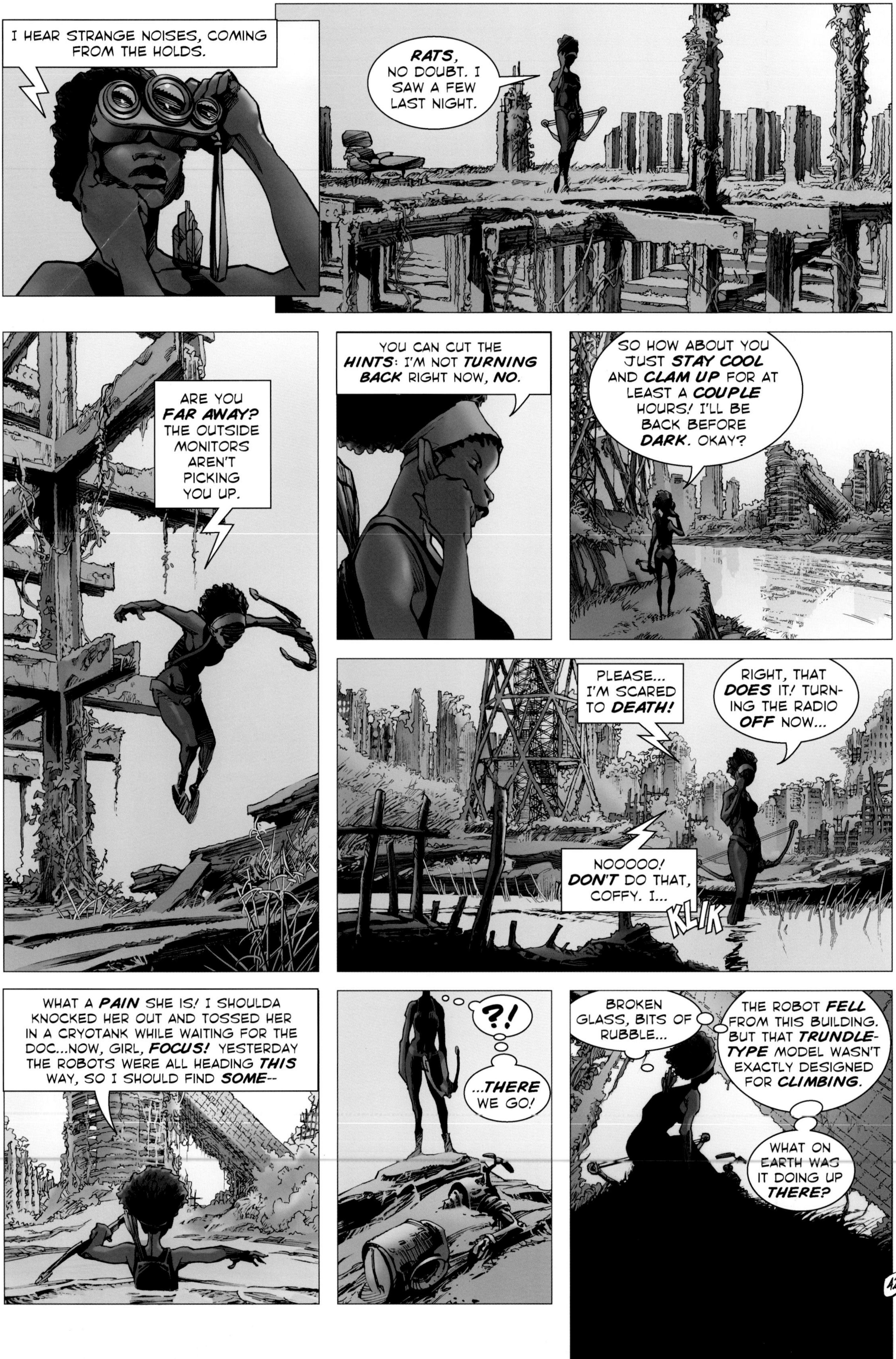

I HEAR STRANGE NOISES, COMING FROM THE HOLDS.
RATS, NO DOUBT. I SAW A FEW LAST NIGHT.
ARE YOU FAR AWAY? THE OUTSIDE MONITORS AREN'T PICKING YOU UP.
YOU CAN CUT THE HINTS: I'M NOT TURNING BACK RIGHT NOW, NO.
SO HOW ABOUT YOU JUST STAY COOL AND CLAM UP FOR AT LEAST A COUPLE HOURS! I'LL BE BACK BEFORE DARK. OKAY?
PLEASE... I'M SCARED TO DEATH!
RIGHT, THAT DOES IT! TURNING THE RADIO OFF NOW...
NOOOOO! DON'T DO THAT, COFFY. I...
KLIK
WHAT A PAIN SHE IS! I SHOULDA KNOCKED HER OUT AND TOSSED HER IN A CRYOTANK WHILE WAITING FOR THE DOC...NOW, GIRL, FOCUS! YESTERDAY THE ROBOTS WERE ALL HEADING THIS WAY, SO I SHOULD FIND SOME--
?!
...THERE WE GO!
BROKEN GLASS, BITS OF RUBBLE...
THE ROBOT FELL FROM THIS BUILDING. BUT THAT TRUNDLE-TYPE MODEL WASN'T EXACTLY DESIGNED FOR CLIMBING.
WHAT ON EARTH WAS IT DOING UP THERE?

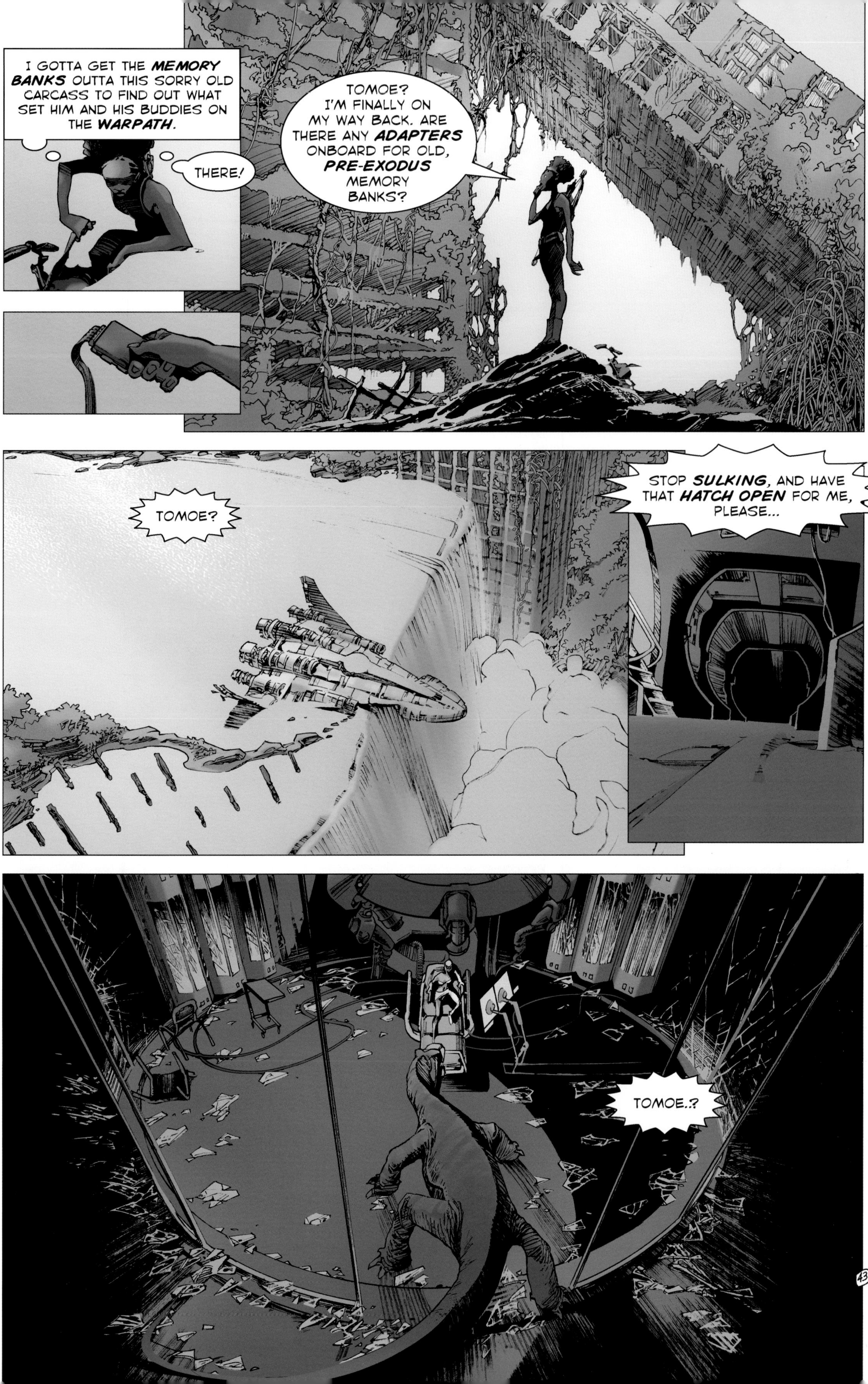
I GOTTA GET THE MEMORY BANKS OUTTA THIS SORRY OLD CARCASS TO FIND OUT WHAT SET HIM AND HIS BUDDIES ON THE WARPATH.
THERE!
TOMOE? I'M FINALLY ON MY WAY BACK. ARE THERE ANY ADAPTERS ONBOARD FOR OLD, PRE-EXODUS MEMORY BANKS?
TOMOE?
STOP SULKING, AND HAVE THAT HATCH OPEN FOR ME, PLEASE...
TOMOE..?

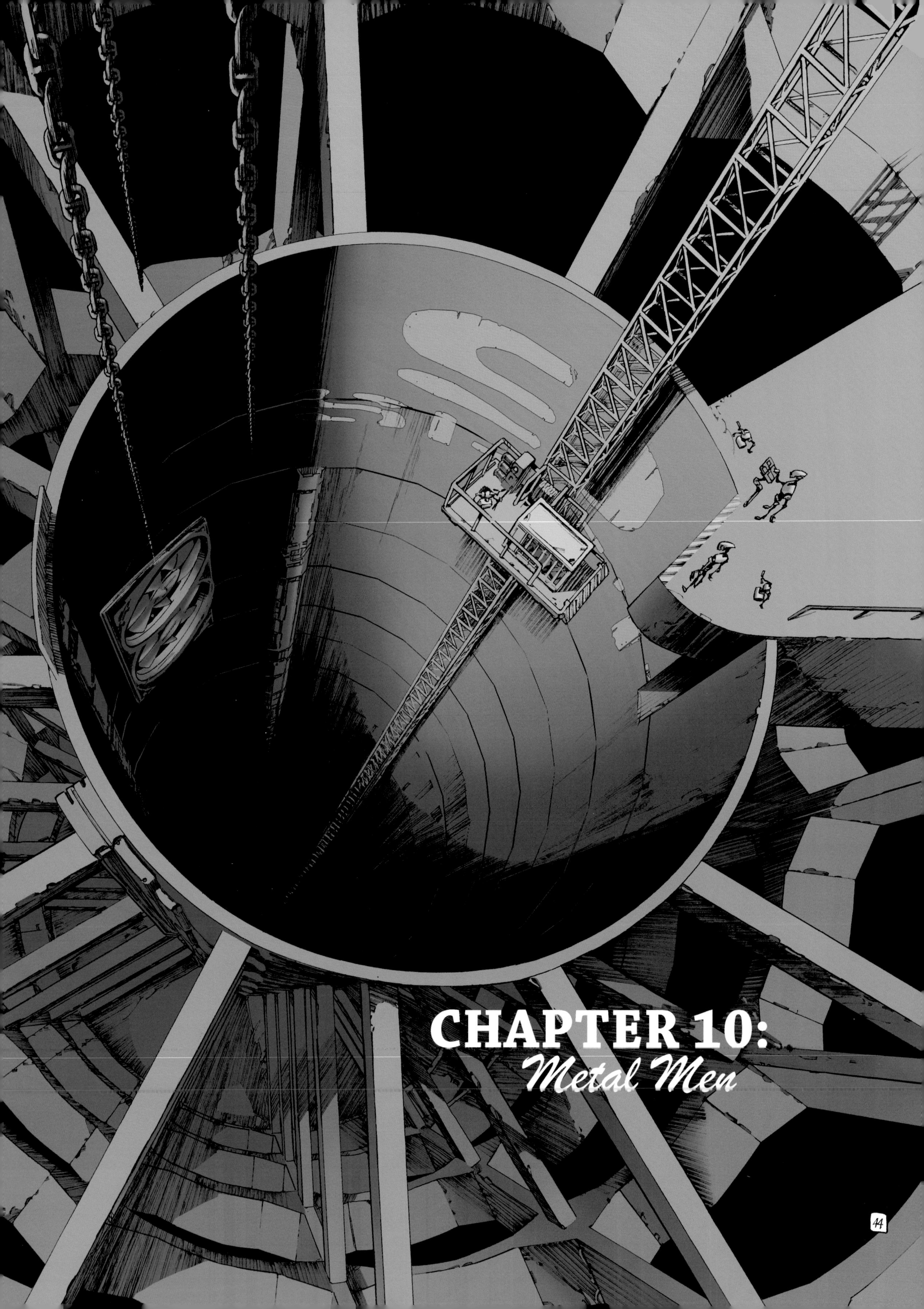
CHAPTER 10:
Metal Men

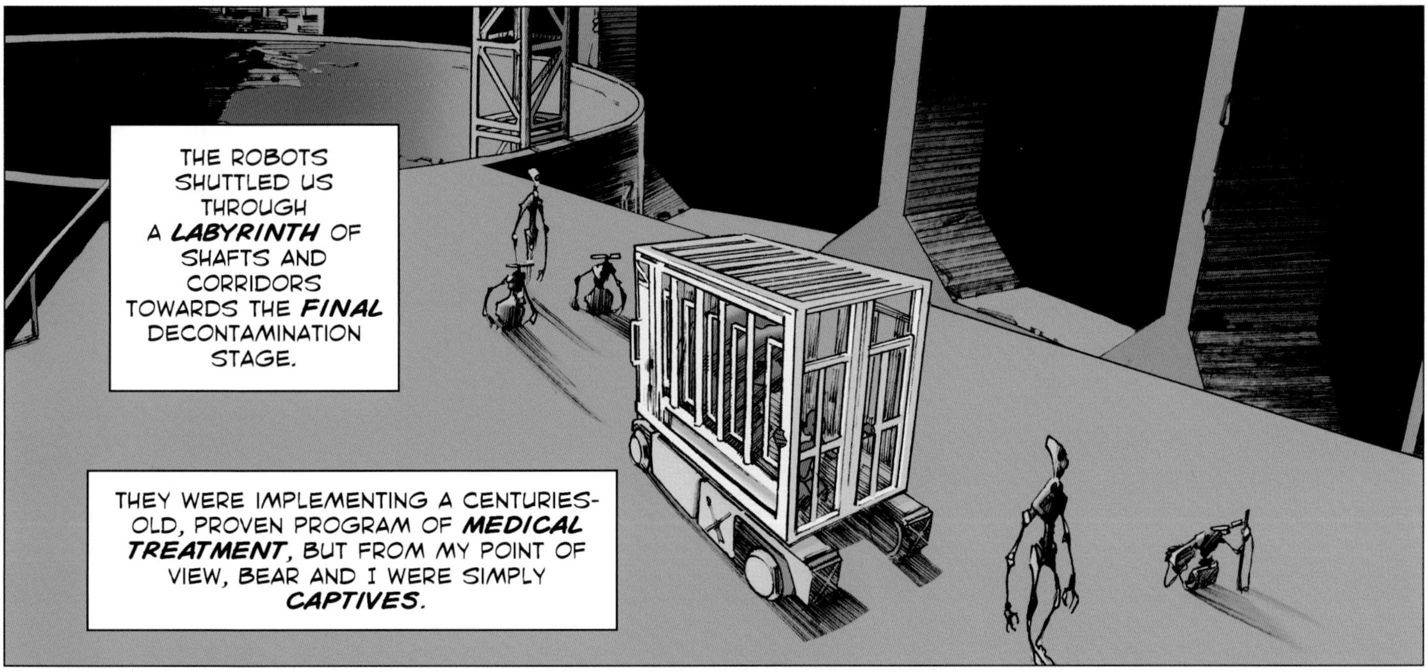
THE ROBOTS SHUTTLED US THROUGH A LABYRINTH OF SHAFTS AND CORRIDORS TOWARDS THE FINAL DECONTAMINATION STAGE.
THEY WERE IMPLEMENTING A CENTURIES-OLD, PROVEN PROGRAM OF MEDICAL TREATMENT, BUT FROM MY POINT OF VIEW, BEAR AND I WERE SIMPLY CAPTIVES.
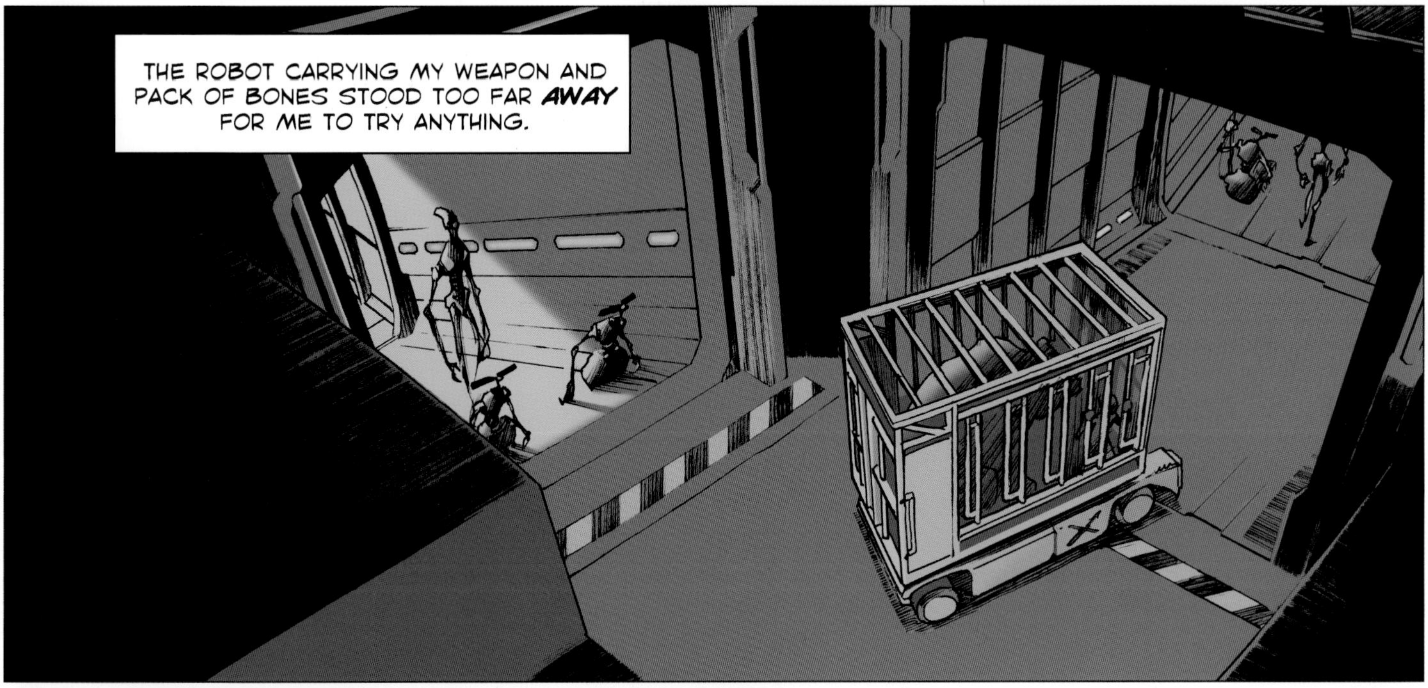
THE ROBOT CARRYING MY WEAPON AND PACK OF BONES STOOD TOO FAR AWAY FOR ME TO TRY ANYTHING.
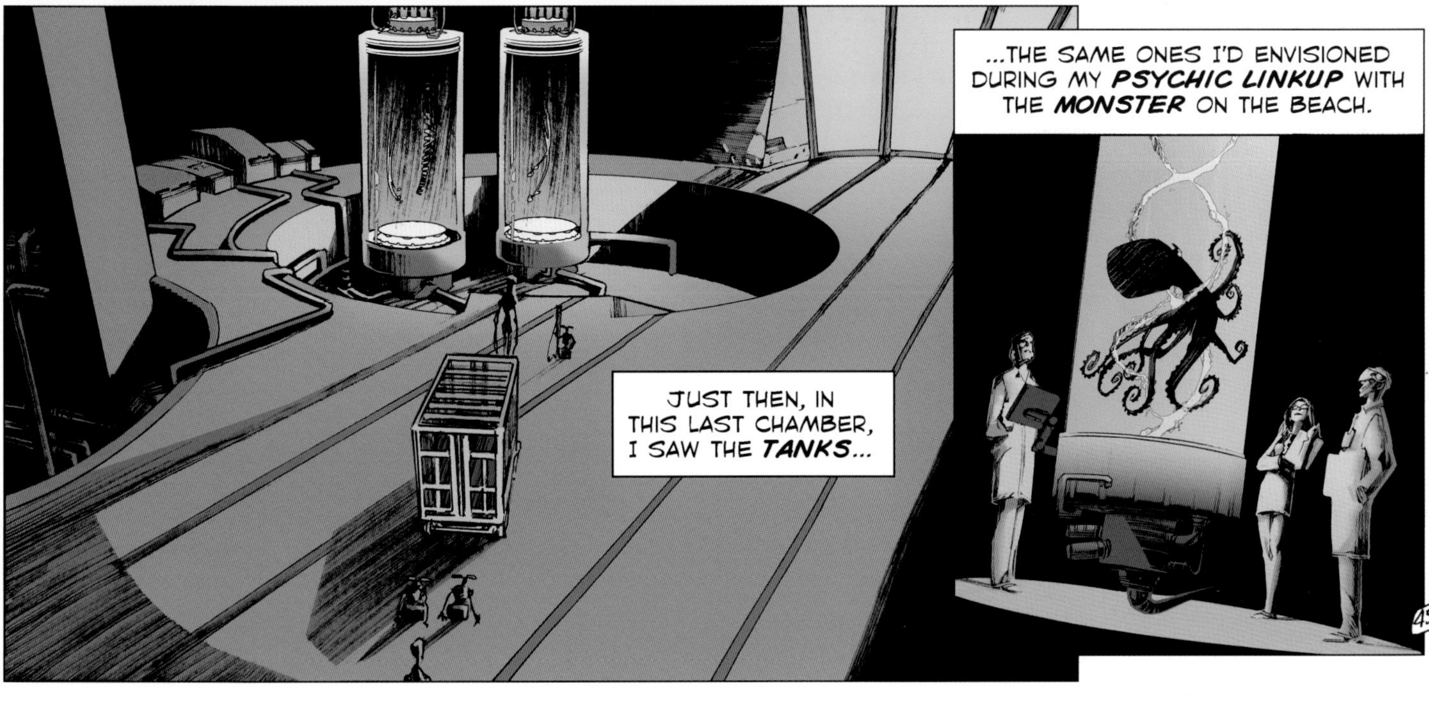
JUST THEN, IN THIS LAST CHAMBER, I SAW THE TANKS...
...THE SAME ONES I'D ENVISIONED DURING MY PSYCHIC LINKUP WITH THE MONSTER ON THE BEACH.

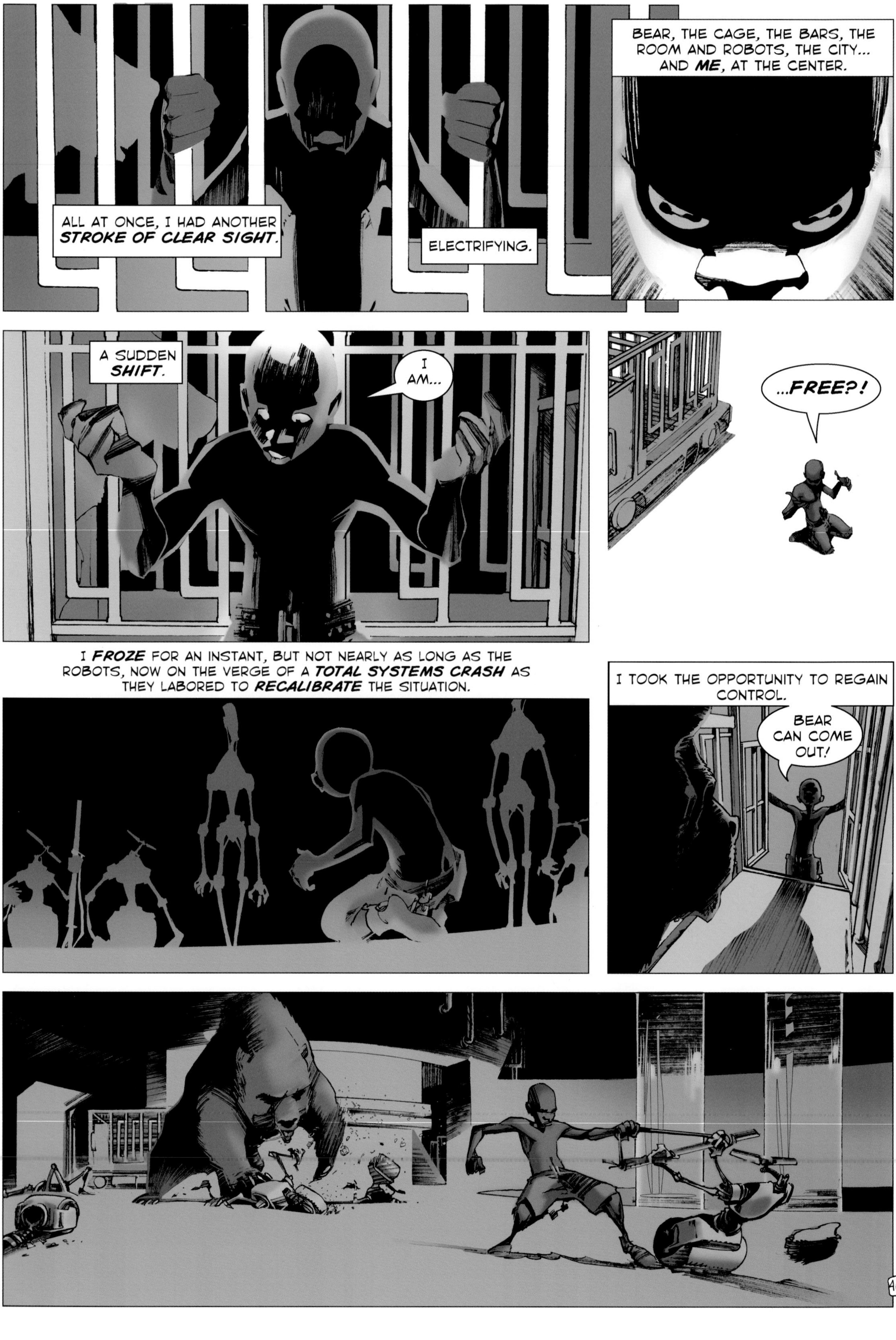
ALL AT ONCE, I HAD ANOTHER *STROKE OF CLEAR SIGHT*.
ELECTRIFYING.
BEAR, THE CAGE, THE BARS, THE ROOM AND ROBOTS, THE CITY... AND *ME*, AT THE CENTER.
A SUDDEN *SHIFT*.
I AM...
...*FREE?!*
I *FROZE* FOR AN INSTANT, BUT NOT NEARLY AS LONG AS THE ROBOTS, NOW ON THE VERGE OF A *TOTAL SYSTEMS CRASH* AS THEY LABORED TO *RECALIBRATE* THE SITUATION.
I TOOK THE OPPORTUNITY TO REGAIN CONTROL.
BEAR CAN COME OUT!

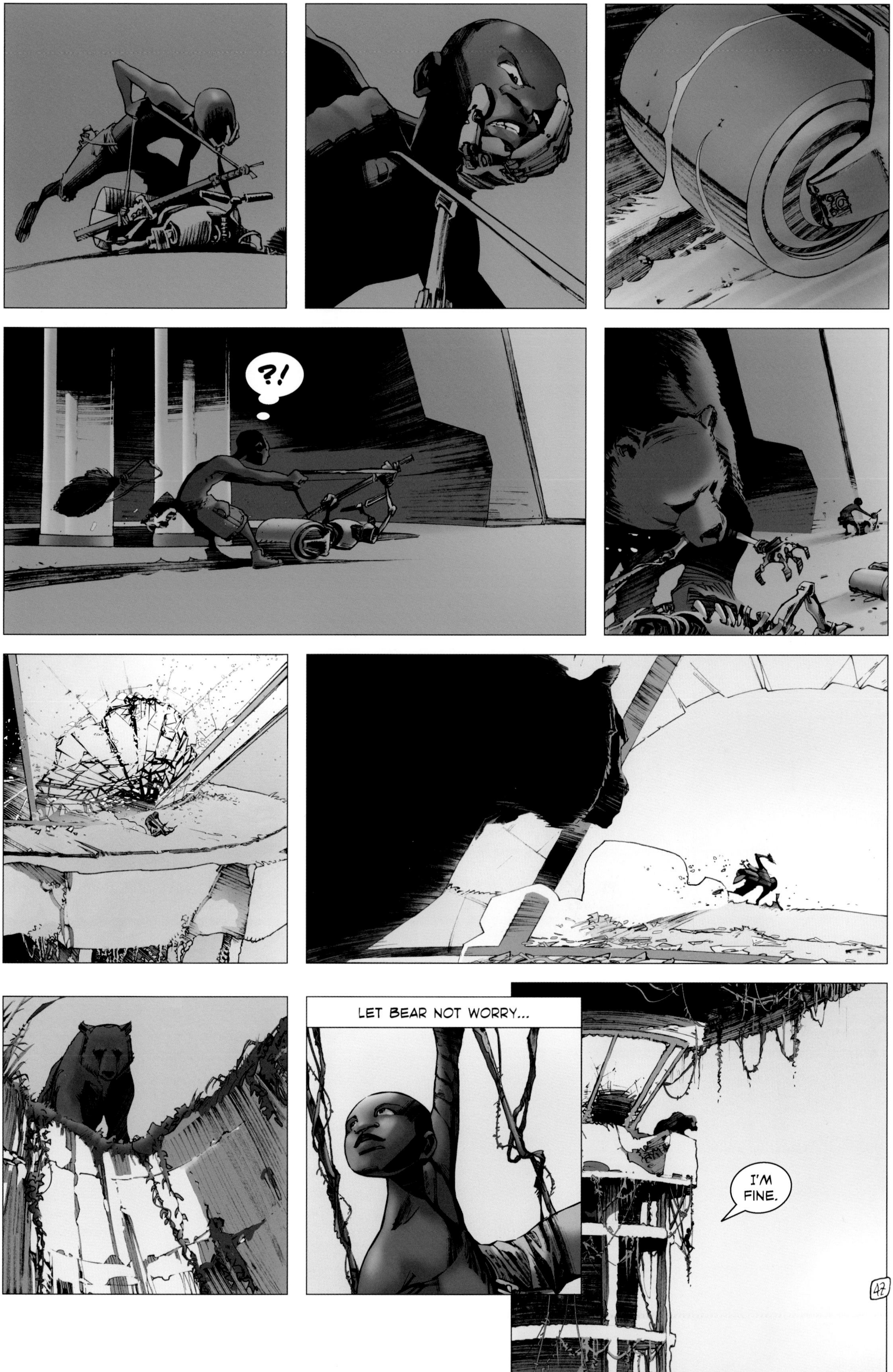
?!
LET BEAR NOT WORRY...
I'M FINE.

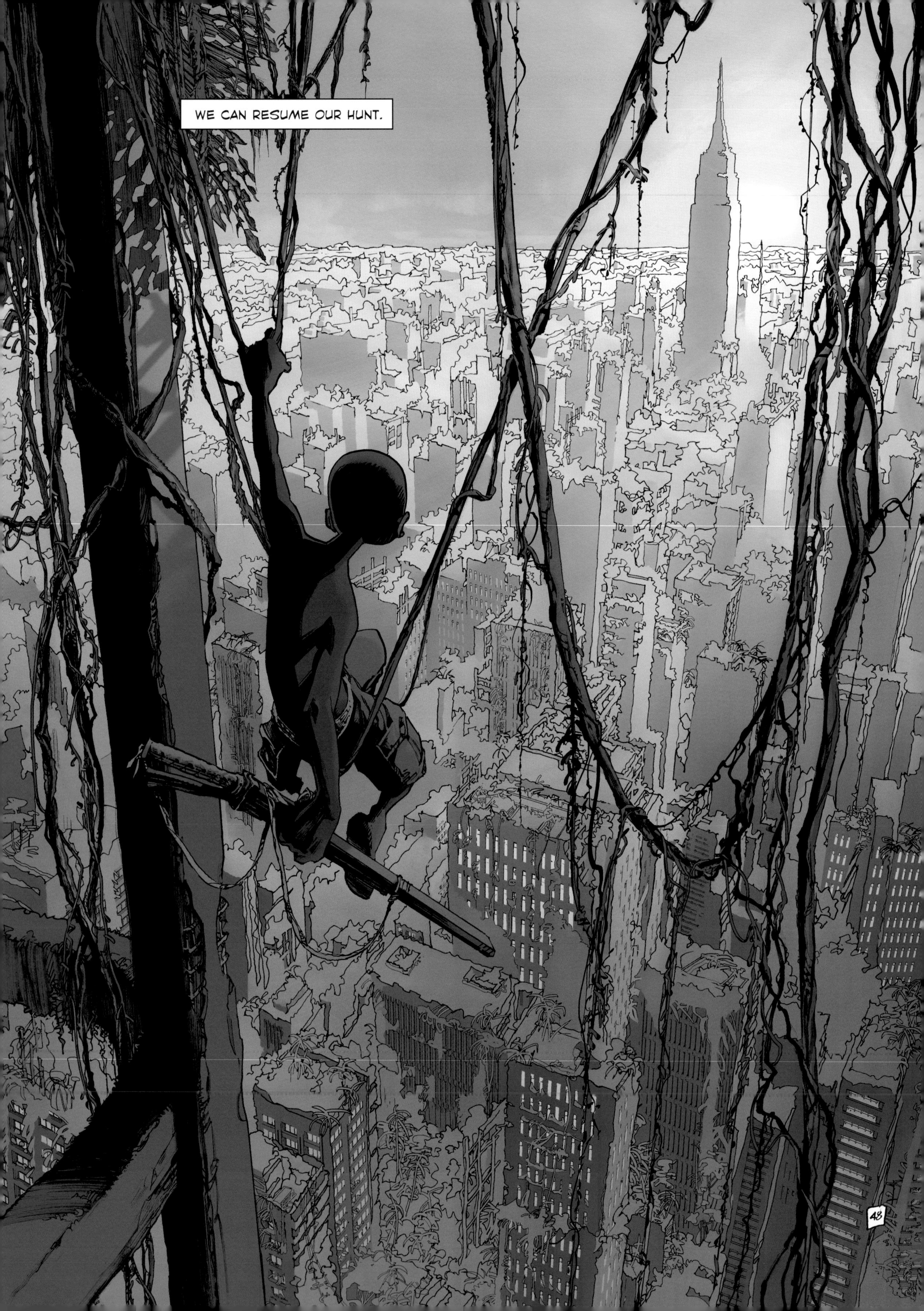
WE CAN RESUME OUR HUNT.

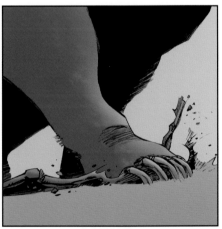

BEAR MAKES TOO MUCH **NOISE** AND FRIGHTENS OFF THE GAME!

DARK CHILD IS **SORRY**. BEAR DID NOT BREAK THAT BRANCH ON PURPOSE.

01

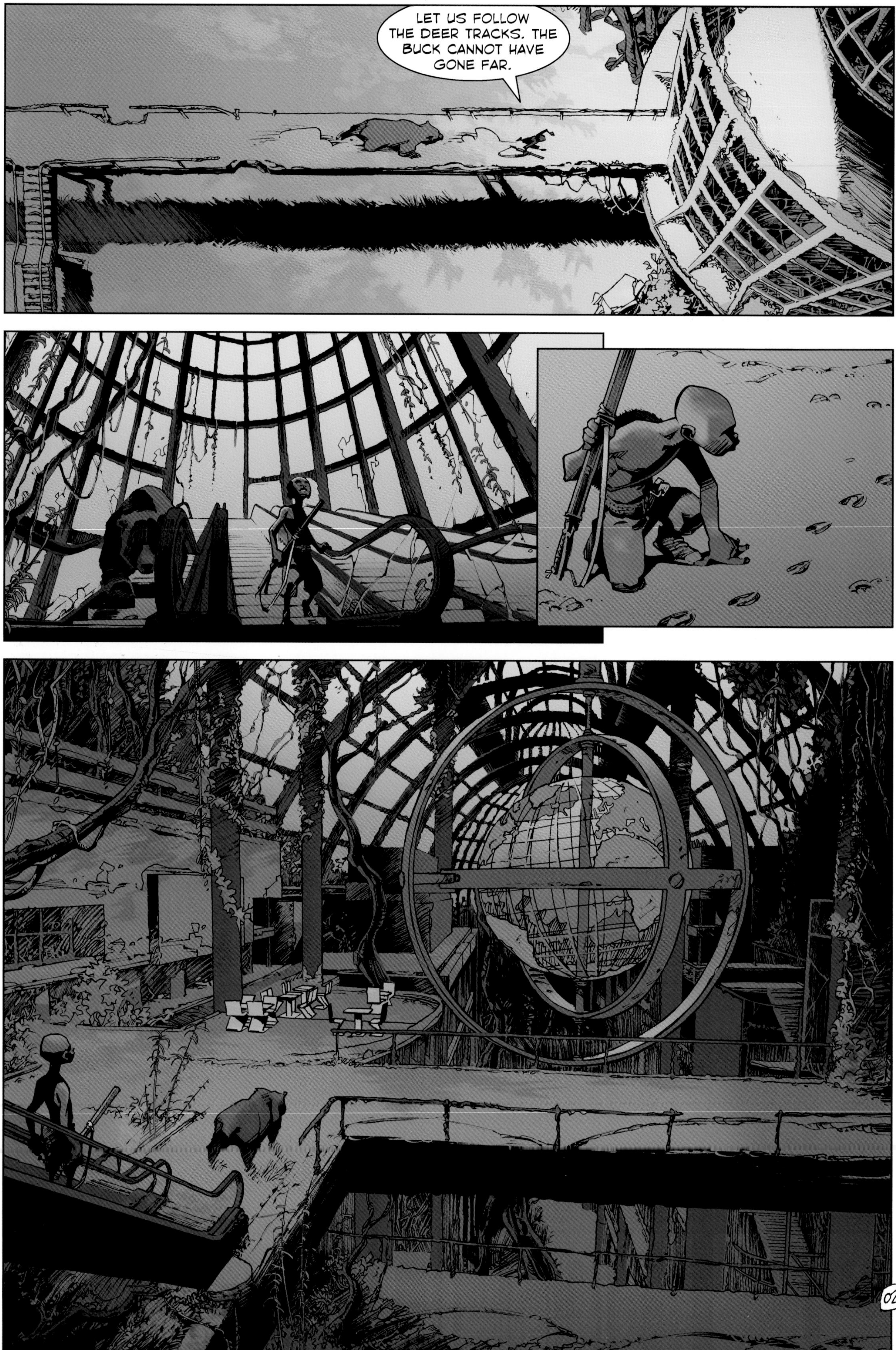
LET US FOLLOW THE DEER TRACKS. THE BUCK CANNOT HAVE GONE FAR.

GOOD DAY, SIR. WOULD YOU RATHER SEE A MENU OR JUST ORDER **TODAY'S SPECIAL?**

A **TALKING IMAGE**, AS IN SANTIAG!

ARE YOU A TINY GODDESS?

TODAY WE'RE OFFERING A VARIETY OF **PRIME CHOICE RECONSTITUTED** FISH.

YES! FISH! DARK CHILD AND BEAR WERE TRAILING A YOUNG BUCK, BUT **FISH** WILL DO!

I MUST INFORM YOU, SIR: **PETS** ARE **NOT** ALLOWED...

HOWEVER, **THIS** ANIMAL-- **URSUS ARCTOS MIDDENDORFFI--** DOES NOT APPEAR ON THE COMPANY LIST OF **PROHIBITED** SPECIES...

PLEASE BE SEATED. THE **MEZZANINE** IS ESPECIALLY ATTRACTIVE AT THIS TIME OF YEAR...

DARK CHILD IS HUNGRY! WHERE IS THE FISH?

I WILL TAKE YOUR ORDER WHEN YOU ARE PROPERLY SEATED.

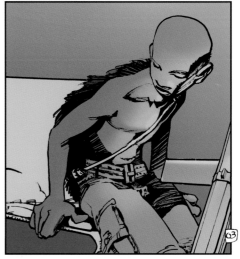

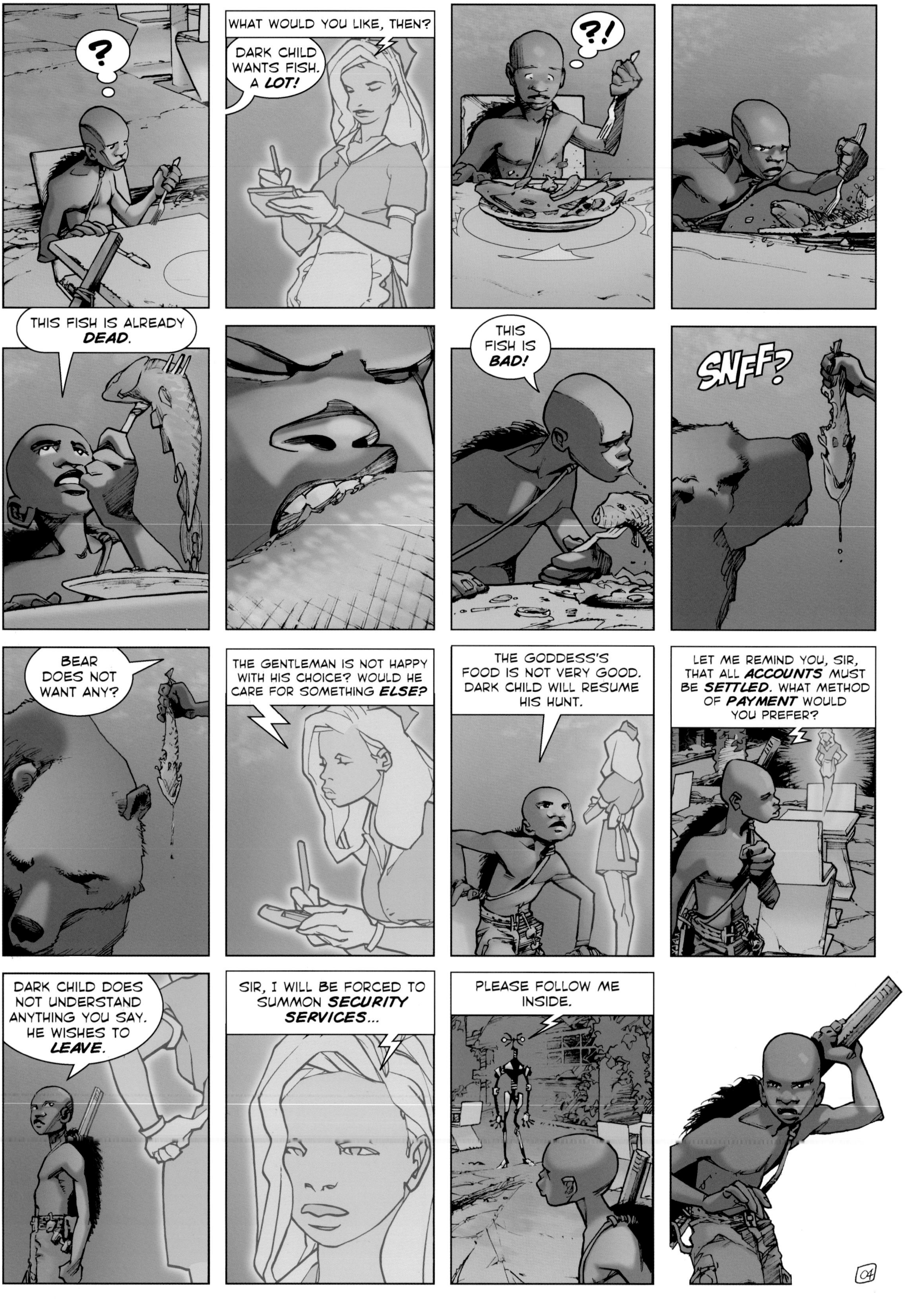

?
WHAT WOULD YOU LIKE, THEN?
DARK CHILD WANTS FISH. A *LOT!*
?!
THIS FISH IS ALREADY *DEAD*.
THIS FISH IS *BAD!*
SNFF?
BEAR DOES NOT WANT ANY?
THE GENTLEMAN IS NOT HAPPY WITH HIS CHOICE? WOULD HE CARE FOR SOMETHING *ELSE?*
THE GODDESS'S FOOD IS NOT VERY GOOD. DARK CHILD WILL RESUME HIS HUNT.
LET ME REMIND YOU, SIR, THAT ALL *ACCOUNTS* MUST BE *SETTLED*. WHAT METHOD OF *PAYMENT* WOULD YOU PREFER?
DARK CHILD DOES NOT UNDERSTAND ANYTHING YOU SAY. HE WISHES TO *LEAVE*.
SIR, I WILL BE FORCED TO SUMMON *SECURITY SERVICES*...
PLEASE FOLLOW ME INSIDE.

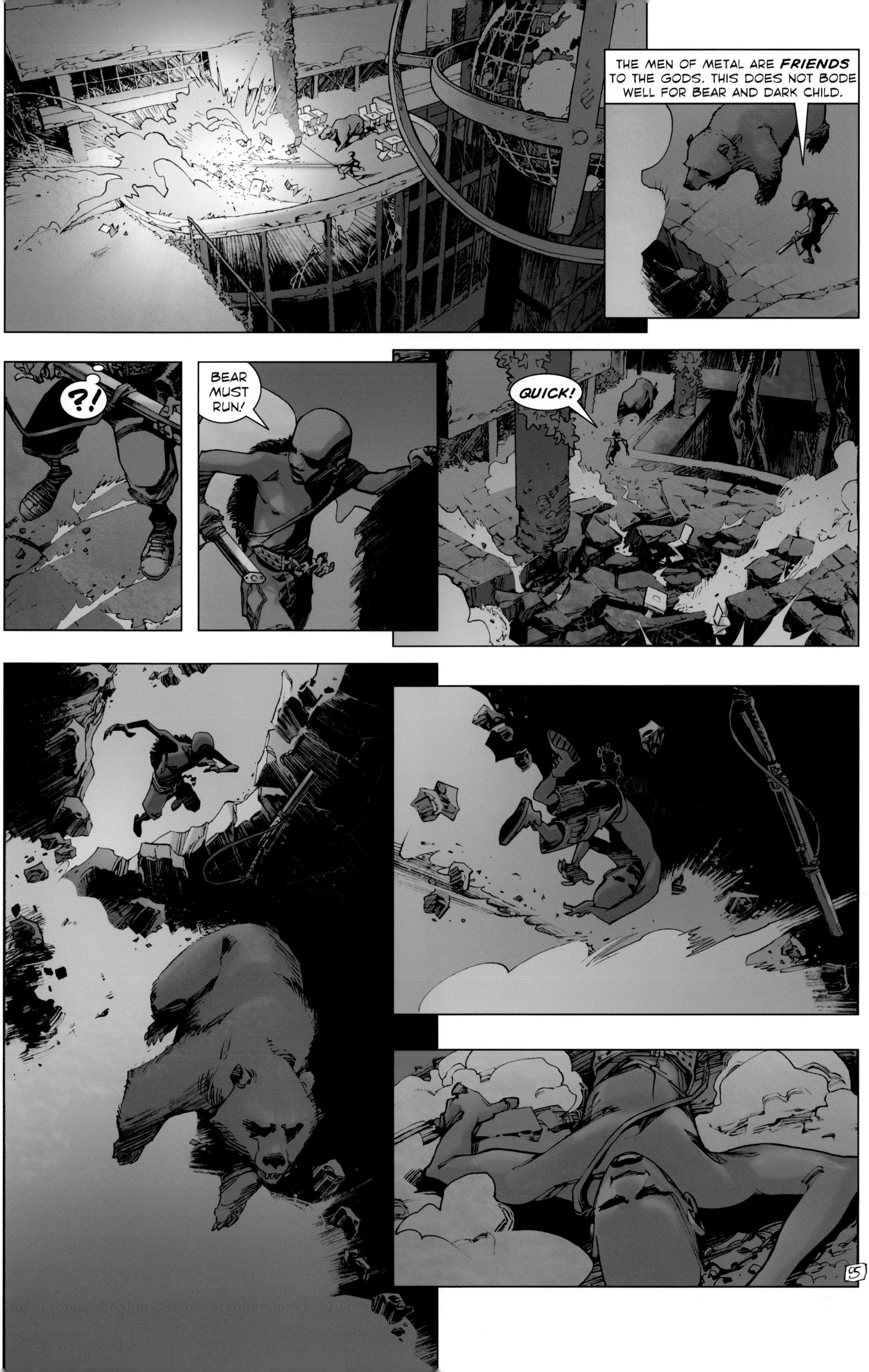
THE MEN OF METAL ARE FRIENDS TO THE GODS. THIS DOES NOT BODE WELL FOR BEAR AND DARK CHILD.
?!
BEAR MUST RUN!
QUICK!

CHAPTER 11: *Doc Gen-4*

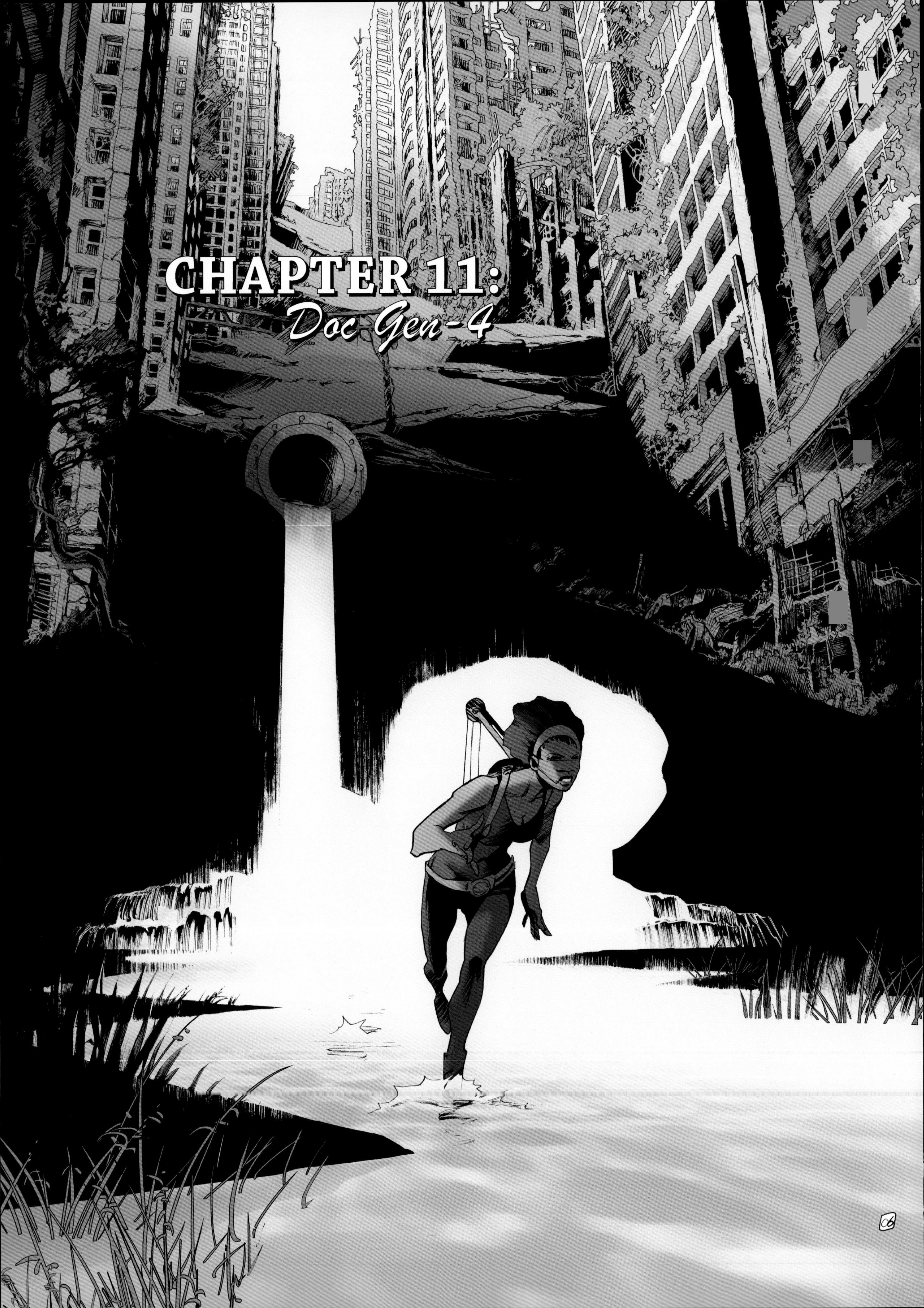

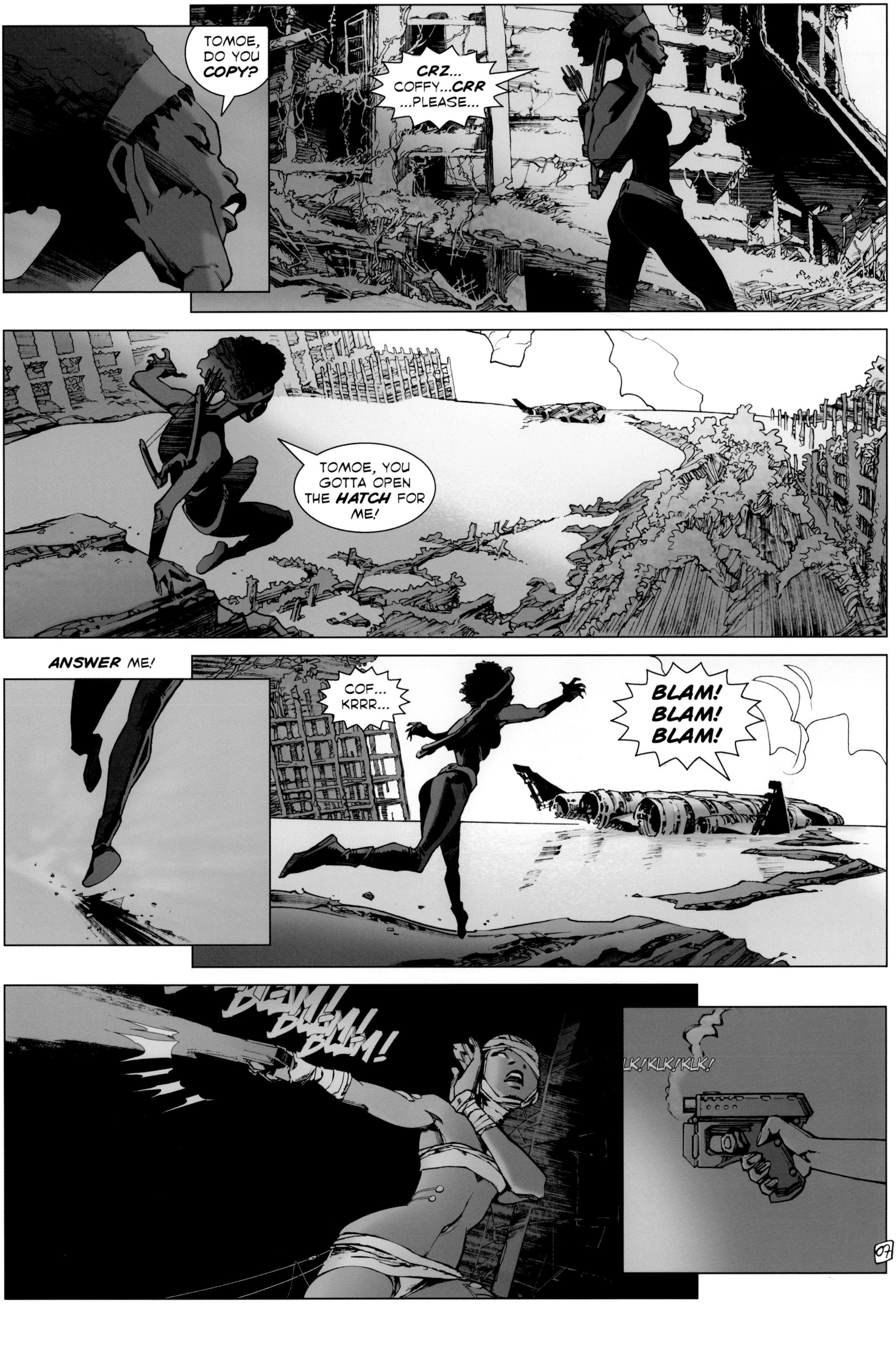
TOMOE, DO YOU COPY?
CRZ... COFFY...CRR ...PLEASE...
TOMOE, YOU GOTTA OPEN THE HATCH FOR ME!
ANSWER ME!
COF... KRRR...
BLAM! BLAM! BLAM!
LK!KLK!KLK!

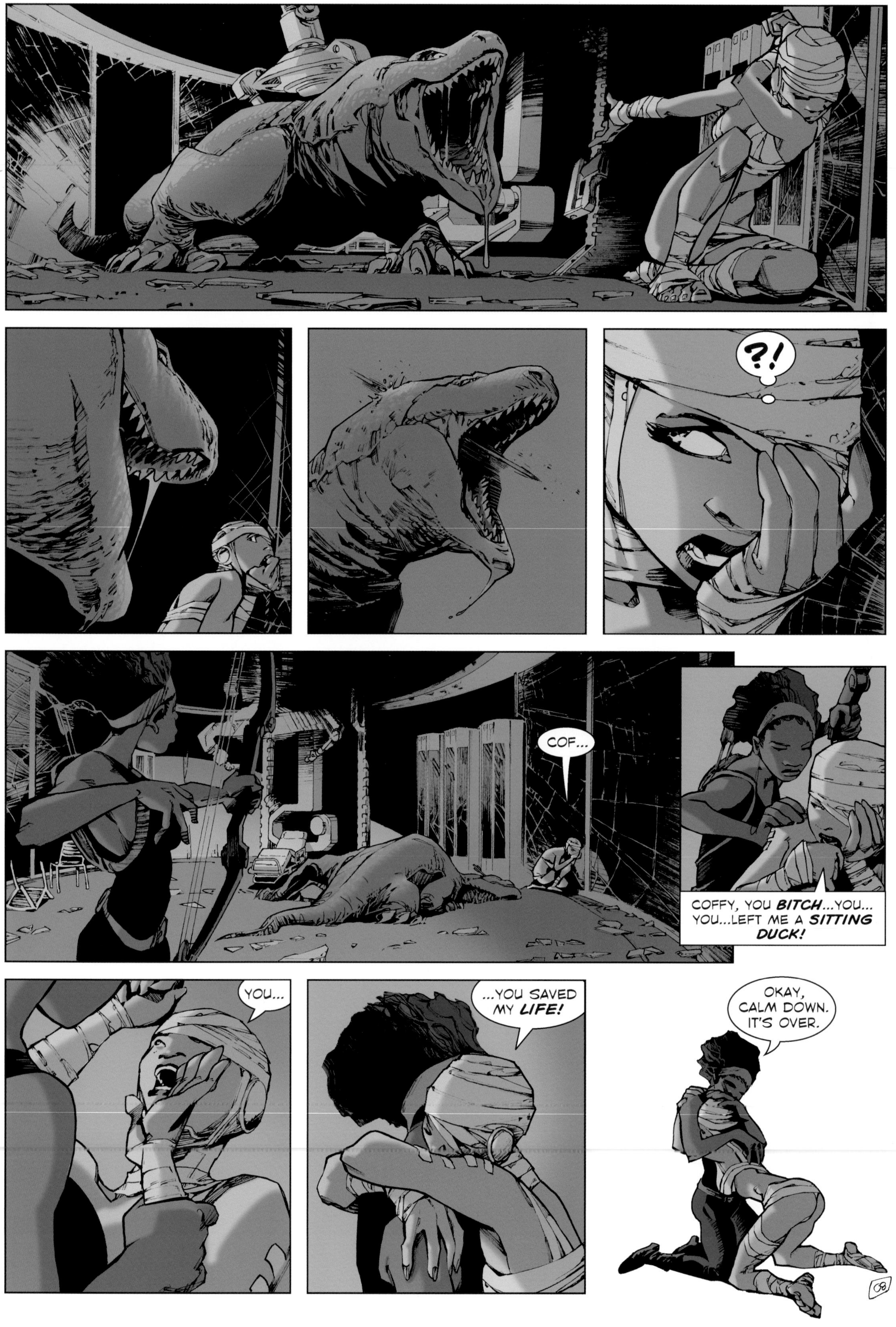
?!
COF...
COFFY, YOU **BITCH**...YOU... YOU...LEFT ME A **SITTING DUCK!**
YOU...
...YOU SAVED MY **LIFE!**
OKAY, CALM DOWN. IT'S OVER.

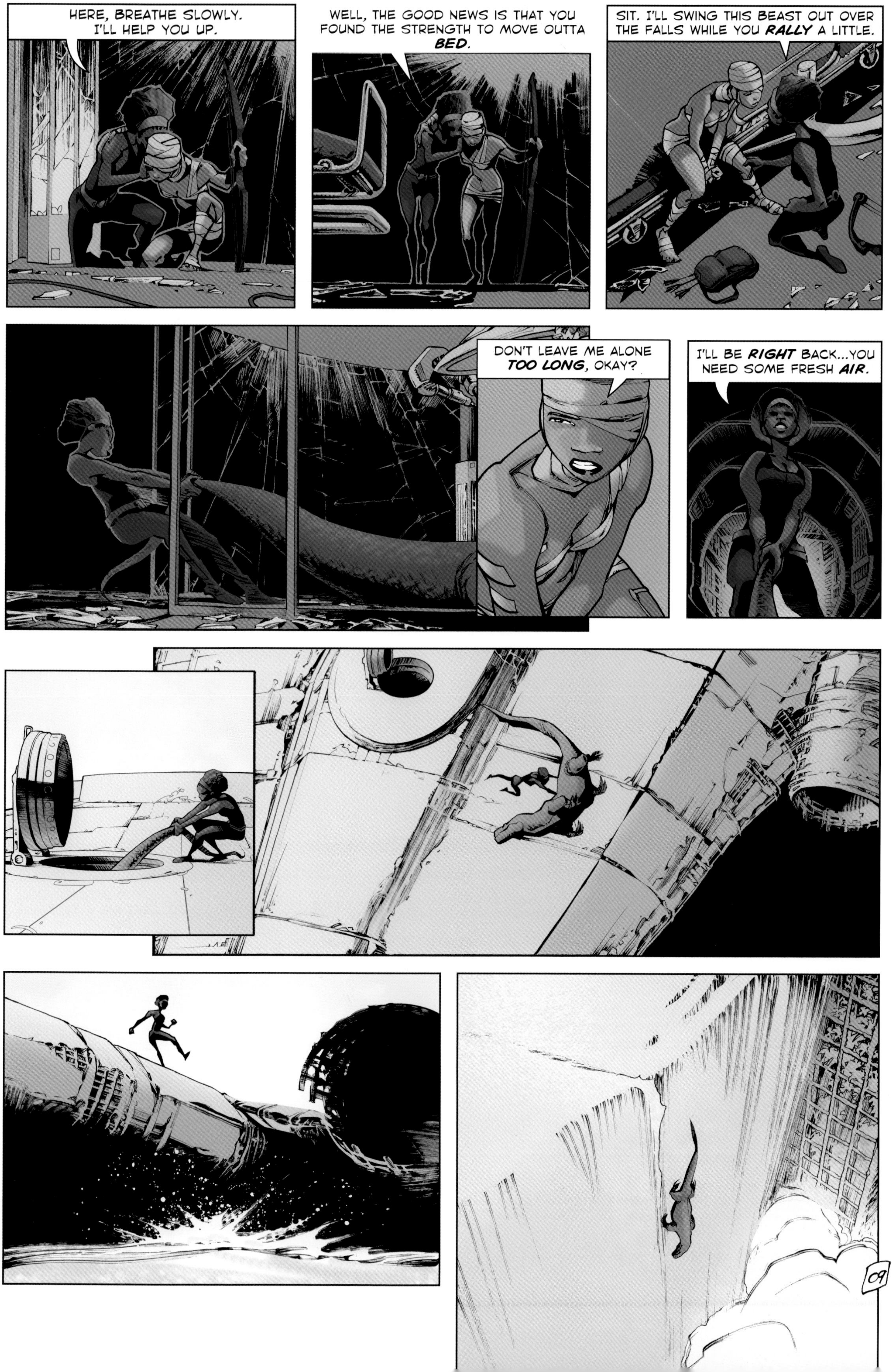
HERE, BREATHE SLOWLY. I'LL HELP YOU UP.
WELL, THE GOOD NEWS IS THAT YOU FOUND THE STRENGTH TO MOVE OUTTA BED.
SIT. I'LL SWING THIS BEAST OUT OVER THE FALLS WHILE YOU RALLY A LITTLE.
DON'T LEAVE ME ALONE TOO LONG, OKAY?
I'LL BE RIGHT BACK...YOU NEED SOME FRESH AIR.

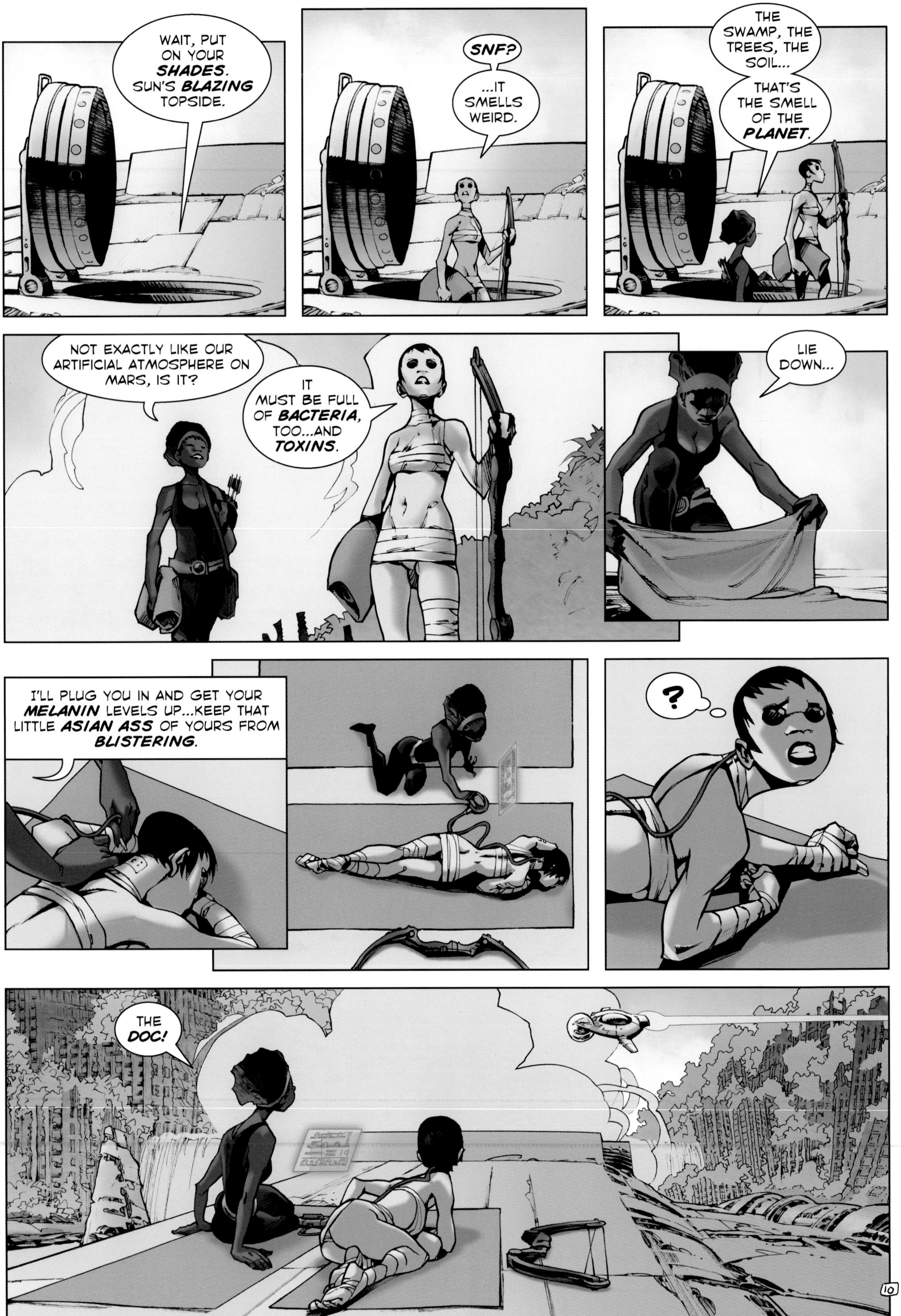

WAIT, PUT ON YOUR SHADES. SUN'S BLAZING TOPSIDE.
SNF?
...IT SMELLS WEIRD.
THE SWAMP, THE TREES, THE SOIL...
THAT'S THE SMELL OF THE PLANET.
NOT EXACTLY LIKE OUR ARTIFICIAL ATMOSPHERE ON MARS, IS IT?
IT MUST BE FULL OF BACTERIA, TOO...AND TOXINS.
LIE DOWN...
I'LL PLUG YOU IN AND GET YOUR MELANIN LEVELS UP...KEEP THAT LITTLE ASIAN ASS OF YOURS FROM BLISTERING.
?
THE DOC!

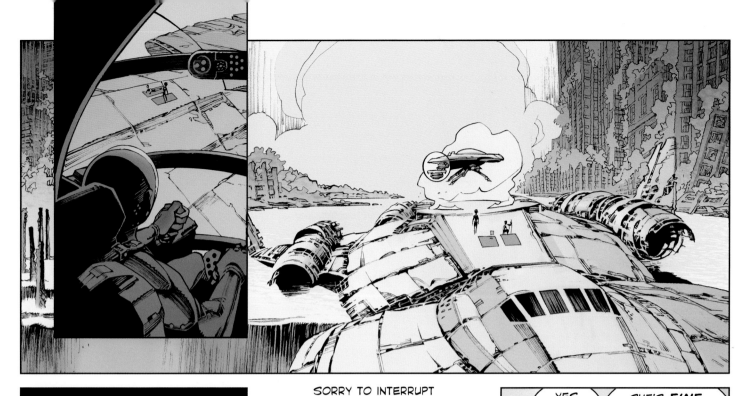

HEY, DOC. ABOUT *TIME* YOU GOT BACK.

SORRY TO INTERRUPT YOUR *SUNBATHING*, LADIES, BUT I'LL NEED A HAND UNLOADING THESE SPARE PARTS.

FEELING BETTER, TOMOE?

YES, AT LAST! I—

SHE'S *FINE*. DID YOU GET WHAT WE NEED TO FIX THE *TRANSPONDER*?

I *CANNIBALIZED* EVERY DEAD DEVICE I COULD *FIND* BETWEEN HERE AND *OLD ARGENTINA*: SPENT HOURS SORTING THROUGH COMPONENTS AND *COBBLING* PIECES TOGETHER.

MIGHT WORK.

NOT TO MENTION...I MET SOME *EARTHERS*.

WHAT?!

?!

I'M TALKING ABOUT EARTHERS FROM *EARTH*. NOT EARTHERS FROM *MARS*, LIKE US.

11

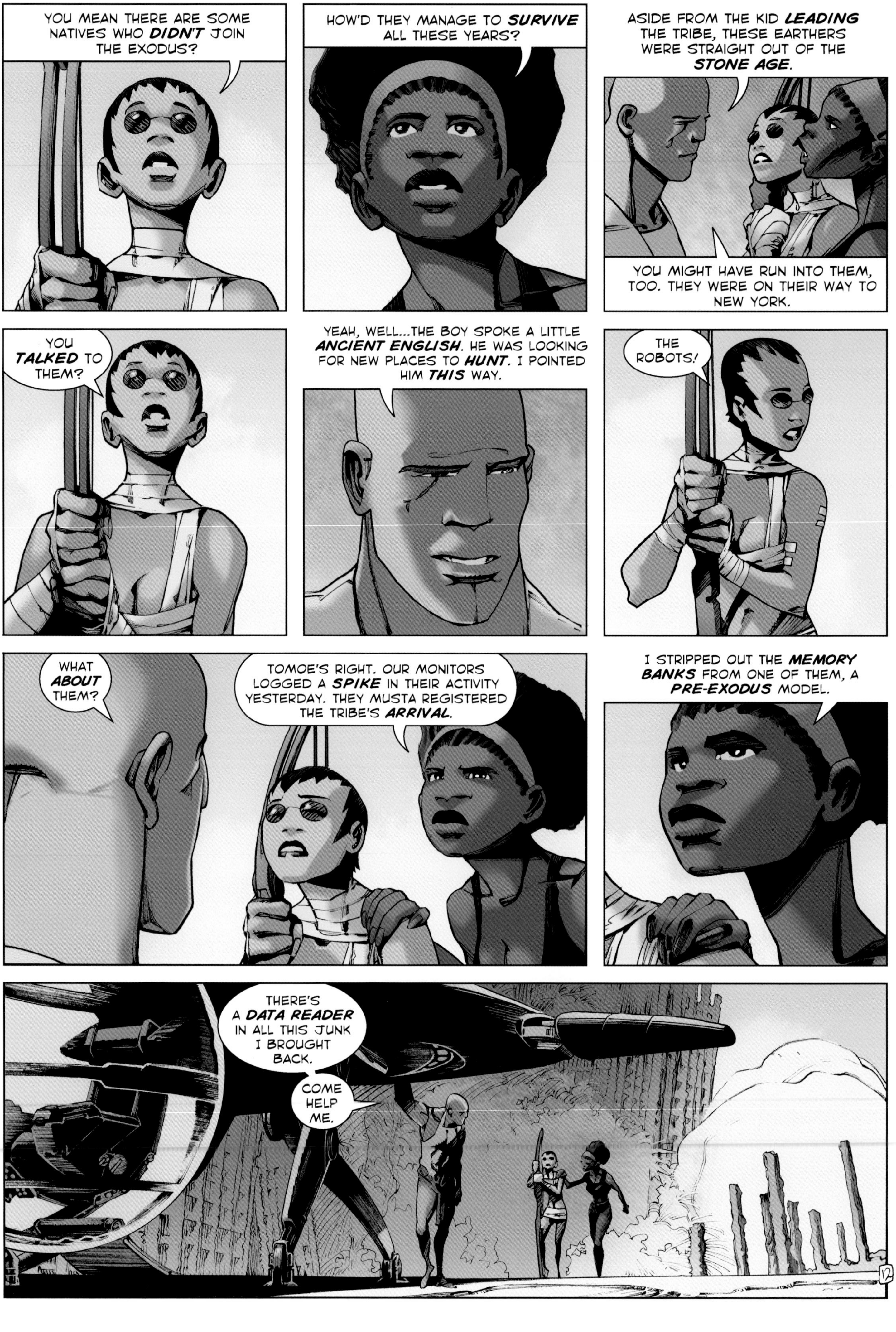
YOU MEAN THERE ARE SOME NATIVES WHO DIDN'T JOIN THE EXODUS?
HOW'D THEY MANAGE TO SURVIVE ALL THESE YEARS?
ASIDE FROM THE KID LEADING THE TRIBE, THESE EARTHERS WERE STRAIGHT OUT OF THE STONE AGE.
YOU MIGHT HAVE RUN INTO THEM, TOO. THEY WERE ON THEIR WAY TO NEW YORK.
YOU TALKED TO THEM?
YEAH, WELL...THE BOY SPOKE A LITTLE ANCIENT ENGLISH. HE WAS LOOKING FOR NEW PLACES TO HUNT. I POINTED HIM THIS WAY.
THE ROBOTS!
WHAT ABOUT THEM?
TOMOE'S RIGHT. OUR MONITORS LOGGED A SPIKE IN THEIR ACTIVITY YESTERDAY. THEY MUSTA REGISTERED THE TRIBE'S ARRIVAL.
I STRIPPED OUT THE MEMORY BANKS FROM ONE OF THEM, A PRE-EXODUS MODEL.
THERE'S A DATA READER IN ALL THIS JUNK I BROUGHT BACK.
COME HELP ME.

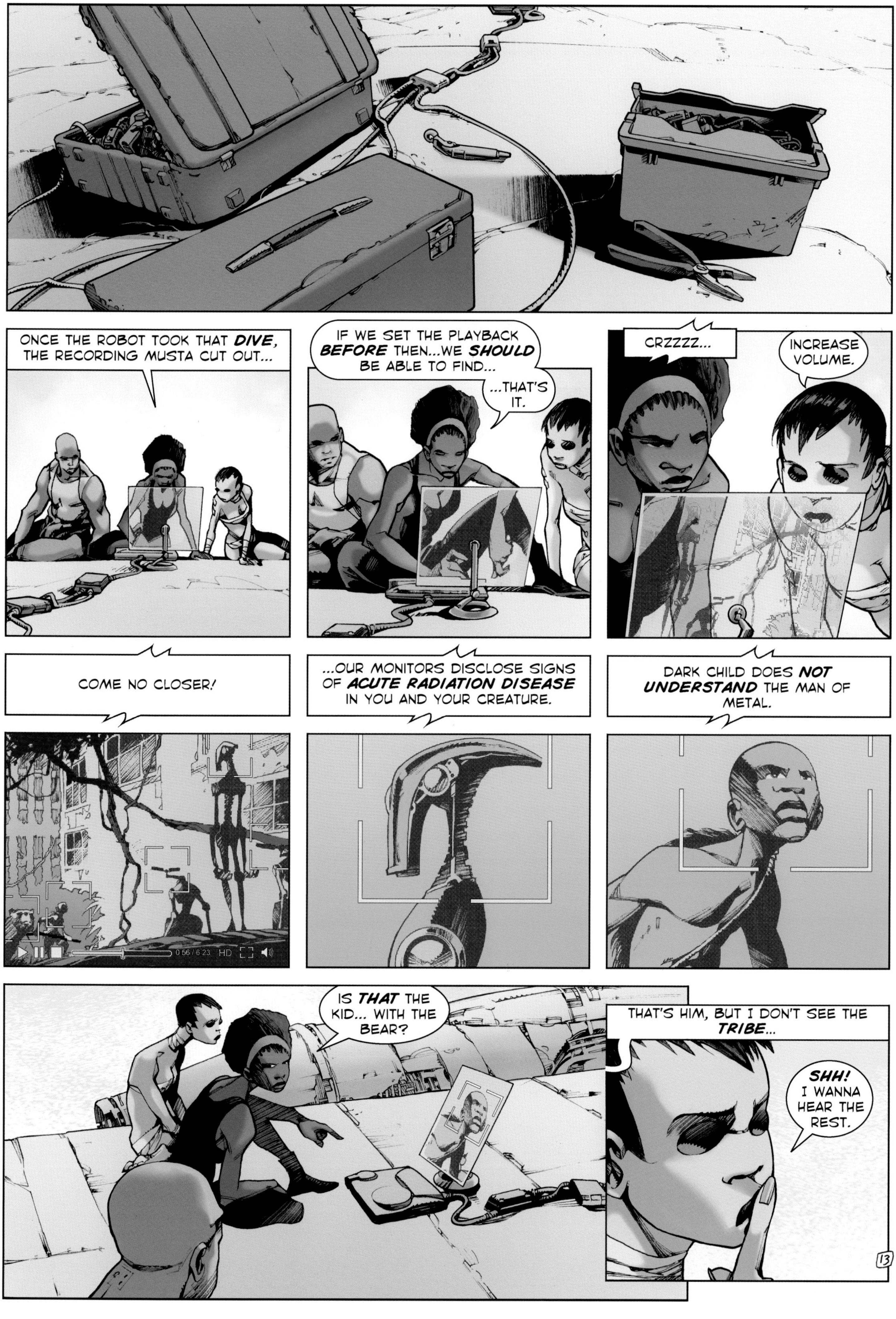
ONCE THE ROBOT TOOK THAT *DIVE*, THE RECORDING MUSTA CUT OUT...
IF WE SET THE PLAYBACK *BEFORE* THEN...WE *SHOULD* BE ABLE TO FIND...
...THAT'S IT.
CRZZZZ...
INCREASE VOLUME.
COME NO CLOSER!
...OUR MONITORS DISCLOSE SIGNS OF *ACUTE RADIATION DISEASE* IN YOU AND YOUR CREATURE.
DARK CHILD DOES *NOT UNDERSTAND* THE MAN OF METAL.
IS *THAT* THE KID... WITH THE BEAR?
THAT'S HIM, BUT I DON'T SEE THE *TRIBE*...
SHH! I WANNA HEAR THE REST.

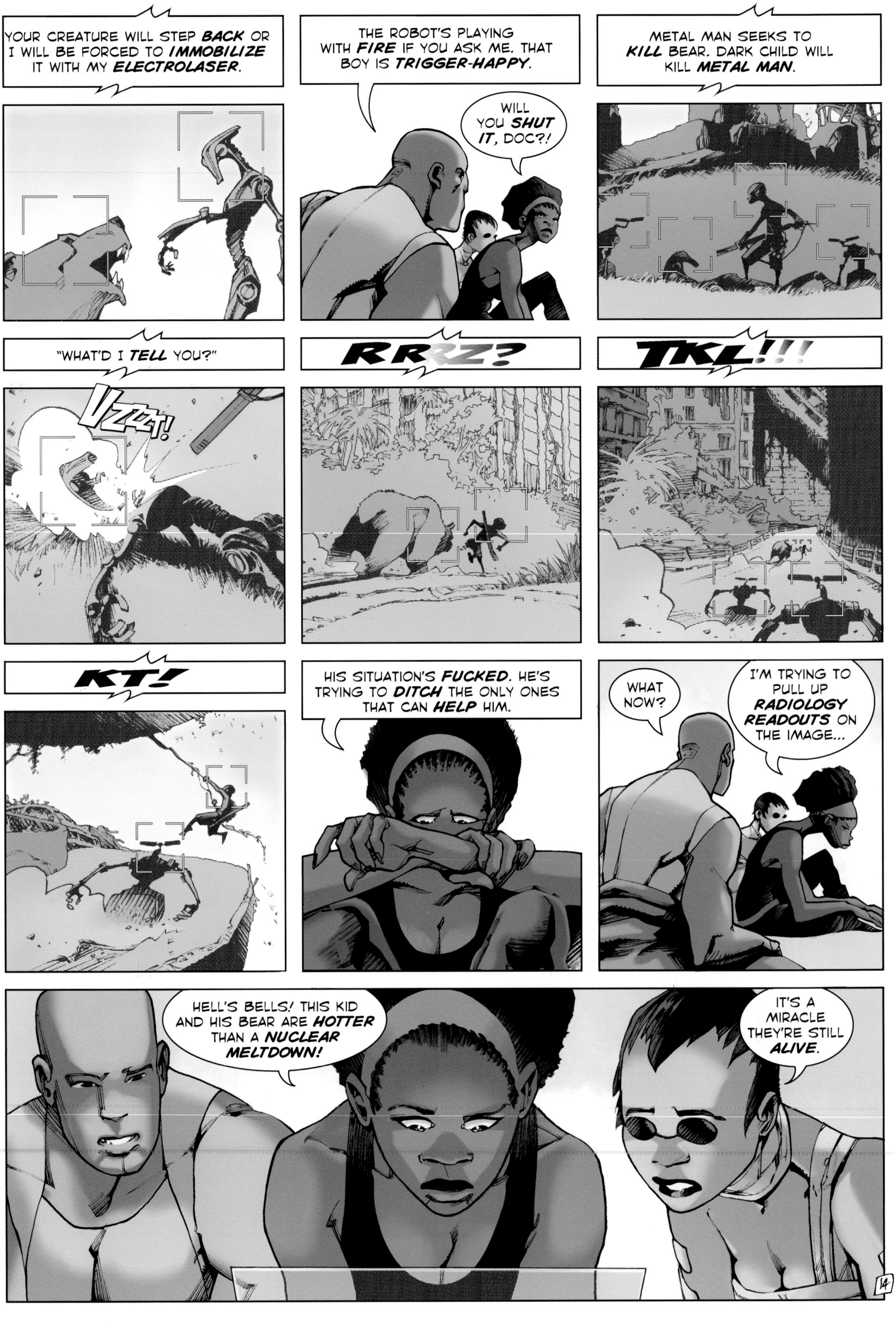
YOUR CREATURE WILL STEP BACK OR I WILL BE FORCED TO IMMOBILIZE IT WITH MY ELECTROLASER.
THE ROBOT'S PLAYING WITH FIRE IF YOU ASK ME. THAT BOY IS TRIGGER-HAPPY.
WILL YOU SHUT IT, DOC?!
METAL MAN SEEKS TO KILL BEAR. DARK CHILD WILL KILL METAL MAN.
"WHAT'D I TELL YOU?"
VZZZT!
RRRZ?
TKL!!!
KT!
HIS SITUATION'S FUCKED. HE'S TRYING TO DITCH THE ONLY ONES THAT CAN HELP HIM.
WHAT NOW?
I'M TRYING TO PULL UP RADIOLOGY READOUTS ON THE IMAGE...
HELL'S BELLS! THIS KID AND HIS BEAR ARE HOTTER THAN A NUCLEAR MELTDOWN!
IT'S A MIRACLE THEY'RE STILL ALIVE.

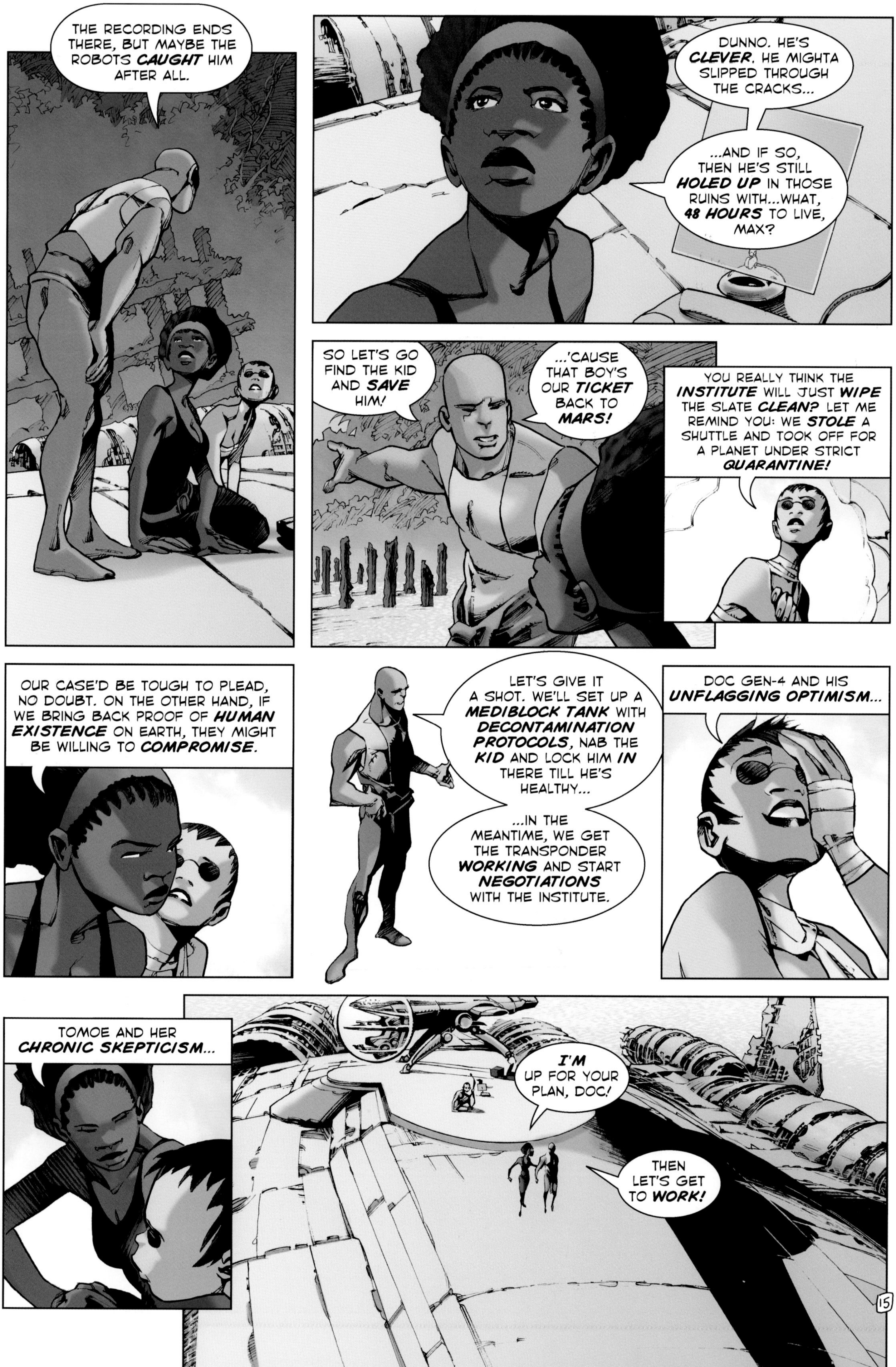
THE RECORDING ENDS THERE, BUT MAYBE THE ROBOTS CAUGHT HIM AFTER ALL.
DUNNO. HE'S CLEVER. HE MIGHTA SLIPPED THROUGH THE CRACKS...
...AND IF SO, THEN HE'S STILL HOLED UP IN THOSE RUINS WITH...WHAT, 48 HOURS TO LIVE, MAX?
SO LET'S GO FIND THE KID AND SAVE HIM!
...'CAUSE THAT BOY'S OUR TICKET BACK TO MARS!
YOU REALLY THINK THE INSTITUTE WILL JUST WIPE THE SLATE CLEAN? LET ME REMIND YOU: WE STOLE A SHUTTLE AND TOOK OFF FOR A PLANET UNDER STRICT QUARANTINE!
OUR CASE'D BE TOUGH TO PLEAD, NO DOUBT. ON THE OTHER HAND, IF WE BRING BACK PROOF OF HUMAN EXISTENCE ON EARTH, THEY MIGHT BE WILLING TO COMPROMISE.
LET'S GIVE IT A SHOT. WE'LL SET UP A MEDIBLOCK TANK WITH DECONTAMINATION PROTOCOLS, NAB THE KID AND LOCK HIM IN THERE TILL HE'S HEALTHY...
...IN THE MEANTIME, WE GET THE TRANSPONDER WORKING AND START NEGOTIATIONS WITH THE INSTITUTE.
DOC GEN-4 AND HIS UNFLAGGING OPTIMISM...
TOMOE AND HER CHRONIC SKEPTICISM...
I'M UP FOR YOUR PLAN, DOC!
THEN LET'S GET TO WORK!
15

CHAPTER 12:
Bear

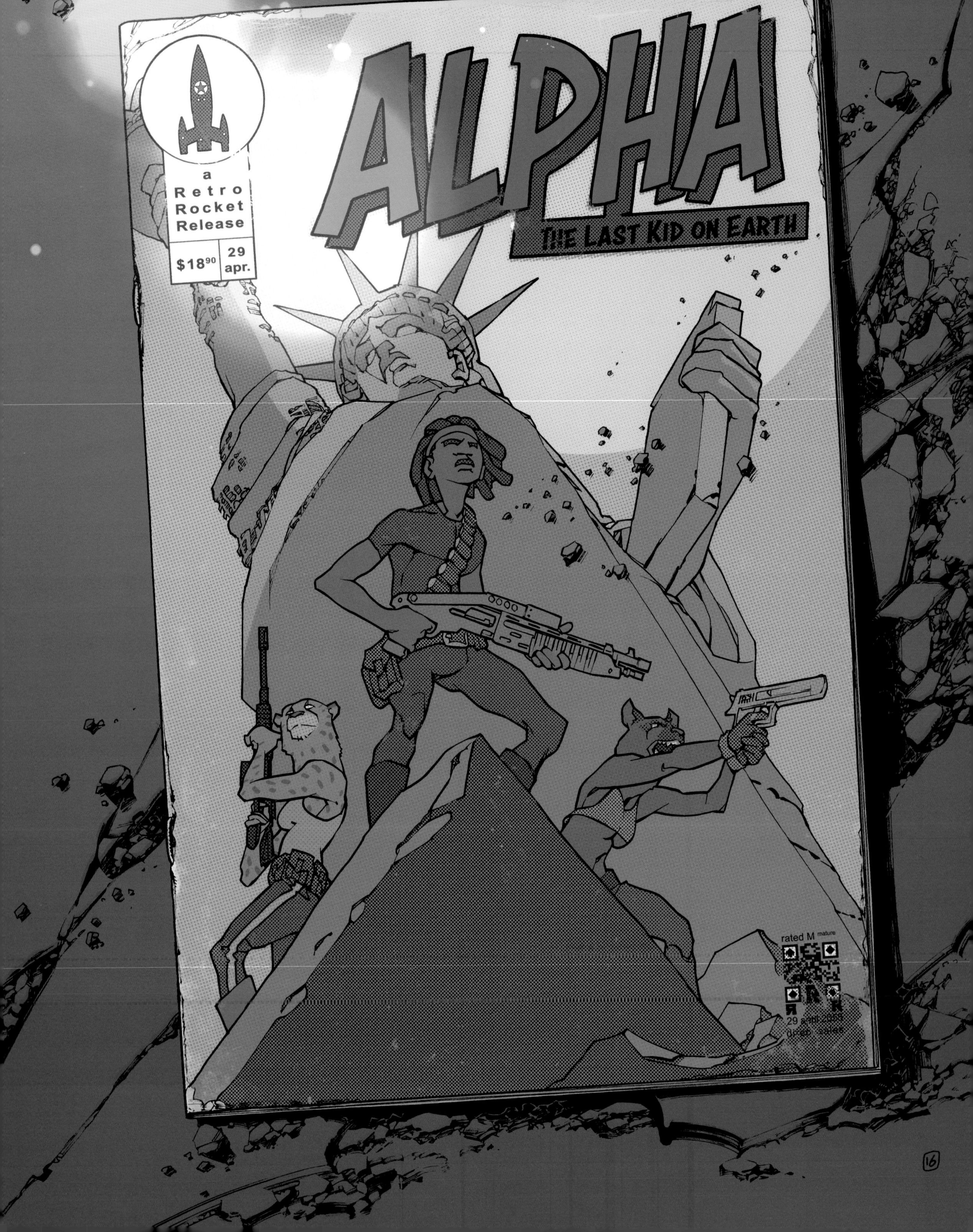
ALPHA
THE LAST KID ON EARTH
a
Retro
Rocket
Release
$18.90
29
apr.
rated M mature

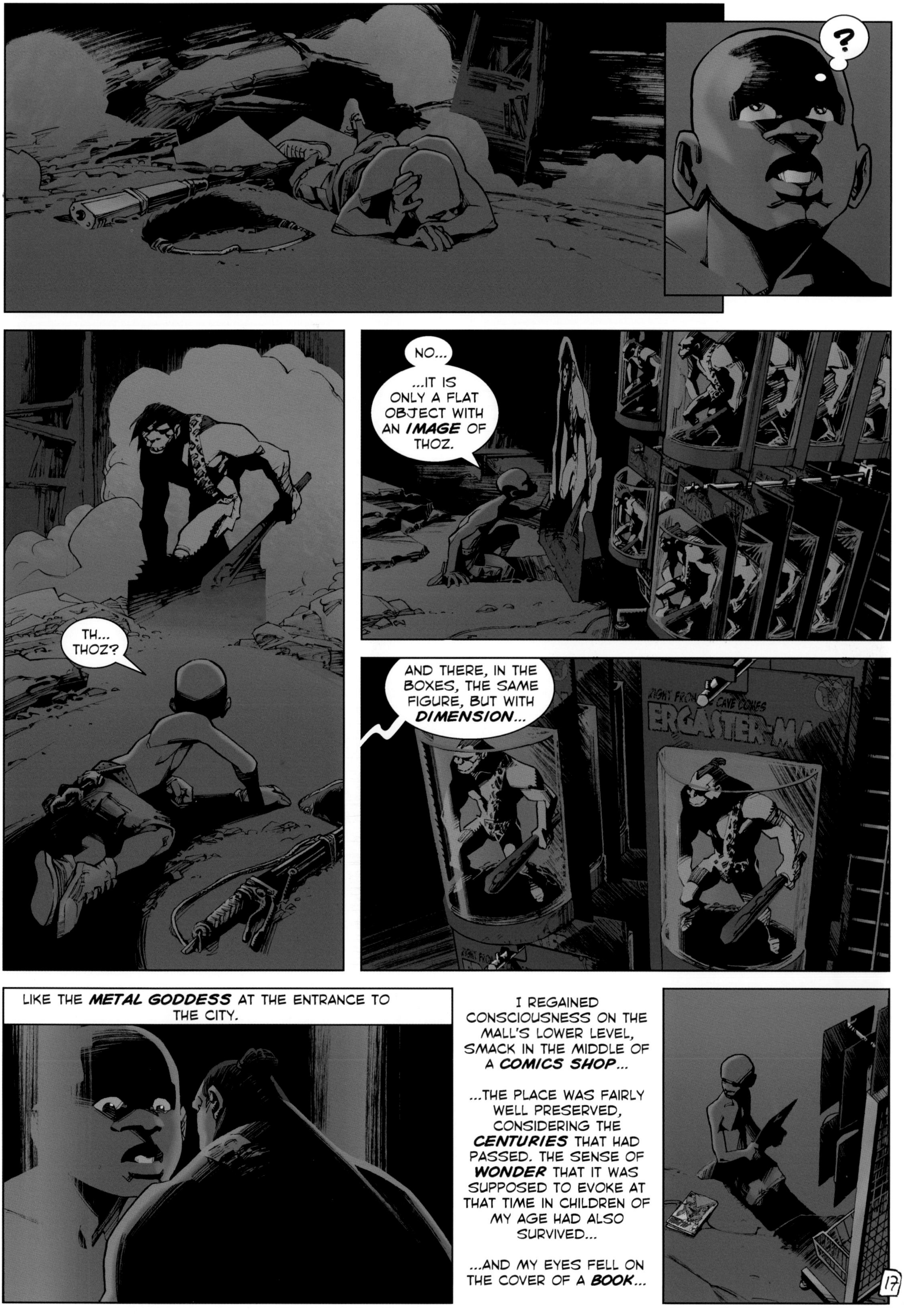
?
TH... THOZ?
NO...
...IT IS ONLY A FLAT OBJECT WITH AN IMAGE OF THOZ.
AND THERE, IN THE BOXES, THE SAME FIGURE, BUT WITH DIMENSION...
ERGASTER-MA
LIKE THE METAL GODDESS AT THE ENTRANCE TO THE CITY.
I REGAINED CONSCIOUSNESS ON THE MALL'S LOWER LEVEL, SMACK IN THE MIDDLE OF A COMICS SHOP...
...THE PLACE WAS FAIRLY WELL PRESERVED, CONSIDERING THE CENTURIES THAT HAD PASSED. THE SENSE OF WONDER THAT IT WAS SUPPOSED TO EVOKE AT THAT TIME IN CHILDREN OF MY AGE HAD ALSO SURVIVED...
...AND MY EYES FELL ON THE COVER OF A BOOK...

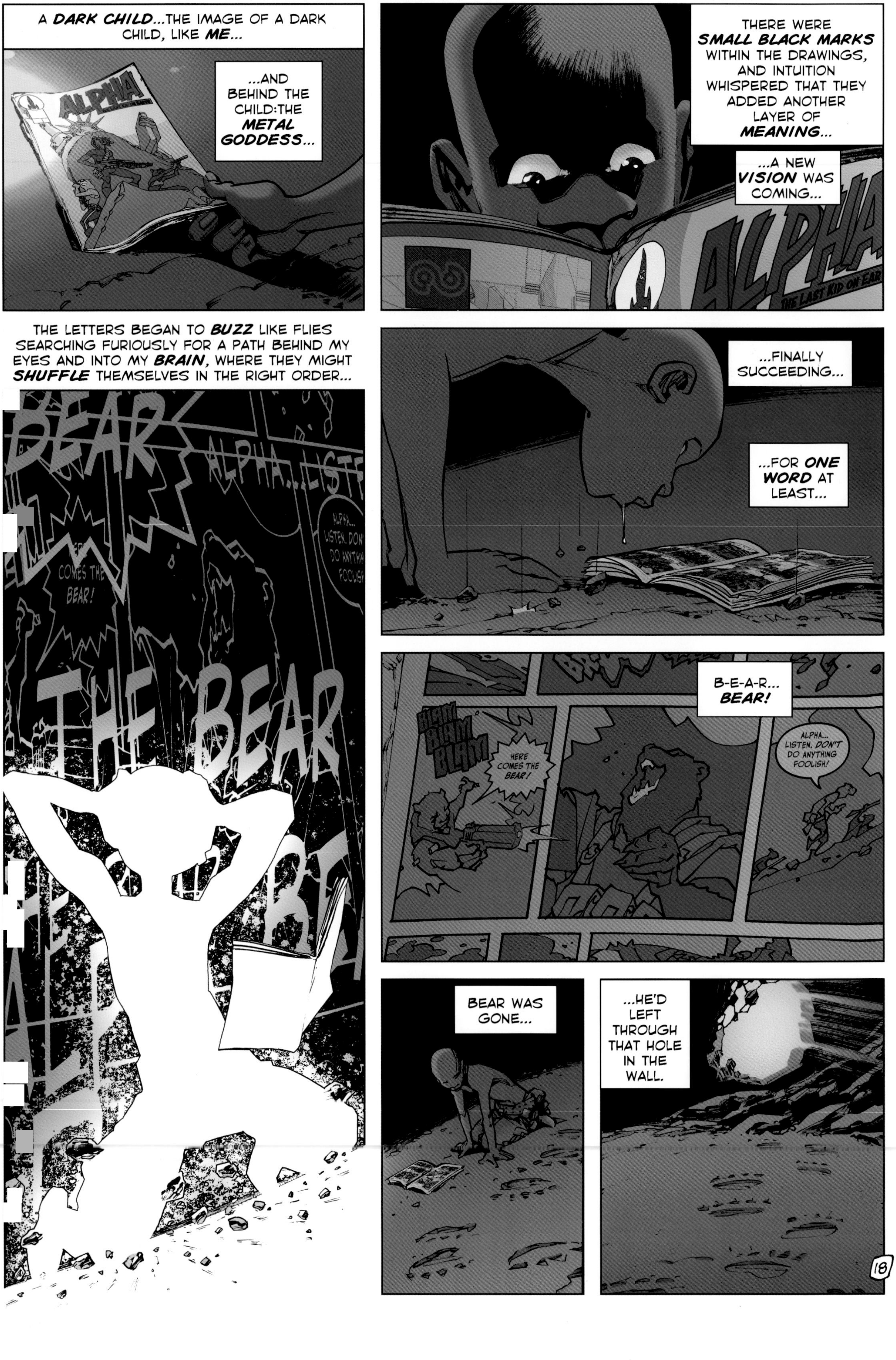

A DARK CHILD...THE IMAGE OF A DARK CHILD, LIKE ME...
...AND BEHIND THE CHILD:THE METAL GODDESS...
ALPHA
THERE WERE SMALL BLACK MARKS WITHIN THE DRAWINGS, AND INTUITION WHISPERED THAT THEY ADDED ANOTHER LAYER OF MEANING...
...A NEW VISION WAS COMING...
ALPHA
THE LAST KID ON EAR
THE LETTERS BEGAN TO BUZZ LIKE FLIES SEARCHING FURIOUSLY FOR A PATH BEHIND MY EYES AND INTO MY BRAIN, WHERE THEY MIGHT SHUFFLE THEMSELVES IN THE RIGHT ORDER...
BEAR
ALPHA...LISTE
COMES THE BEAR!
ALPHA... LISTEN. DON'T DO ANYTHIN FOOLISH
THE BEAR
...FINALLY SUCCEEDING...
...FOR ONE WORD AT LEAST...
B-E-A-R... BEAR!
BLAM BLAM BLAM
HERE COMES THE BEAR!
ALPHA... LISTEN. DON'T DO ANYTHING FOOLISH!
BEAR WAS GONE...
...HE'D LEFT THROUGH THAT HOLE IN THE WALL.

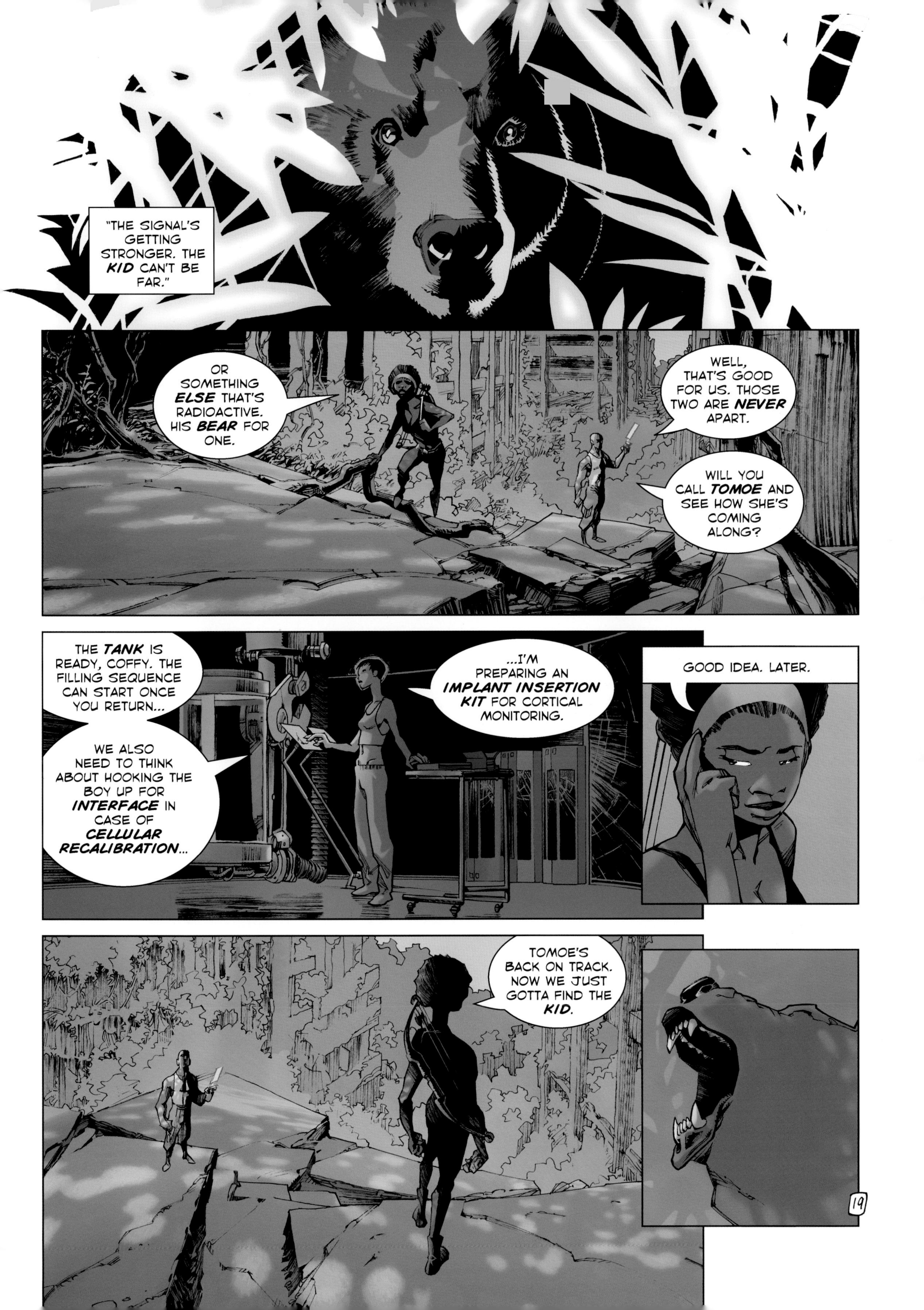
"THE SIGNAL'S GETTING STRONGER. THE KID CAN'T BE FAR."
OR SOMETHING ELSE THAT'S RADIOACTIVE. HIS BEAR FOR ONE.
WELL, THAT'S GOOD FOR US. THOSE TWO ARE NEVER APART.
WILL YOU CALL TOMOE AND SEE HOW SHE'S COMING ALONG?
THE TANK IS READY, COFFY. THE FILLING SEQUENCE CAN START ONCE YOU RETURN...
WE ALSO NEED TO THINK ABOUT HOOKING THE BOY UP FOR INTERFACE IN CASE OF CELLULAR RECALIBRATION...
...I'M PREPARING AN IMPLANT INSERTION KIT FOR CORTICAL MONITORING.
GOOD IDEA. LATER.
TOMOE'S BACK ON TRACK. NOW WE JUST GOTTA FIND THE KID.
19

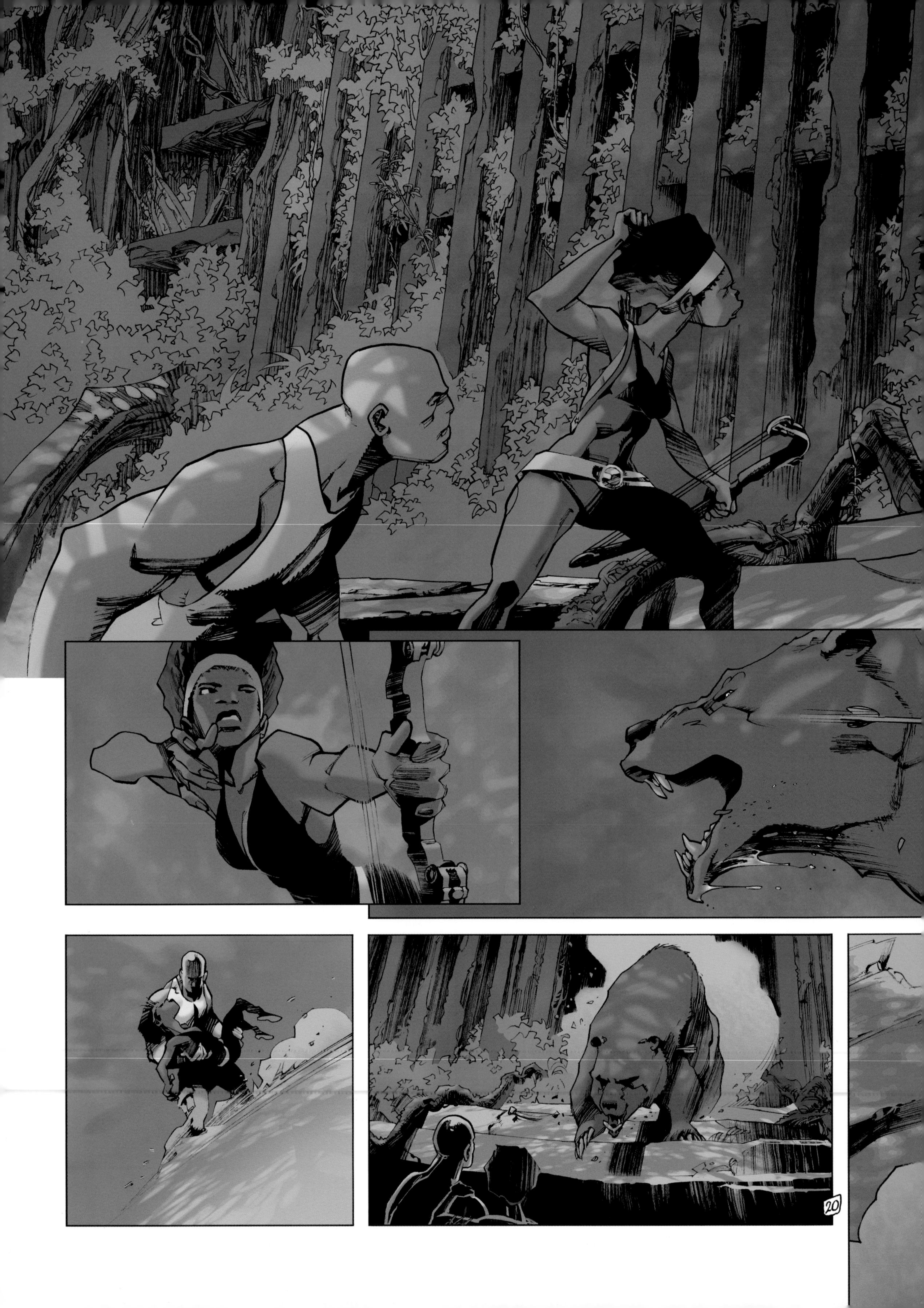

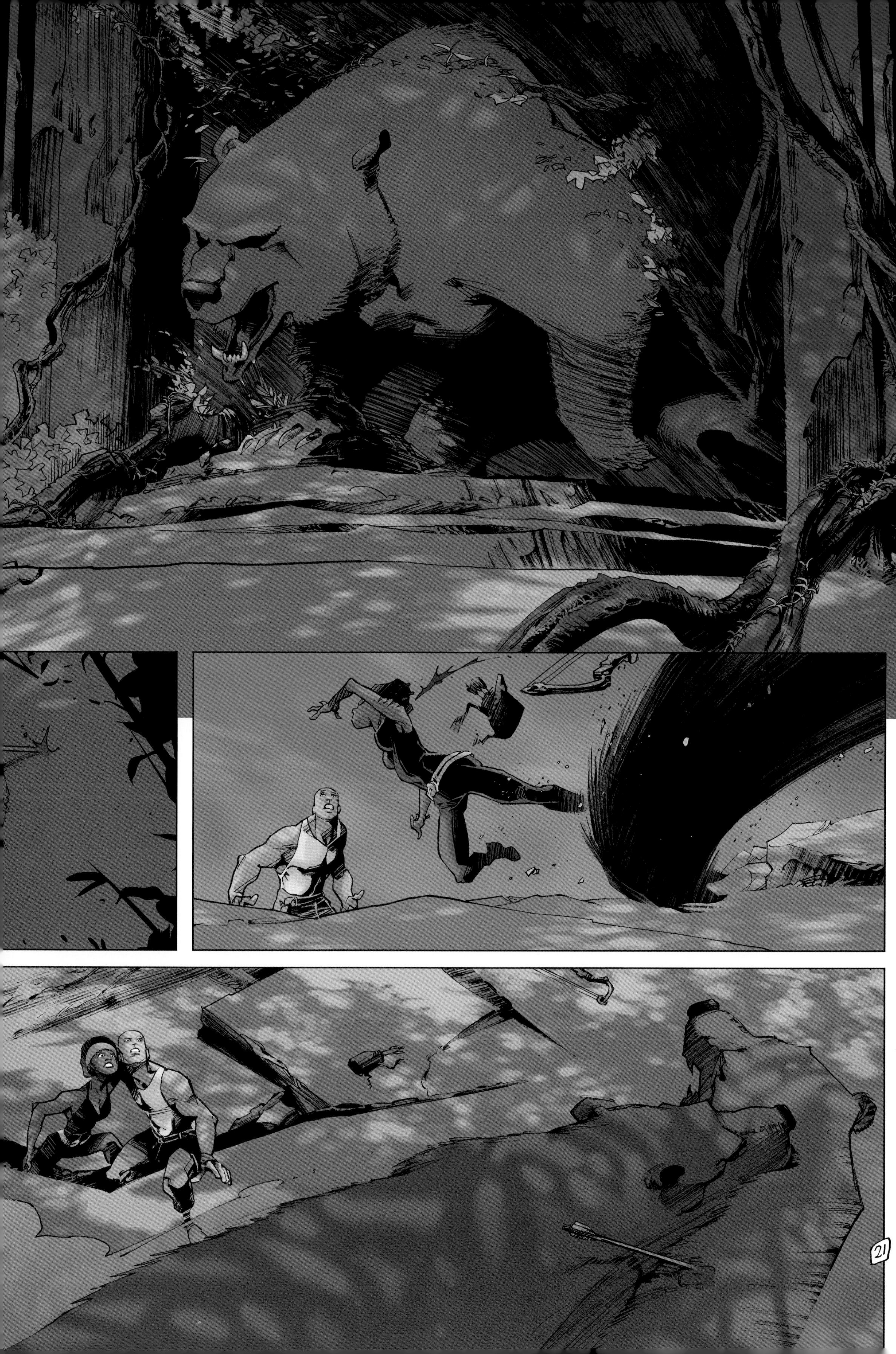

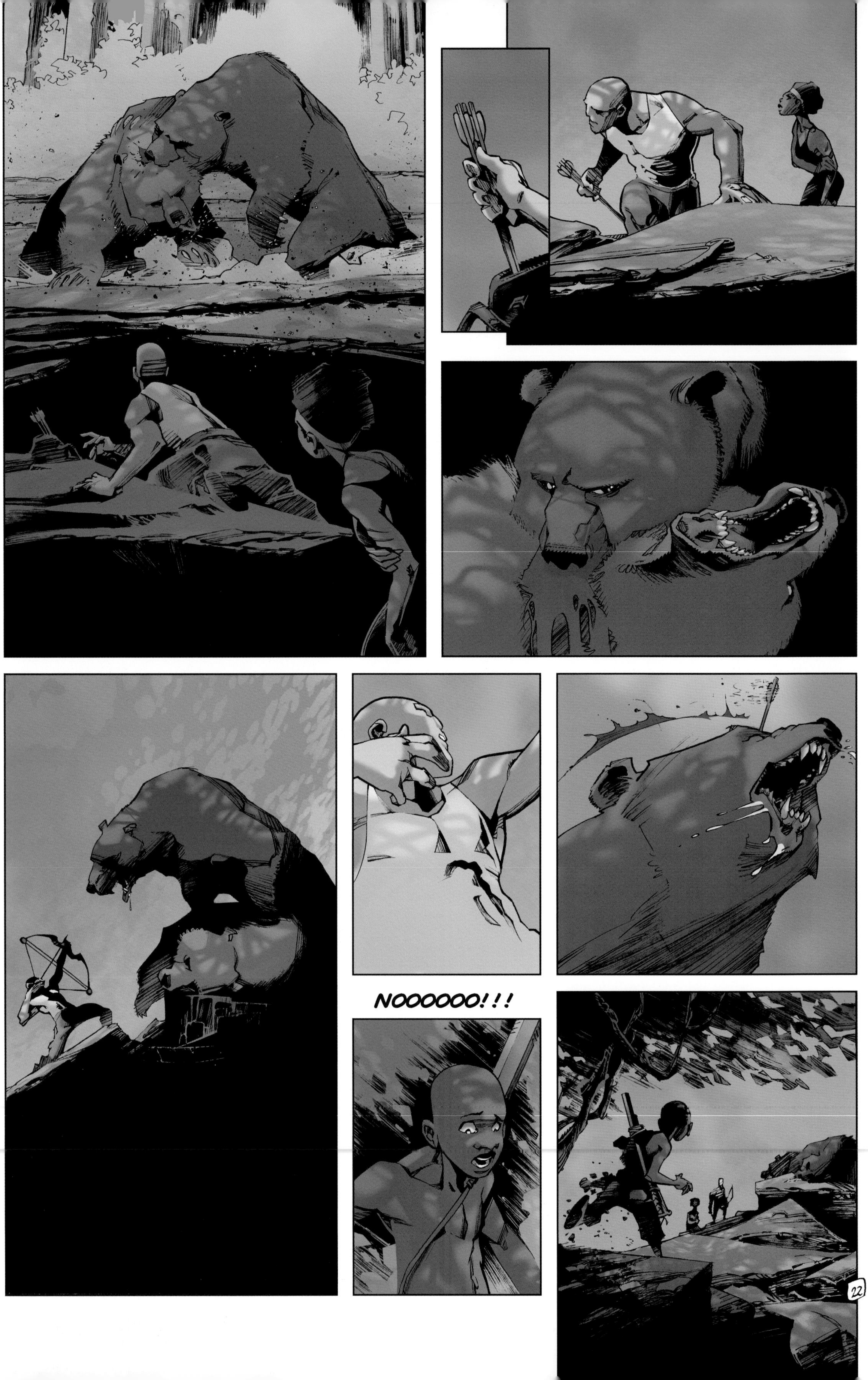
NOOOOOO!!!

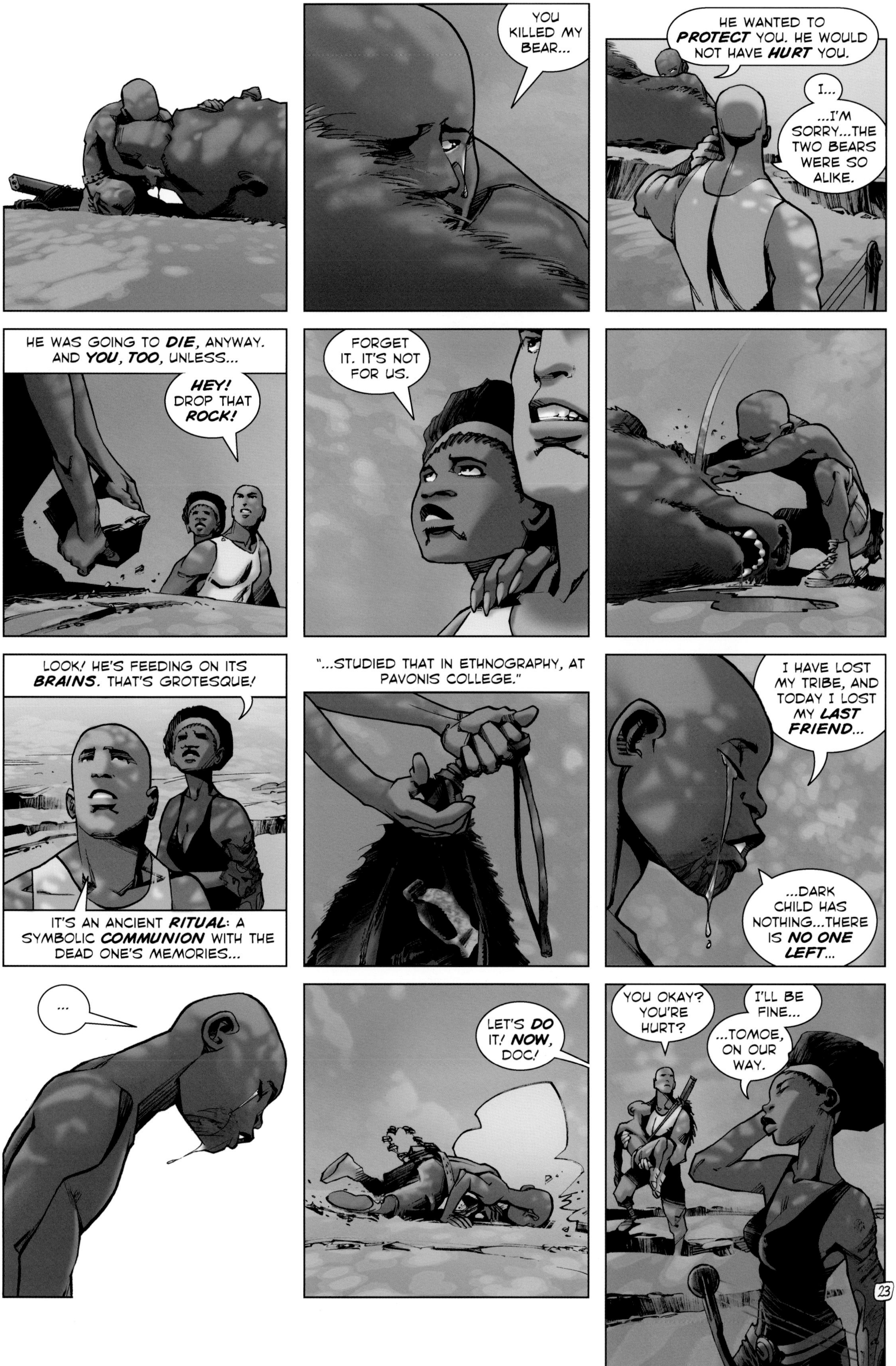

YOU KILLED MY BEAR...
HE WANTED TO PROTECT YOU. HE WOULD NOT HAVE HURT YOU.
I...
...I'M SORRY...THE TWO BEARS WERE SO ALIKE.
HE WAS GOING TO DIE, ANYWAY. AND YOU, TOO, UNLESS...
HEY! DROP THAT ROCK!
FORGET IT. IT'S NOT FOR US.
LOOK! HE'S FEEDING ON ITS BRAINS. THAT'S GROTESQUE!
IT'S AN ANCIENT RITUAL: A SYMBOLIC COMMUNION WITH THE DEAD ONE'S MEMORIES...
"...STUDIED THAT IN ETHNOGRAPHY, AT PAVONIS COLLEGE."
I HAVE LOST MY TRIBE, AND TODAY I LOST MY LAST FRIEND...
...DARK CHILD HAS NOTHING...THERE IS NO ONE LEFT...
...
LET'S DO IT! NOW, DOC!
YOU OKAY? YOU'RE HURT?
I'LL BE FINE...
...TOMOE, ON OUR WAY.

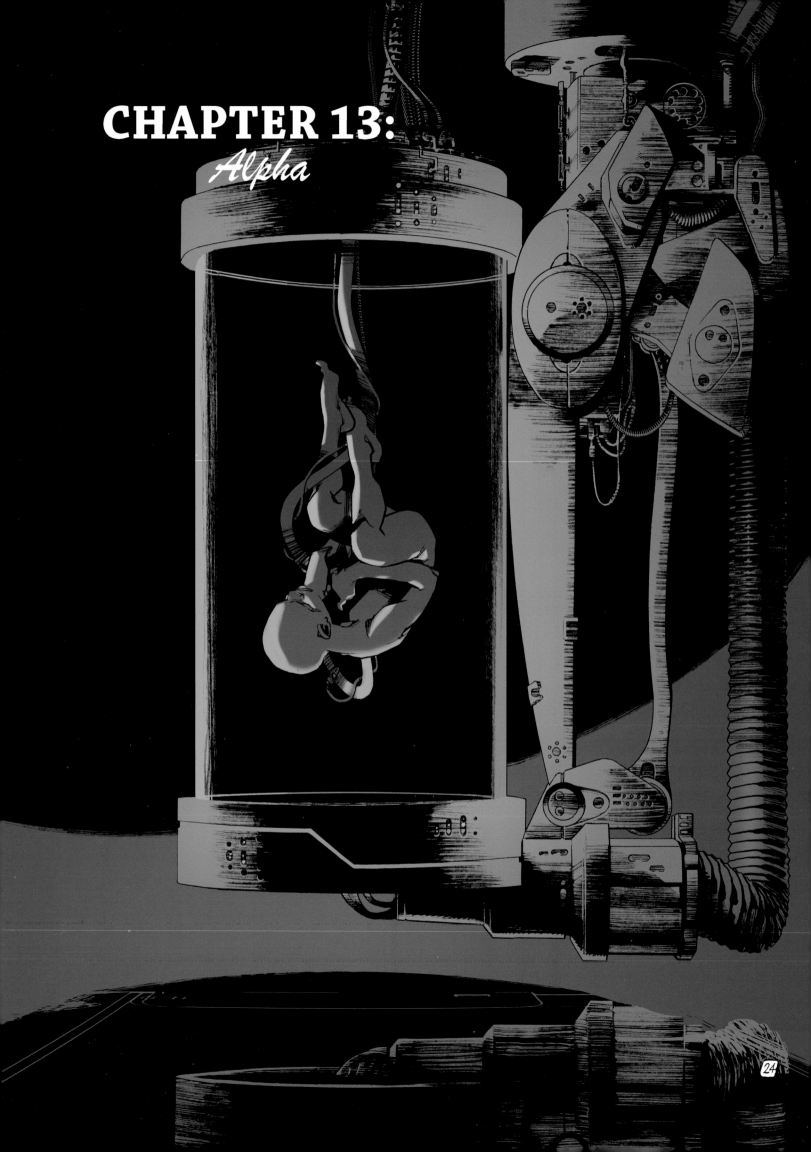

CHAPTER 13:
Alpha

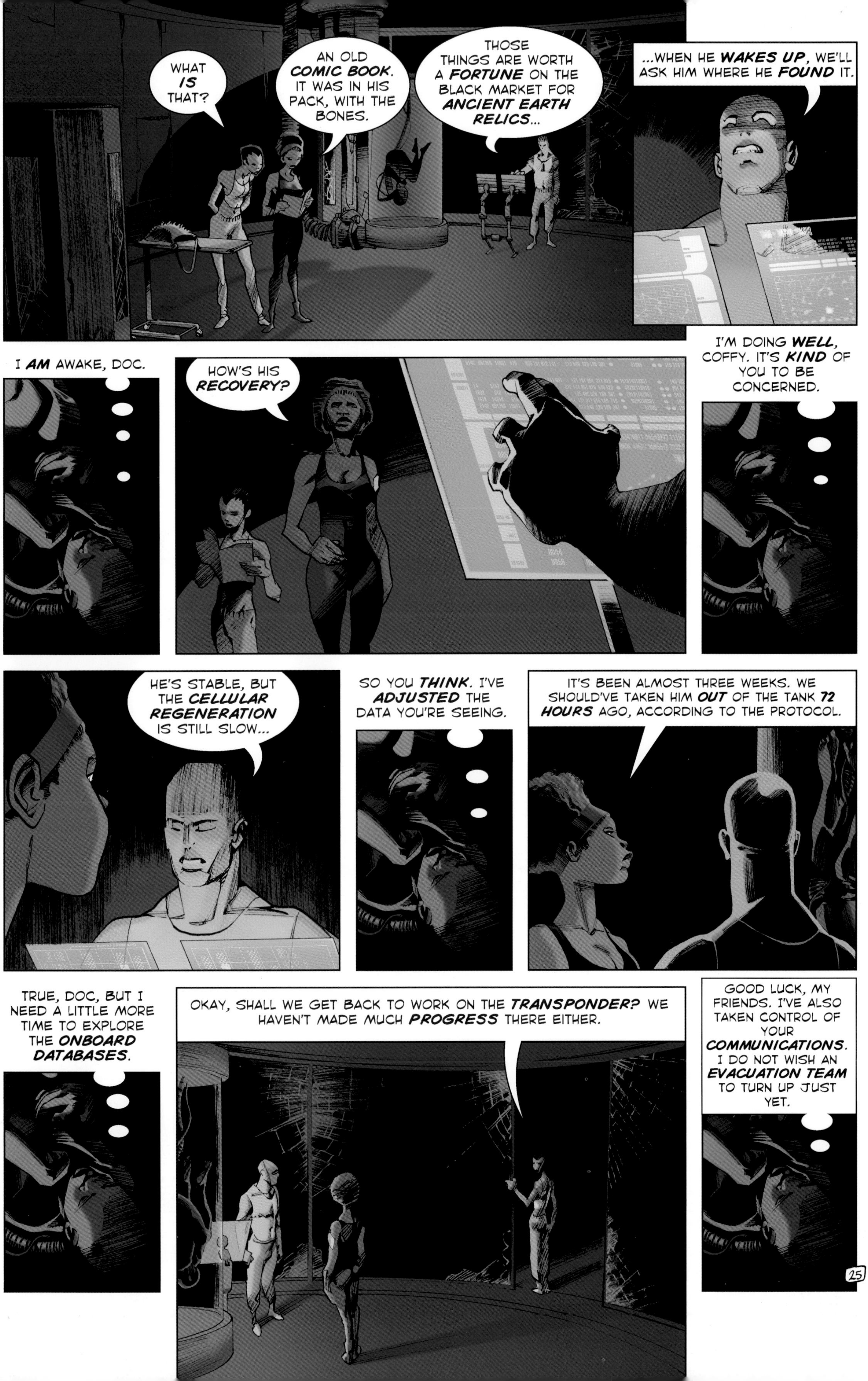
WHAT IS THAT?
AN OLD COMIC BOOK. IT WAS IN HIS PACK, WITH THE BONES.
THOSE THINGS ARE WORTH A FORTUNE ON THE BLACK MARKET FOR ANCIENT EARTH RELICS...
...WHEN HE WAKES UP, WE'LL ASK HIM WHERE HE FOUND IT.
I AM AWAKE, DOC.
HOW'S HIS RECOVERY?
I'M DOING WELL, COFFY. IT'S KIND OF YOU TO BE CONCERNED.
HE'S STABLE, BUT THE CELLULAR REGENERATION IS STILL SLOW...
SO YOU THINK. I'VE ADJUSTED THE DATA YOU'RE SEEING.
IT'S BEEN ALMOST THREE WEEKS. WE SHOULD'VE TAKEN HIM OUT OF THE TANK 72 HOURS AGO, ACCORDING TO THE PROTOCOL.
TRUE, DOC, BUT I NEED A LITTLE MORE TIME TO EXPLORE THE ONBOARD DATABASES.
OKAY, SHALL WE GET BACK TO WORK ON THE TRANSPONDER? WE HAVEN'T MADE MUCH PROGRESS THERE EITHER.
GOOD LUCK, MY FRIENDS. I'VE ALSO TAKEN CONTROL OF YOUR COMMUNICATIONS. I DO NOT WISH AN EVACUATION TEAM TO TURN UP JUST YET.

THEREUPON, I WAS LEFT ALONE TO RESUME EXPLORING THIS NEW UNIVERSE INTO WHICH I'D BEEN PLUNGED...
...WHEN THEY'D IMPLANTED THE NEURAL ANALYSIS INTERFACE, THEY HAD NEGLECTED TO BLOCK ACCESS FROM THE TANK TO THE SHIP'S SYSTEMS...WHY WORRY ABOUT A RADIOACTIVE, SEMI-CONSCIOUS CHILD, AFTER ALL?
I WAS A GHOST IN THEIR MACHINE, BUT MADE THE ROUNDS AS IF IT WERE MINE.
SO WHERE WAS I BEFORE BEING INTERRUPTED BY THE THREE MARTIANS?
...ECOLOGICAL CRISIS > ENVIRONMENTAL CATASTROPHE ...AH, HERE: > 2011 JAPAN, FUKUSHIMA DAIICHI NUCLEAR DISASTER.
Source: BarsoomMedia.orb> [archive 04-12-2011]
The nuclear accident has now been rated at Level 7 on the INES scale, which makes it comparable to the Chernobyl disaster...
>
HITACHI
General Electric
TOSHIBA
原発にもメーカー責任を
...in light of the nuclear industry's arrogance as well as the criminal negligence of regulatory authorities, world opinion has turned openly pessimistic.
Source: BarsoomMedia.orb>[archive 04-29-2055]
The solution to our problem of nuclear waste has been found: at 7,000 meters below sea level, in the oceanic subduction zones...
>
subducting plate
trench
sea level
continental plate
athenosphere
mantle
...the basic principle is to exploit continental tectonic plates at the thinnest point of the Earth's crust. The waste is deposited in the upper mantle, where it is slowly drawn towards the lower regions of magma...
>
...though at those inaccessible depths, it won't be robots doing the work, but some rather unexpected helpers, is that right?
>
Absolutely. Working with a type of cephalopod already adapted to that extreme environment, a team of engineers has succeeded in mutating a new species of super-octopod: 80-foot-long giants that are gentle as lambs and obedient as puppets!
>
A nootropic feed with organic interface allows us to communicate with these creatures. In the same way, the animal can transmit its knowledge to a second-generation octopod...
Source: BarsoomMedia.orb> [archive 11-07-2115]
The first icebergs destined for Mars have been towed to the São Tomé space elevator, where they will be broken up and calibrated for geosynchronous orbit...
>
...from there, a magnetic cannon will launch the ice towards the Red Planet to begin the terraforming process. By the end of the year, 270 million tons of water will have been dispatched.

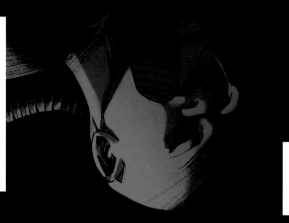

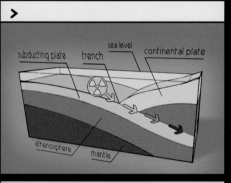

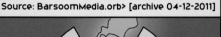

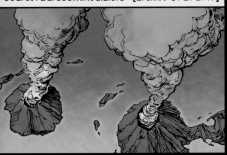

Source: BarsoomMedia.orb> [archive 01-21-2147]
Volcanic activity on Terceira Island has now extended to the entire Archipelago of the Azores, with increasing levels of radioactive sulfur dioxide, evidence that the nuclear waste dumps in Earth's subductive zones have created unexpected hazards to life.
>
Pressure in the magma chambers of our major volcanoes is growing rapidly. With the threat of imminent nuclear eruptions, Europe has raised the alert level to maximum and ordered the evacuation of its entire population.
Source: BarsoomMedia.orb> [archive 06-18-2181]
Now thirty years since the Azores Disaster caused the death of a billion and a half people due to large scale atmospheric dispersion of radioactive isotopes, the International Geophysics Agency has expressed concerns about renewed activity at certain hotspots around the world.
The spokesperson for OffWorld has taken advantage of the situation to resurrect advocacy for the original Exodus Project. By spitting out the poisons we injected beneath its crust, the Earth is now ordering us to leave.
Source: BarsoomMedia.orb> [archive 07-19-2206]
MARS
EXODUS
The AI governing commission at Lagrange points L4 and L5 has agreed to assist in construction of the spacecraft required for the Mars Exodus Project.
>
Construction of two ships to transport humanity's genomic data to the Red Planet should be completed within five years.
Source: BarsoomMedia.orb> [archive 04-29-2208]
Though largely forgotten, they've resurfaced from out of the past! From the middle of the 21st century, to be exact: the mutant octopod workers of the seas!
>
After last century's nuclear eruptions in the Azores, they had effectively been laid off with the termination of the radioactive waste recycling program. It seems the creatures took the situation as an opportunity to reproduce.
>
Korean fishermen spotted a group of these cephalopods not far from Incheon Airport. Similar sightings have been reported near the Japanese island of Tsushima and in the Atlantic waters off the coast of Central America.
27

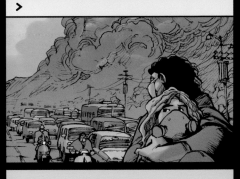

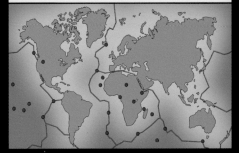

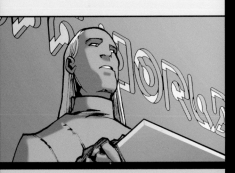

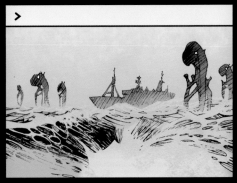

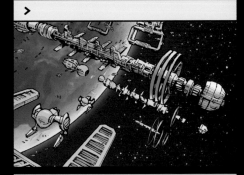

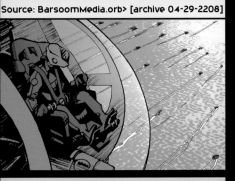

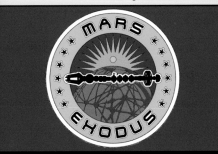

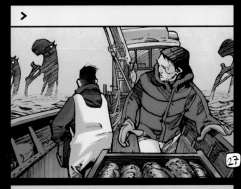

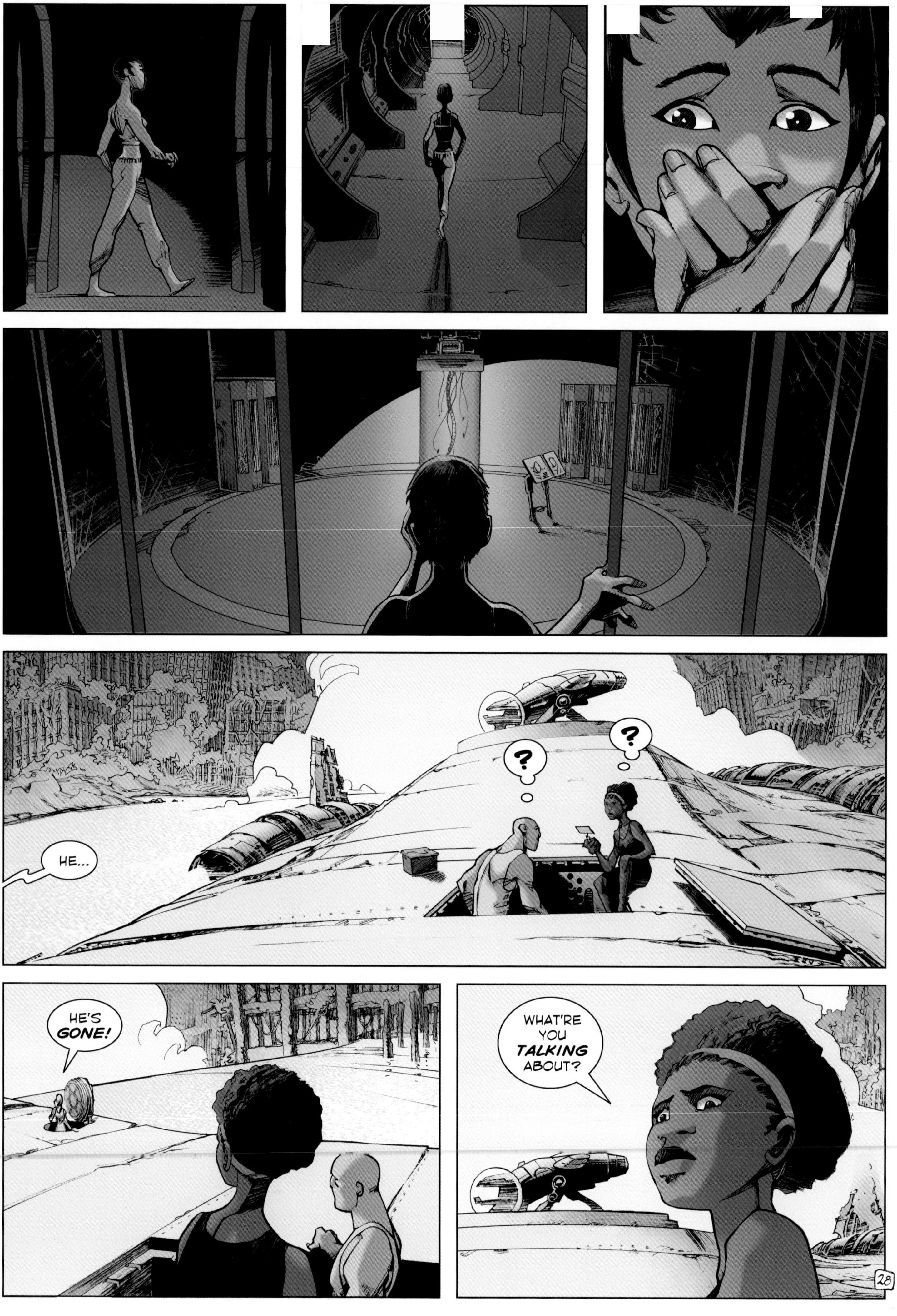
?
?
HE...
HE'S *GONE!*
WHAT'RE YOU *TALKING* ABOUT?

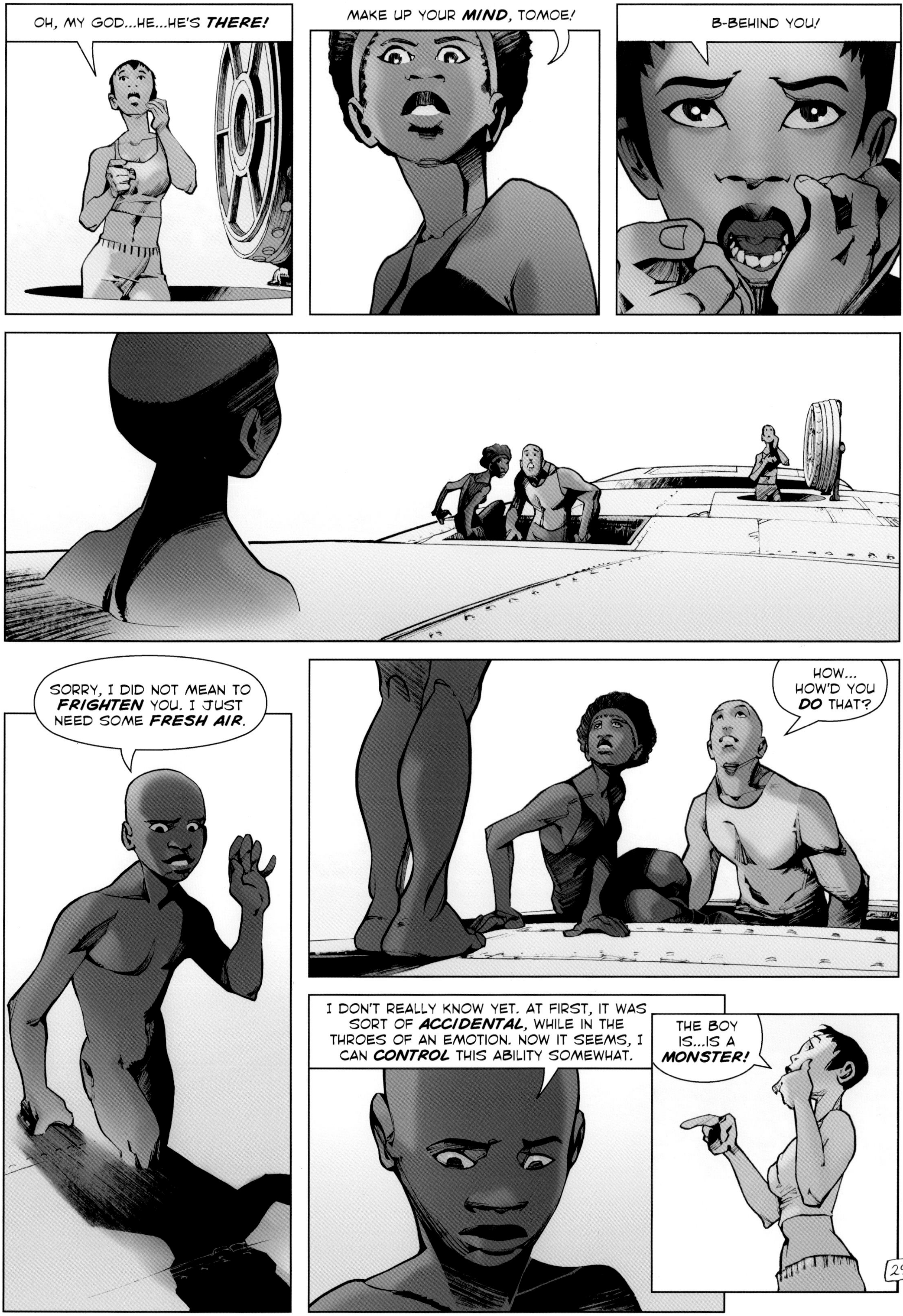
OH, MY GOD...HE...HE'S THERE!
MAKE UP YOUR MIND, TOMOE!
B-BEHIND YOU!
SORRY, I DID NOT MEAN TO FRIGHTEN YOU. I JUST NEED SOME FRESH AIR.
HOW... HOW'D YOU DO THAT?
I DON'T REALLY KNOW YET. AT FIRST, IT WAS SORT OF ACCIDENTAL, WHILE IN THE THROES OF AN EMOTION. NOW IT SEEMS, I CAN CONTROL THIS ABILITY SOMEWHAT.
THE BOY IS...IS A MONSTER!

MONSTERS... THAT IS EXACTLY WHAT MY TRIBE USED TO CALL THE *MUTANT OCTOPODS.*

WHAT ARE YOU SAYING?

I *LEARNED* THINGS WHILE IN THE TANK, INTERFACING WITH THE SHUTTLE'S OPERATING SYSTEM. BUT SOME OF YOUR *ARCHIVES* WERE DAMAGED WHEN YOU CRASHED...

...COFFY WILL FILL ME IN WHEN I RETURN. I UNDERSTAND SHE IS THE *HISTORIAN* OF THE GROUP.

AND HOW DO YOU KNOW *THAT?*

I WAS *LISTENING* TO YOU DURING MY CELLULAR RECONSTRUCTION. YOU SAVED MY *LIFE,* PUTTING ME IN THAT TANK. THANK YOU.

WHEN YOU *RETURN?* WHERE ARE YOU *GOING?*

I HAVE TO ACQUAINT MYSELF WITH MY *NEW ABILITIES,* AND THAT COULD BE DANGEROUS. IT IS BETTER FOR US TO BE *APART,* FOR THE MOMENT.

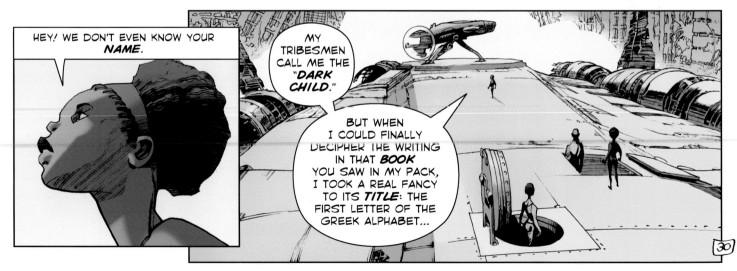

HEY! WE DON'T EVEN KNOW YOUR *NAME.*

MY TRIBESMEN CALL ME THE *"DARK CHILD."*

BUT WHEN I COULD FINALLY DECIPHER THE WRITING IN THAT *BOOK* YOU SAW IN MY PACK, I TOOK A REAL FANCY TO ITS *TITLE:* THE FIRST LETTER OF THE GREEK ALPHABET...

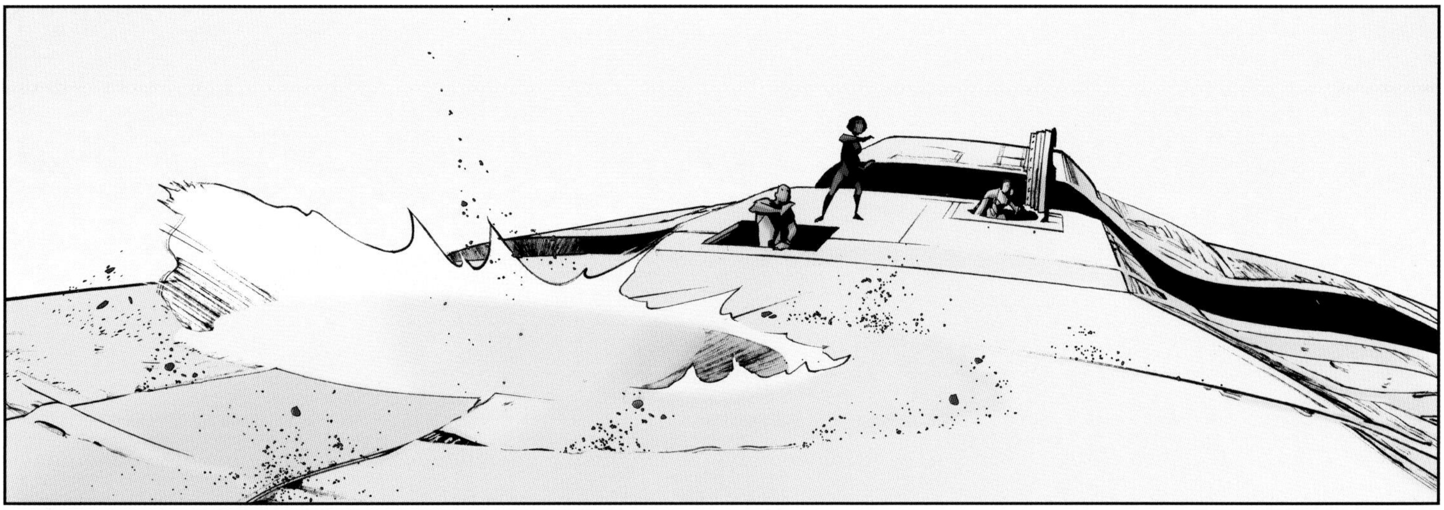

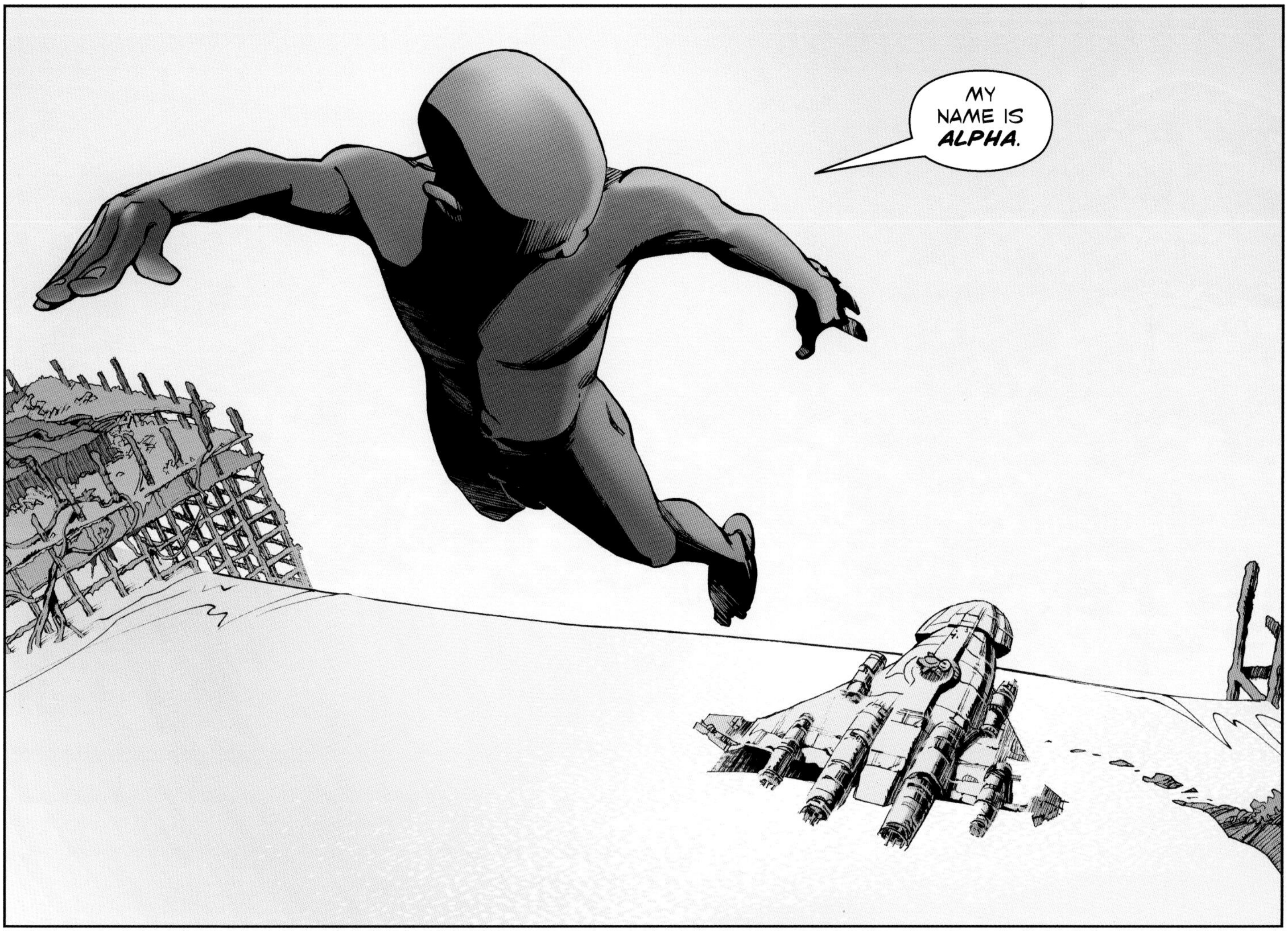
MY NAME IS ALPHA.

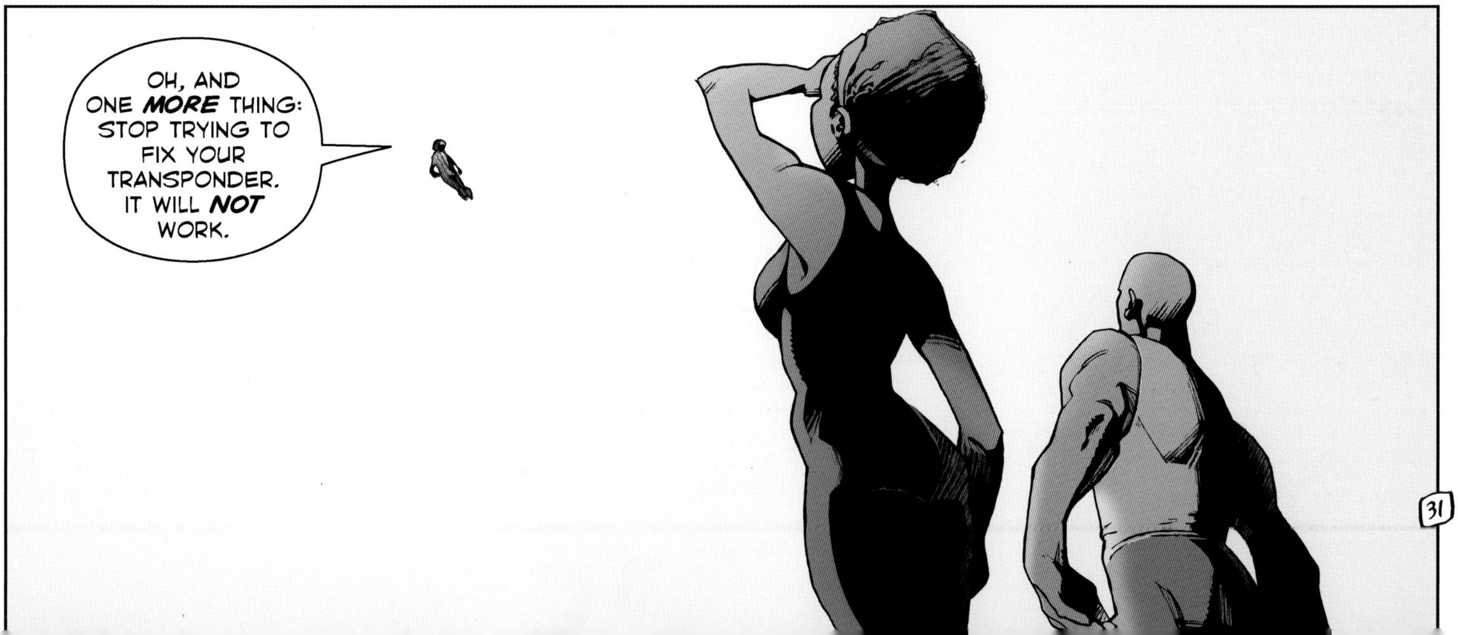
OH, AND ONE MORE THING: STOP TRYING TO FIX YOUR TRANSPONDER. IT WILL NOT WORK.

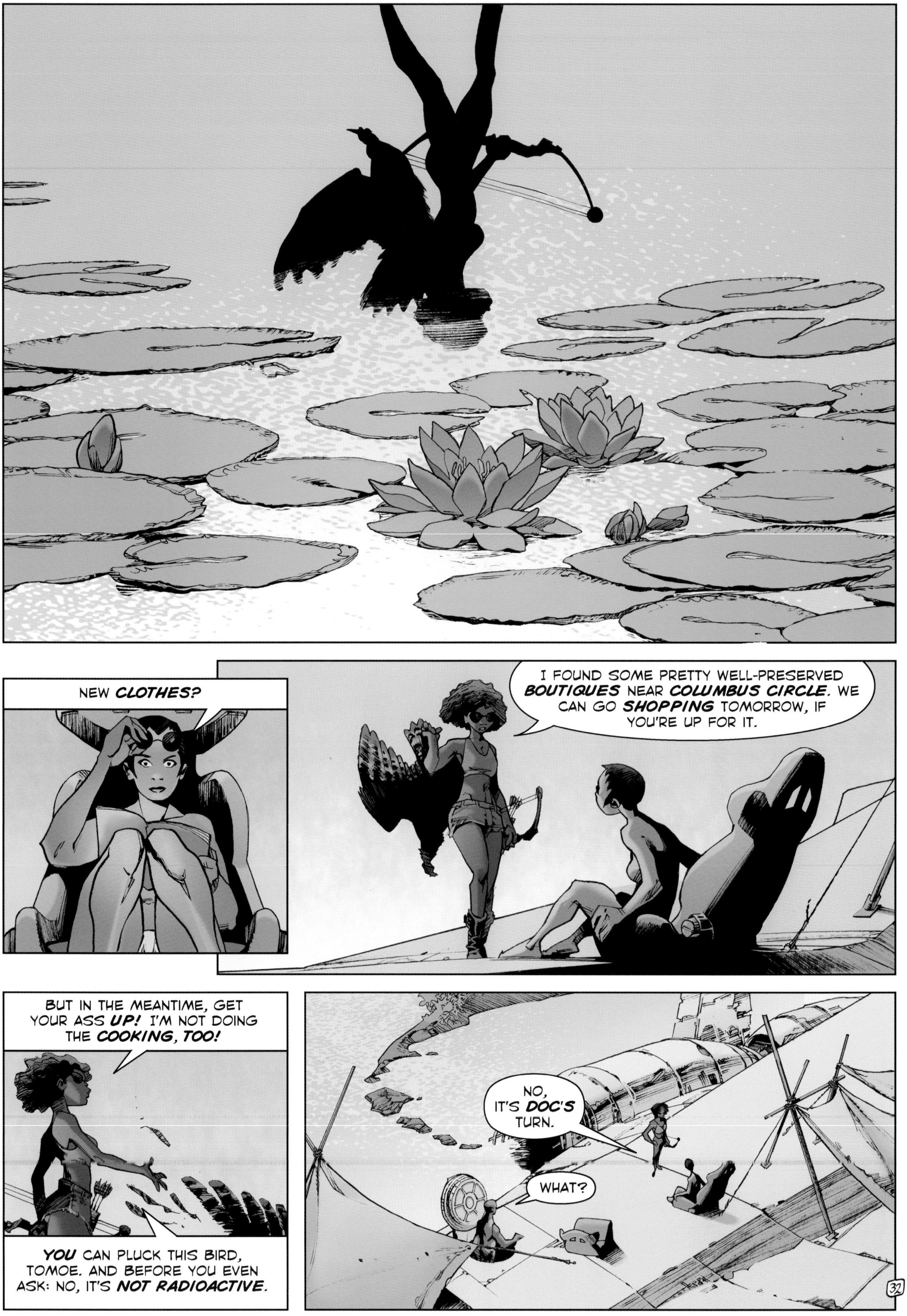
NEW *CLOTHES?*
I FOUND SOME PRETTY WELL-PRESERVED *BOUTIQUES* NEAR *COLUMBUS CIRCLE.* WE CAN GO *SHOPPING* TOMORROW, IF YOU'RE UP FOR IT.
BUT IN THE MEANTIME, GET YOUR ASS *UP!* I'M NOT DOING THE *COOKING, TOO!*
YOU CAN PLUCK THIS BIRD, TOMOE. AND BEFORE YOU EVEN ASK: NO, IT'S *NOT RADIOACTIVE.*
NO, IT'S *DOC'S* TURN.
WHAT?
32

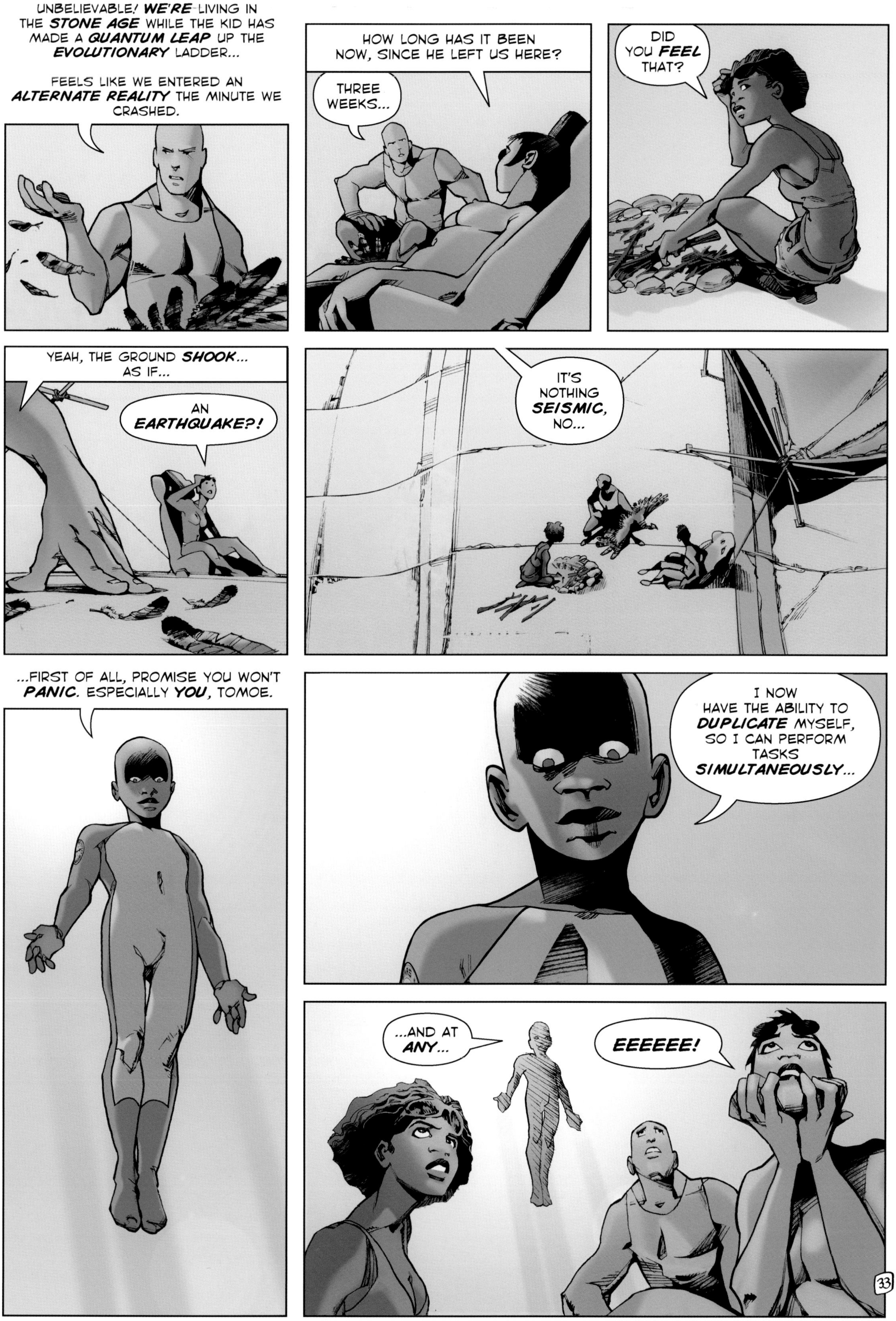
UNBELIEVABLE! WE'RE LIVING IN THE STONE AGE WHILE THE KID HAS MADE A QUANTUM LEAP UP THE EVOLUTIONARY LADDER...
FEELS LIKE WE ENTERED AN ALTERNATE REALITY THE MINUTE WE CRASHED.
HOW LONG HAS IT BEEN NOW, SINCE HE LEFT US HERE?
THREE WEEKS...
DID YOU FEEL THAT?
YEAH, THE GROUND SHOOK... AS IF...
AN EARTHQUAKE?!
IT'S NOTHING SEISMIC, NO...
...FIRST OF ALL, PROMISE YOU WON'T PANIC. ESPECIALLY YOU, TOMOE.
I NOW HAVE THE ABILITY TO DUPLICATE MYSELF, SO I CAN PERFORM TASKS SIMULTANEOUSLY...
...AND AT ANY...
EEEEEE!

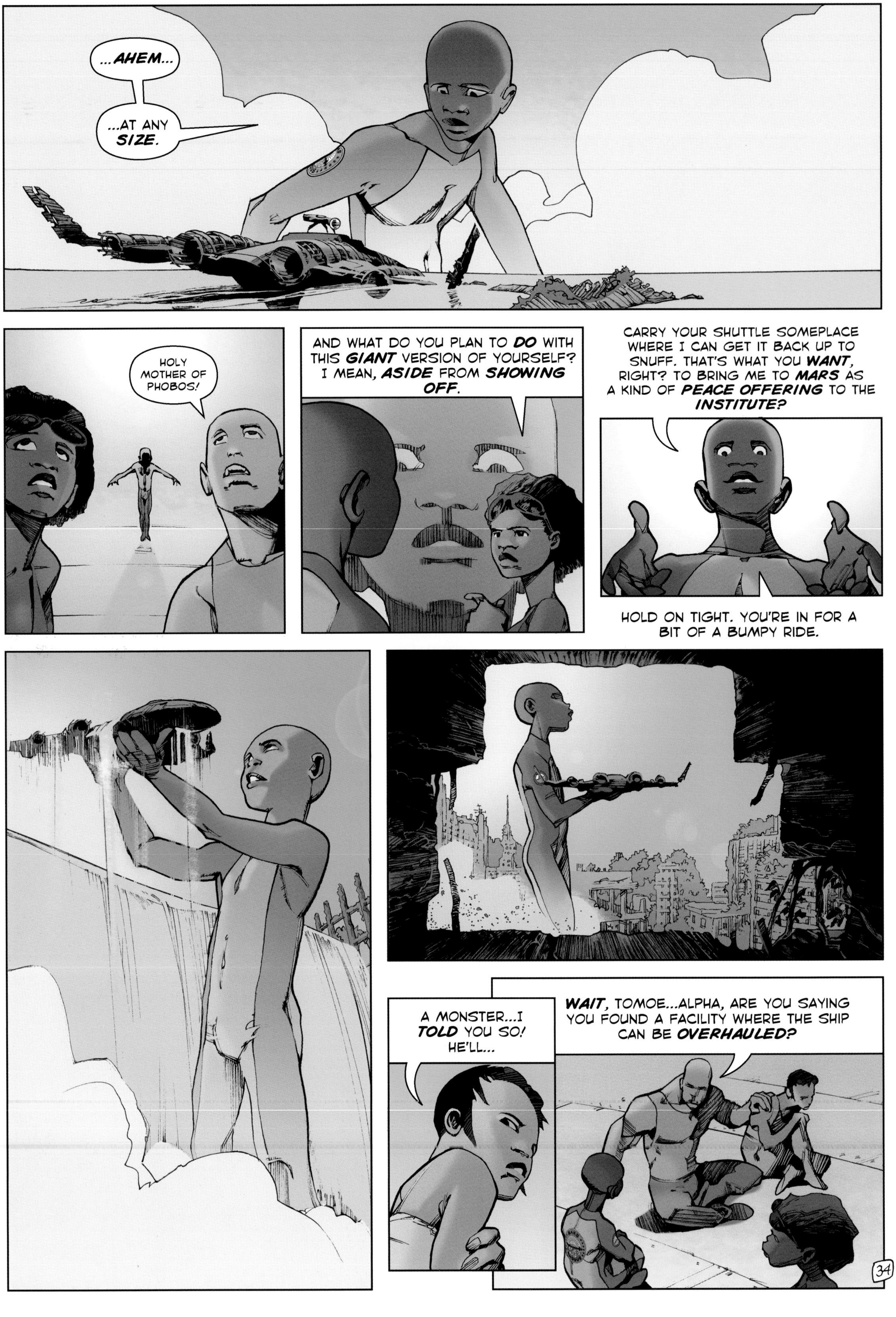
...AHEM...
...AT ANY SIZE.
HOLY MOTHER OF PHOBOS!
AND WHAT DO YOU PLAN TO DO WITH THIS GIANT VERSION OF YOURSELF? I MEAN, ASIDE FROM SHOWING OFF.
CARRY YOUR SHUTTLE SOMEPLACE WHERE I CAN GET IT BACK UP TO SNUFF. THAT'S WHAT YOU WANT, RIGHT? TO BRING ME TO MARS AS A KIND OF PEACE OFFERING TO THE INSTITUTE?
HOLD ON TIGHT. YOU'RE IN FOR A BIT OF A BUMPY RIDE.
A MONSTER...I TOLD YOU SO! HE'LL...
WAIT, TOMOE...ALPHA, ARE YOU SAYING YOU FOUND A FACILITY WHERE THE SHIP CAN BE OVERHAULED?

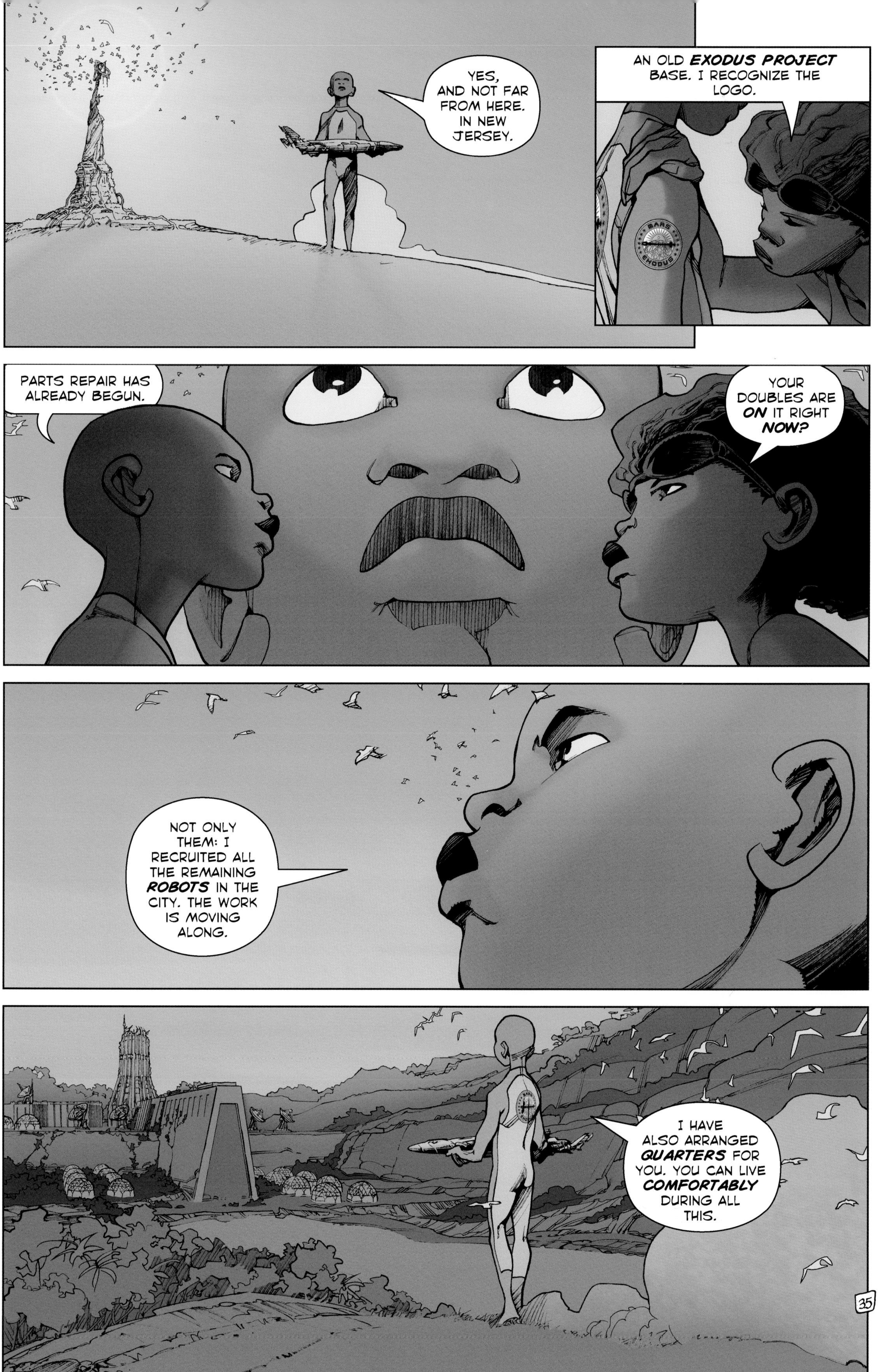

YES, AND NOT FAR FROM HERE. IN NEW JERSEY.
AN OLD ***EXODUS PROJECT*** BASE. I RECOGNIZE THE LOGO.
MARS EXODUS
PARTS REPAIR HAS ALREADY BEGUN.
YOUR DOUBLES ARE ***ON*** IT RIGHT ***NOW?***
NOT ONLY THEM: I RECRUITED ALL THE REMAINING ***ROBOTS*** IN THE CITY. THE WORK IS MOVING ALONG.
I HAVE ALSO ARRANGED ***QUARTERS*** FOR YOU. YOU CAN LIVE ***COMFORTABLY*** DURING ALL THIS.

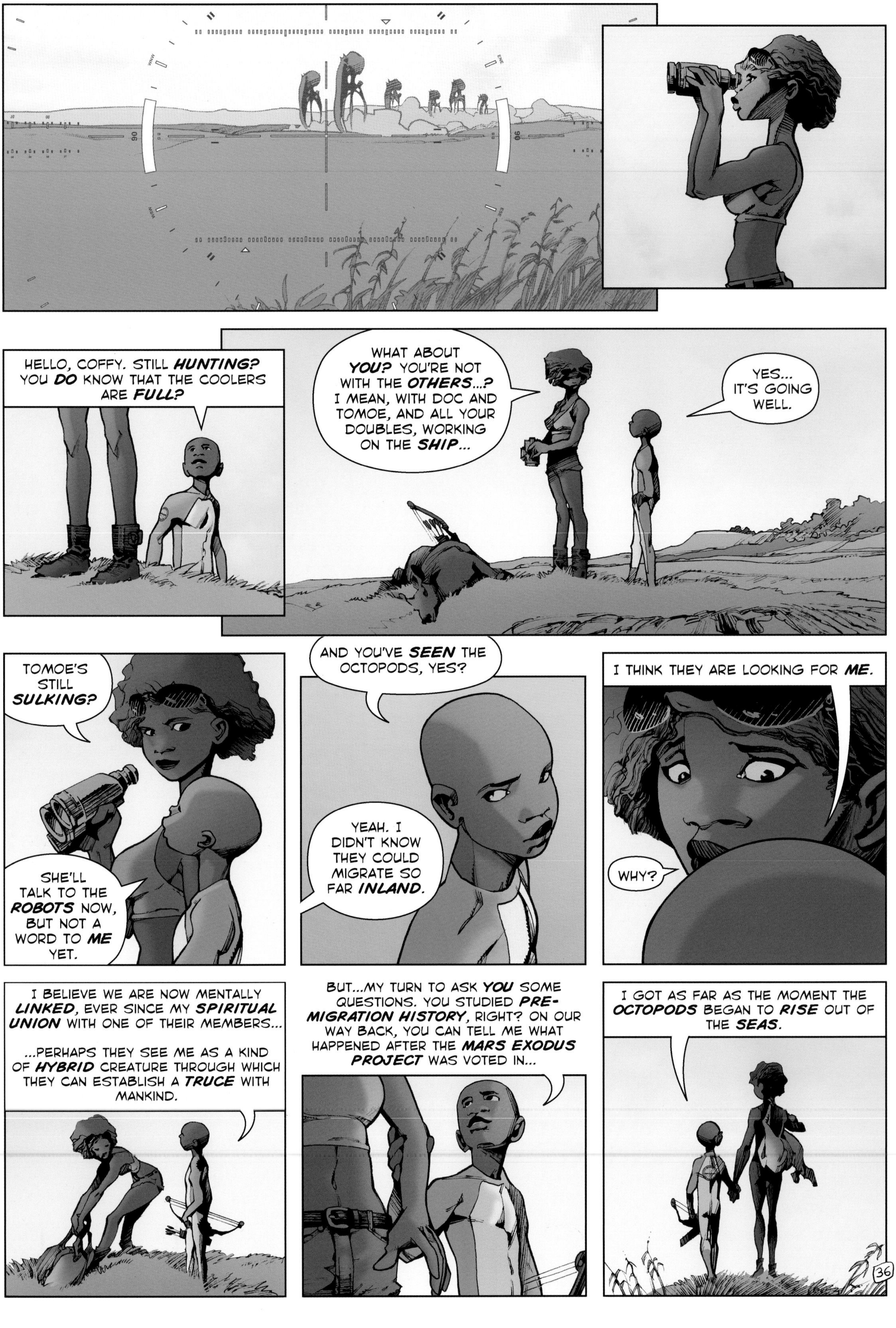
HELLO, COFFY. STILL HUNTING? YOU DO KNOW THAT THE COOLERS ARE FULL?
WHAT ABOUT YOU? YOU'RE NOT WITH THE OTHERS...? I MEAN, WITH DOC AND TOMOE, AND ALL YOUR DOUBLES, WORKING ON THE SHIP...
YES... IT'S GOING WELL.
TOMOE'S STILL SULKING?
SHE'LL TALK TO THE ROBOTS NOW, BUT NOT A WORD TO ME YET.
AND YOU'VE SEEN THE OCTOPODS, YES?
YEAH. I DIDN'T KNOW THEY COULD MIGRATE SO FAR INLAND.
I THINK THEY ARE LOOKING FOR ME.
WHY?
I BELIEVE WE ARE NOW MENTALLY LINKED, EVER SINCE MY SPIRITUAL UNION WITH ONE OF THEIR MEMBERS...
...PERHAPS THEY SEE ME AS A KIND OF HYBRID CREATURE THROUGH WHICH THEY CAN ESTABLISH A TRUCE WITH MANKIND.
BUT...MY TURN TO ASK YOU SOME QUESTIONS. YOU STUDIED PRE-MIGRATION HISTORY, RIGHT? ON OUR WAY BACK, YOU CAN TELL ME WHAT HAPPENED AFTER THE MARS EXODUS PROJECT WAS VOTED IN...
I GOT AS FAR AS THE MOMENT THE OCTOPODS BEGAN TO RISE OUT OF THE SEAS.

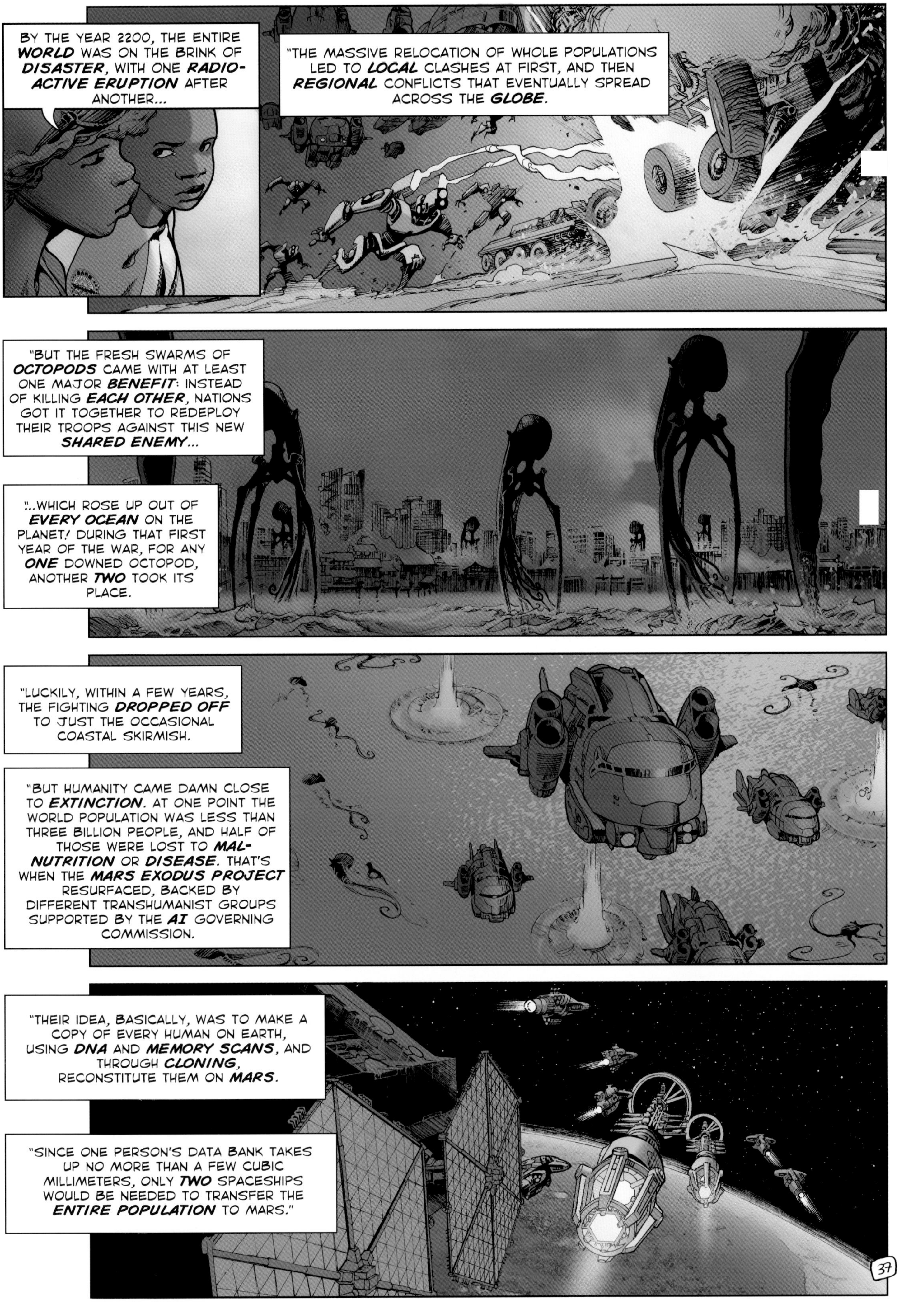
BY THE YEAR 2200, THE ENTIRE WORLD WAS ON THE BRINK OF DISASTER, WITH ONE RADIO-ACTIVE ERUPTION AFTER ANOTHER...
"THE MASSIVE RELOCATION OF WHOLE POPULATIONS LED TO LOCAL CLASHES AT FIRST, AND THEN REGIONAL CONFLICTS THAT EVENTUALLY SPREAD ACROSS THE GLOBE.
"BUT THE FRESH SWARMS OF OCTOPODS CAME WITH AT LEAST ONE MAJOR BENEFIT: INSTEAD OF KILLING EACH OTHER, NATIONS GOT IT TOGETHER TO REDEPLOY THEIR TROOPS AGAINST THIS NEW SHARED ENEMY...
"...WHICH ROSE UP OUT OF EVERY OCEAN ON THE PLANET! DURING THAT FIRST YEAR OF THE WAR, FOR ANY ONE DOWNED OCTOPOD, ANOTHER TWO TOOK ITS PLACE.
"LUCKILY, WITHIN A FEW YEARS, THE FIGHTING DROPPED OFF TO JUST THE OCCASIONAL COASTAL SKIRMISH.
"BUT HUMANITY CAME DAMN CLOSE TO EXTINCTION. AT ONE POINT THE WORLD POPULATION WAS LESS THAN THREE BILLION PEOPLE, AND HALF OF THOSE WERE LOST TO MAL-NUTRITION OR DISEASE. THAT'S WHEN THE MARS EXODUS PROJECT RESURFACED, BACKED BY DIFFERENT TRANSHUMANIST GROUPS SUPPORTED BY THE AI GOVERNING COMMISSION.
"THEIR IDEA, BASICALLY, WAS TO MAKE A COPY OF EVERY HUMAN ON EARTH, USING DNA AND MEMORY SCANS, AND THROUGH CLONING, RECONSTITUTE THEM ON MARS.
"SINCE ONE PERSON'S DATA BANK TAKES UP NO MORE THAN A FEW CUBIC MILLIMETERS, ONLY TWO SPACESHIPS WOULD BE NEEDED TO TRANSFER THE ENTIRE POPULATION TO MARS."
37

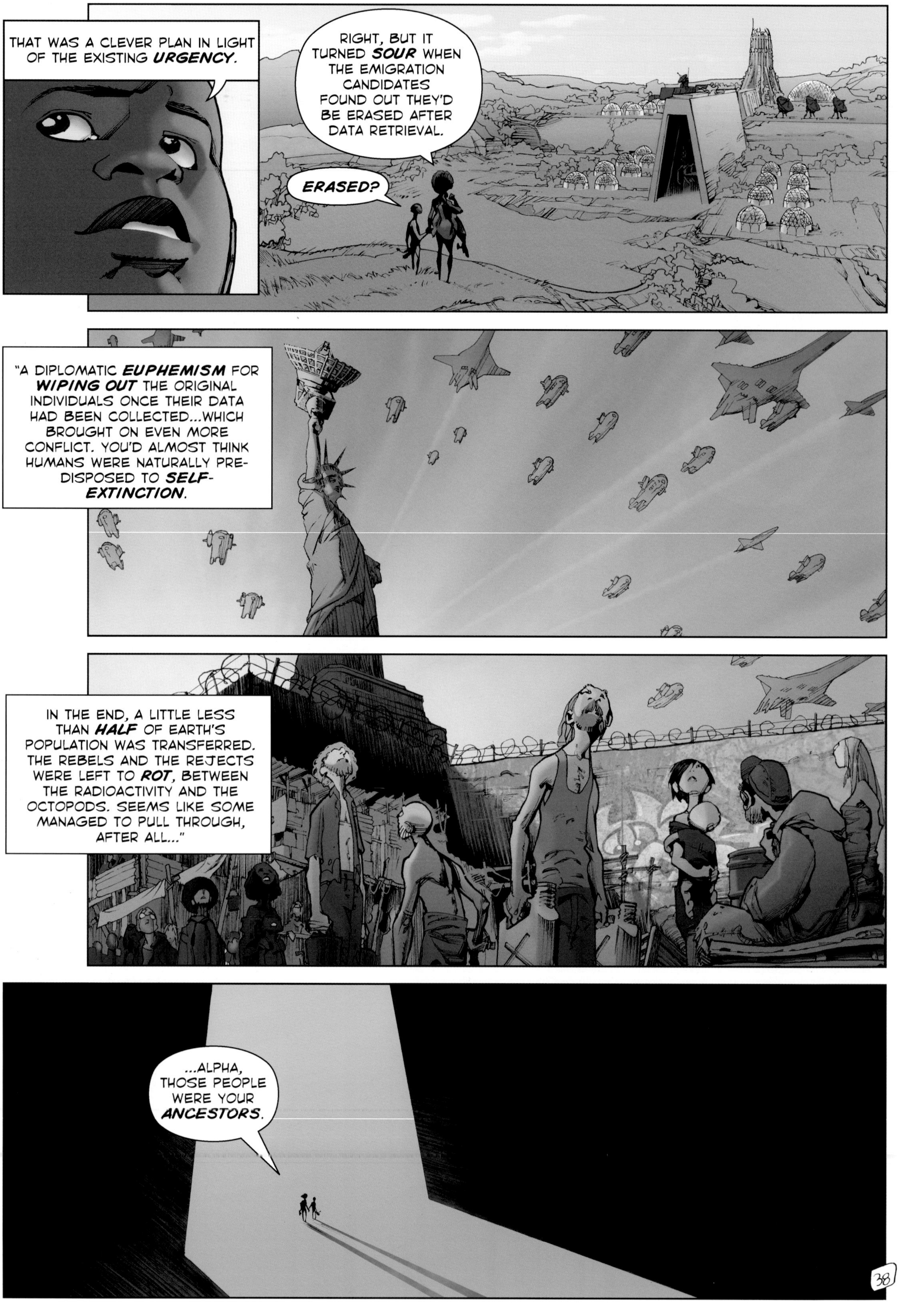
THAT WAS A CLEVER PLAN IN LIGHT OF THE EXISTING URGENCY.
RIGHT, BUT IT TURNED SOUR WHEN THE EMIGRATION CANDIDATES FOUND OUT THEY'D BE ERASED AFTER DATA RETRIEVAL.
ERASED?
"A DIPLOMATIC EUPHEMISM FOR WIPING OUT THE ORIGINAL INDIVIDUALS ONCE THEIR DATA HAD BEEN COLLECTED...WHICH BROUGHT ON EVEN MORE CONFLICT. YOU'D ALMOST THINK HUMANS WERE NATURALLY PRE-DISPOSED TO SELF-EXTINCTION.
IN THE END, A LITTLE LESS THAN HALF OF EARTH'S POPULATION WAS TRANSFERRED. THE REBELS AND THE REJECTS WERE LEFT TO ROT, BETWEEN THE RADIOACTIVITY AND THE OCTOPODS. SEEMS LIKE SOME MANAGED TO PULL THROUGH, AFTER ALL..."
...ALPHA, THOSE PEOPLE WERE YOUR ANCESTORS.

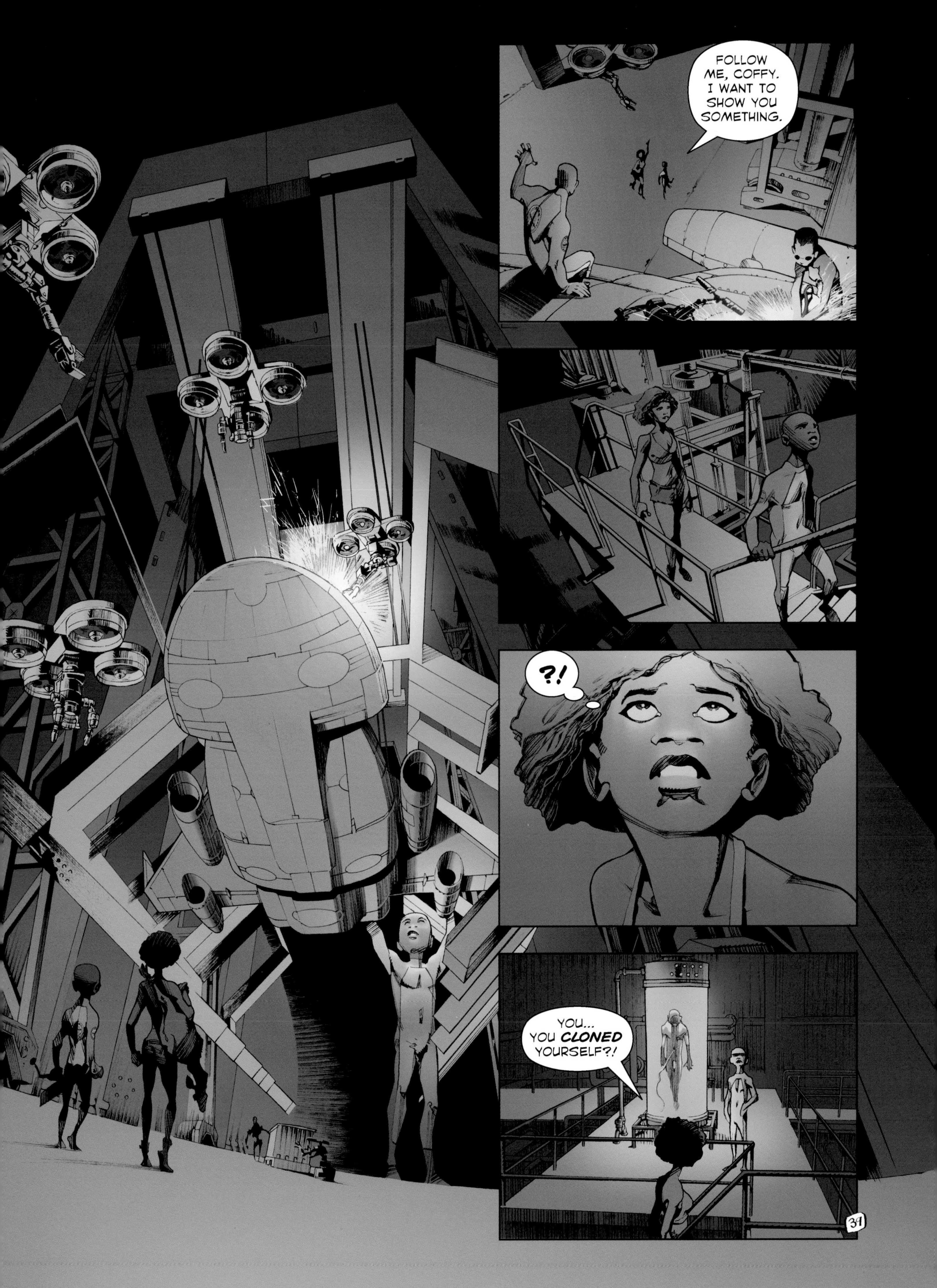
FOLLOW ME, COFFY. I WANT TO SHOW YOU SOMETHING.
?!
YOU... YOU CLONED YOURSELF?!

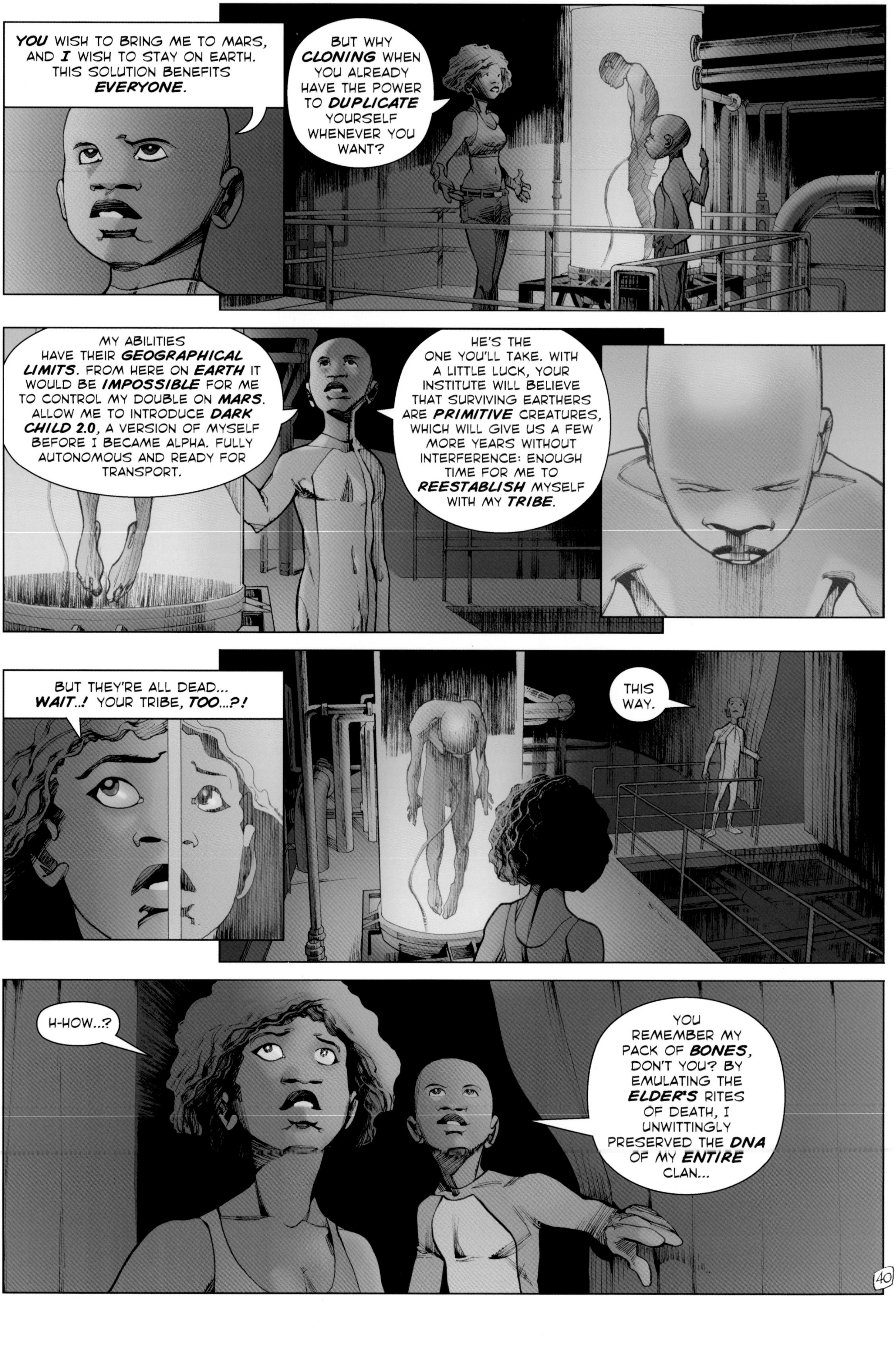
YOU WISH TO BRING ME TO MARS, AND I WISH TO STAY ON EARTH. THIS SOLUTION BENEFITS EVERYONE.
BUT WHY CLONING WHEN YOU ALREADY HAVE THE POWER TO DUPLICATE YOURSELF WHENEVER YOU WANT?
MY ABILITIES HAVE THEIR GEOGRAPHICAL LIMITS. FROM HERE ON EARTH IT WOULD BE IMPOSSIBLE FOR ME TO CONTROL MY DOUBLE ON MARS. ALLOW ME TO INTRODUCE DARK CHILD 2.0, A VERSION OF MYSELF BEFORE I BECAME ALPHA. FULLY AUTONOMOUS AND READY FOR TRANSPORT.
HE'S THE ONE YOU'LL TAKE. WITH A LITTLE LUCK, YOUR INSTITUTE WILL BELIEVE THAT SURVIVING EARTHERS ARE PRIMITIVE CREATURES, WHICH WILL GIVE US A FEW MORE YEARS WITHOUT INTERFERENCE: ENOUGH TIME FOR ME TO REESTABLISH MYSELF WITH MY TRIBE.
BUT THEY'RE ALL DEAD... WAIT..! YOUR TRIBE, TOO...?!
THIS WAY.
H-HOW...?
YOU REMEMBER MY PACK OF BONES, DON'T YOU? BY EMULATING THE ELDER'S RITES OF DEATH, I UNWITTINGLY PRESERVED THE DNA OF MY ENTIRE CLAN...

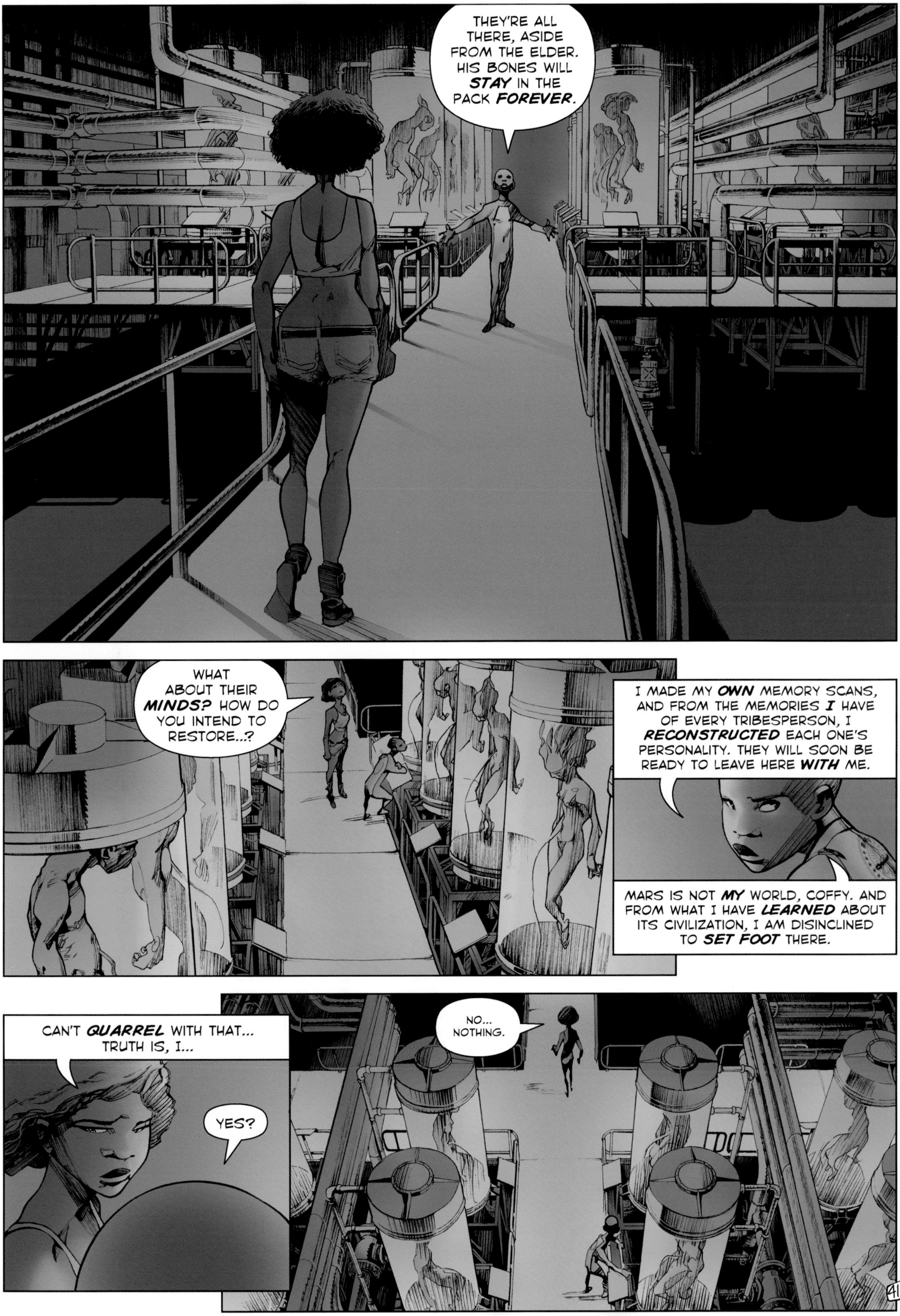
THEY'RE ALL THERE, ASIDE FROM THE ELDER. HIS BONES WILL STAY IN THE PACK FOREVER.
WHAT ABOUT THEIR MINDS? HOW DO YOU INTEND TO RESTORE...?
I MADE MY OWN MEMORY SCANS, AND FROM THE MEMORIES I HAVE OF EVERY TRIBESPERSON, I RECONSTRUCTED EACH ONE'S PERSONALITY. THEY WILL SOON BE READY TO LEAVE HERE WITH ME.
MARS IS NOT MY WORLD, COFFY. AND FROM WHAT I HAVE LEARNED ABOUT ITS CIVILIZATION, I AM DISINCLINED TO SET FOOT THERE.
CAN'T QUARREL WITH THAT... TRUTH IS, I...
YES?
NO... NOTHING.

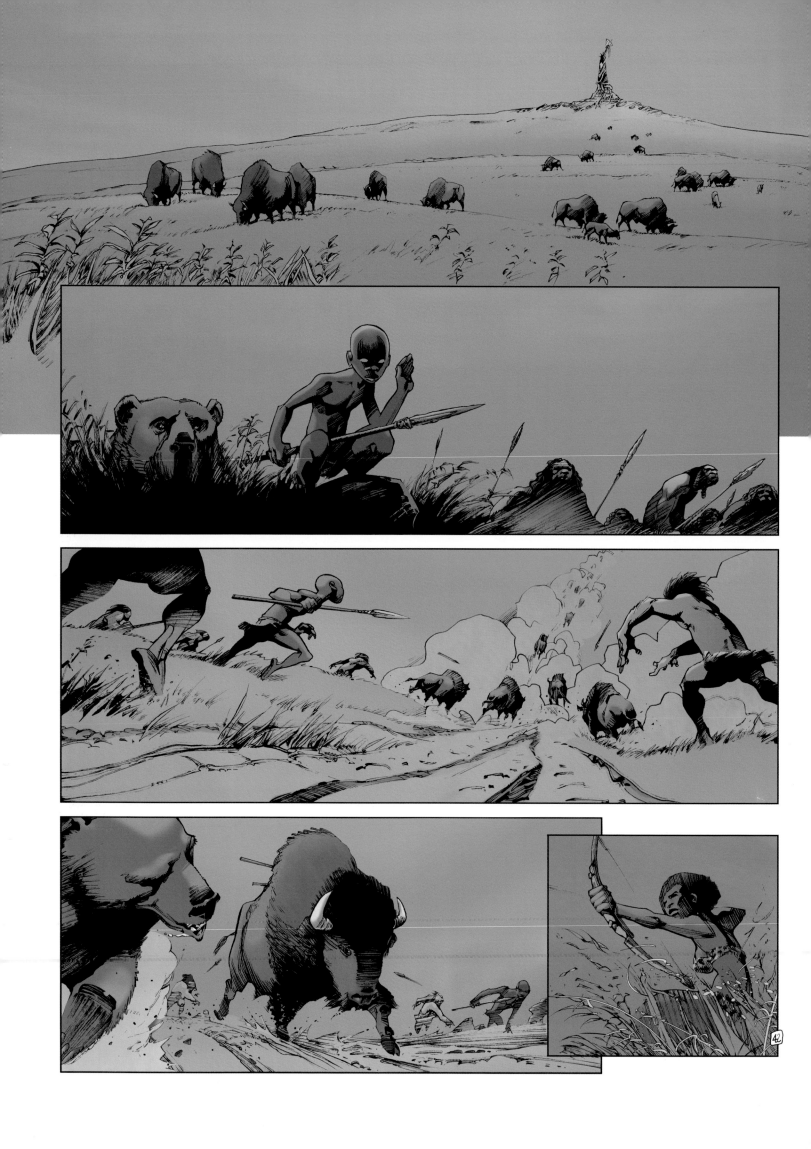

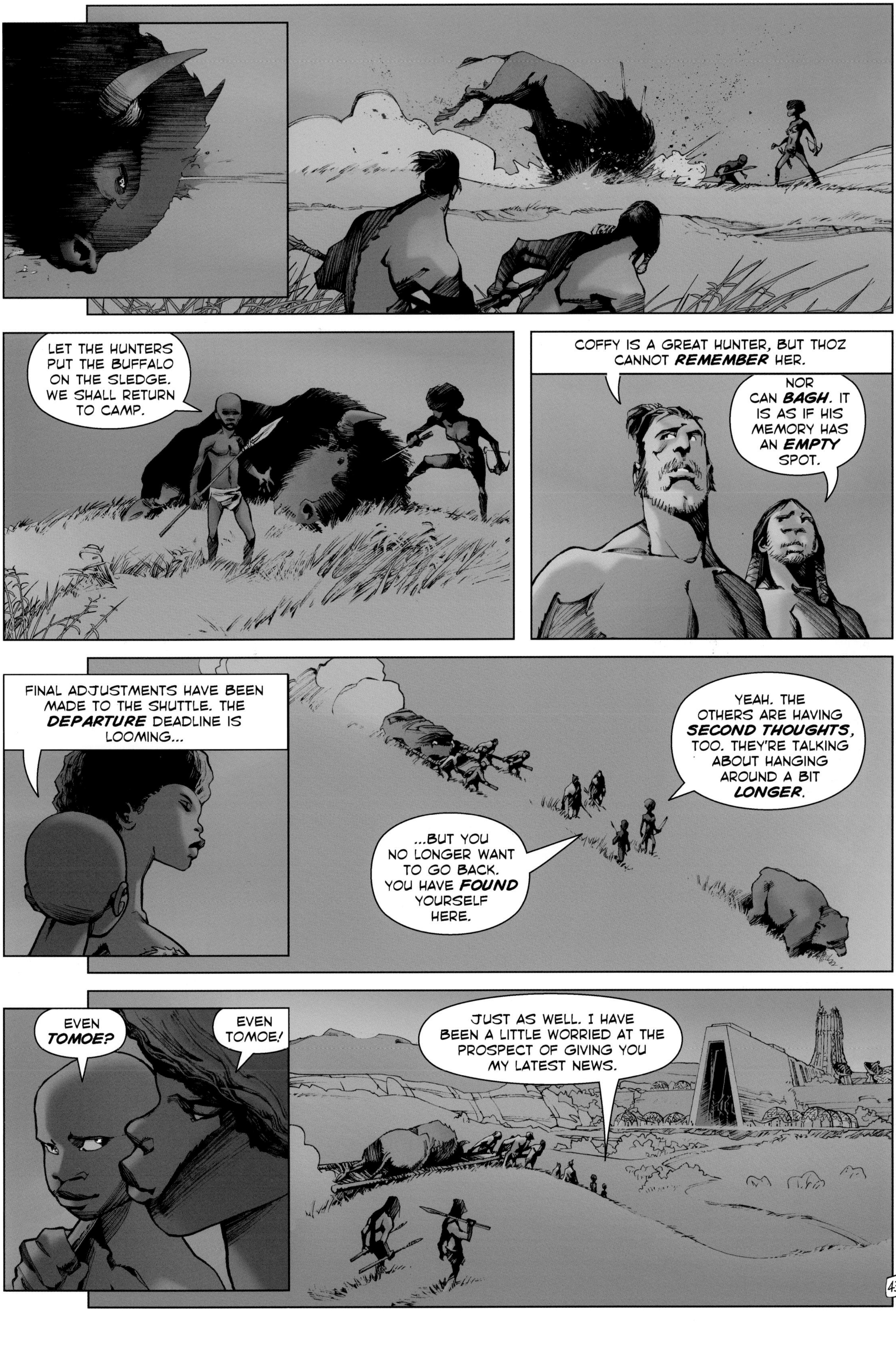

LET THE HUNTERS PUT THE BUFFALO ON THE SLEDGE. WE SHALL RETURN TO CAMP.
COFFY IS A GREAT HUNTER, BUT THOZ CANNOT REMEMBER HER.
NOR CAN BAGH. IT IS AS IF HIS MEMORY HAS AN EMPTY SPOT.
FINAL ADJUSTMENTS HAVE BEEN MADE TO THE SHUTTLE. THE DEPARTURE DEADLINE IS LOOMING...
YEAH. THE OTHERS ARE HAVING SECOND THOUGHTS, TOO. THEY'RE TALKING ABOUT HANGING AROUND A BIT LONGER.
...BUT YOU NO LONGER WANT TO GO BACK. YOU HAVE FOUND YOURSELF HERE.
EVEN TOMOE?
EVEN TOMOE!
JUST AS WELL. I HAVE BEEN A LITTLE WORRIED AT THE PROSPECT OF GIVING YOU MY LATEST NEWS.

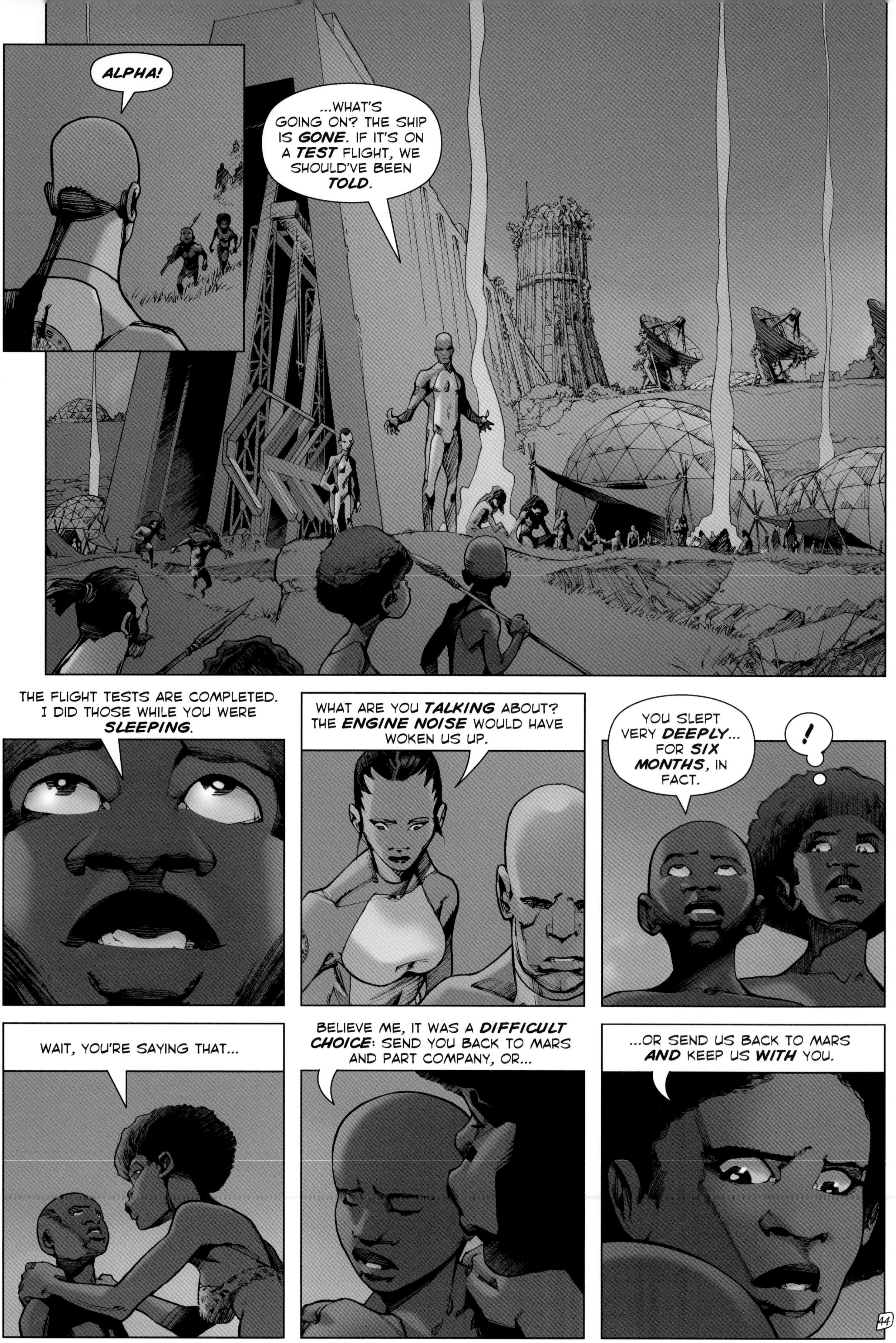
ALPHA!
...WHAT'S GOING ON? THE SHIP IS GONE. IF IT'S ON A TEST FLIGHT, WE SHOULD'VE BEEN TOLD.
THE FLIGHT TESTS ARE COMPLETED. I DID THOSE WHILE YOU WERE SLEEPING.
WHAT ARE YOU TALKING ABOUT? THE ENGINE NOISE WOULD HAVE WOKEN US UP.
YOU SLEPT VERY DEEPLY... FOR SIX MONTHS, IN FACT.
!
WAIT, YOU'RE SAYING THAT...
BELIEVE ME, IT WAS A DIFFICULT CHOICE: SEND YOU BACK TO MARS AND PART COMPANY, OR...
...OR SEND US BACK TO MARS AND KEEP US WITH YOU.
44

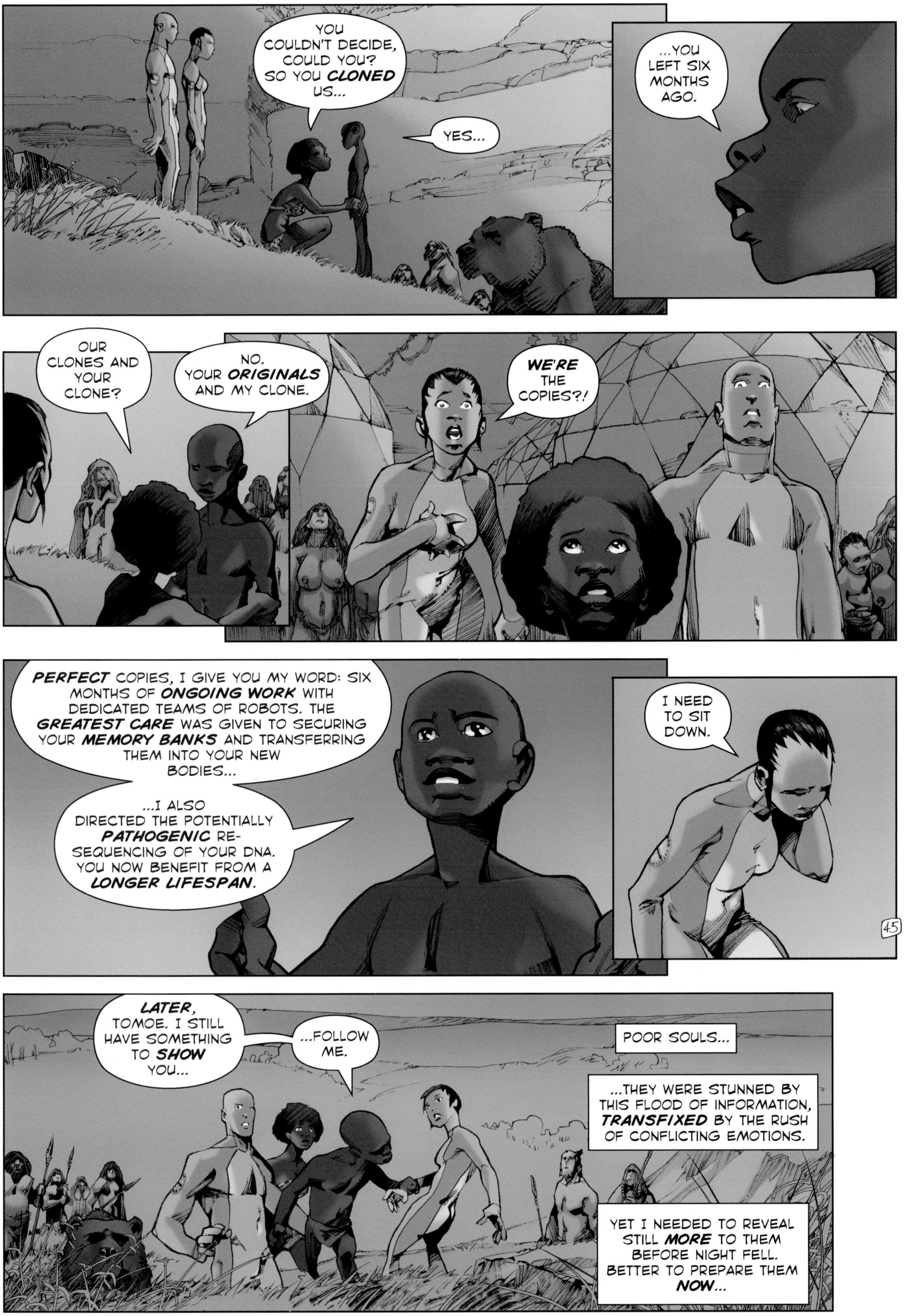
YOU COULDN'T DECIDE, COULD YOU? SO YOU CLONED US...
YES...
...YOU LEFT SIX MONTHS AGO.
OUR CLONES AND YOUR CLONE?
NO. YOUR ORIGINALS AND MY CLONE.
WE'RE THE COPIES?!
PERFECT COPIES, I GIVE YOU MY WORD: SIX MONTHS OF ONGOING WORK WITH DEDICATED TEAMS OF ROBOTS. THE GREATEST CARE WAS GIVEN TO SECURING YOUR MEMORY BANKS AND TRANSFERRING THEM INTO YOUR NEW BODIES...
...I ALSO DIRECTED THE POTENTIALLY PATHOGENIC RE-SEQUENCING OF YOUR DNA. YOU NOW BENEFIT FROM A LONGER LIFESPAN.
I NEED TO SIT DOWN.
LATER, TOMOE. I STILL HAVE SOMETHING TO SHOW YOU...
...FOLLOW ME.
POOR SOULS...
...THEY WERE STUNNED BY THIS FLOOD OF INFORMATION, TRANSFIXED BY THE RUSH OF CONFLICTING EMOTIONS.
YET I NEEDED TO REVEAL STILL MORE TO THEM BEFORE NIGHT FELL. BETTER TO PREPARE THEM NOW...

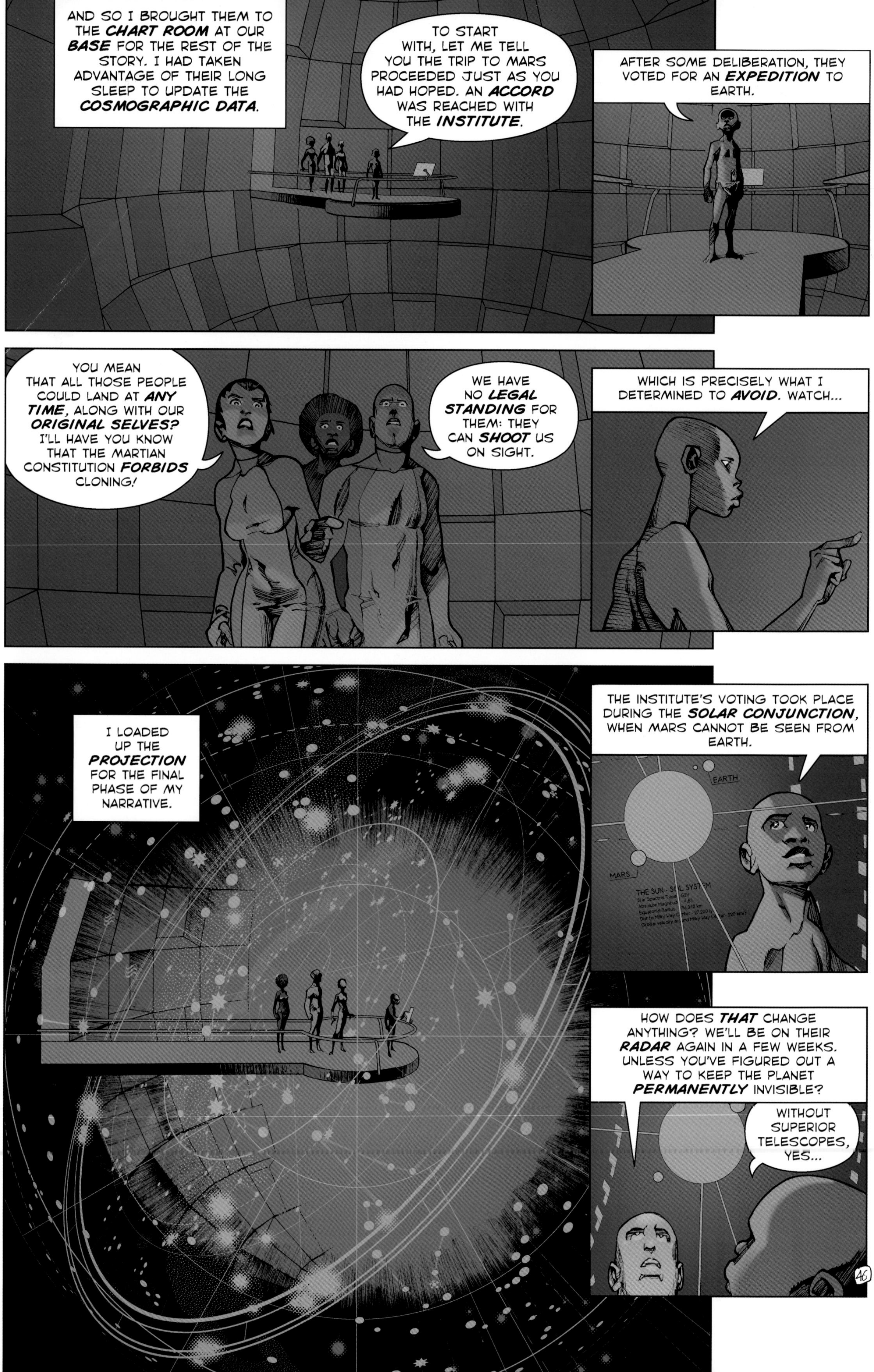
AND SO I BROUGHT THEM TO THE **CHART ROOM** AT OUR **BASE** FOR THE REST OF THE STORY. I HAD TAKEN ADVANTAGE OF THEIR LONG SLEEP TO UPDATE THE **COSMOGRAPHIC DATA**.
TO START WITH, LET ME TELL YOU THE TRIP TO MARS PROCEEDED JUST AS YOU HAD HOPED. AN **ACCORD** WAS REACHED WITH THE **INSTITUTE**.
AFTER SOME DELIBERATION, THEY VOTED FOR AN **EXPEDITION** TO EARTH.
YOU MEAN THAT ALL THOSE PEOPLE COULD LAND AT **ANY TIME**, ALONG WITH OUR **ORIGINAL SELVES?** I'LL HAVE YOU KNOW THAT THE MARTIAN CONSTITUTION **FORBIDS** CLONING!
WE HAVE NO **LEGAL STANDING** FOR THEM: THEY CAN **SHOOT** US ON SIGHT.
WHICH IS PRECISELY WHAT I DETERMINED TO **AVOID**. WATCH...
I LOADED UP THE **PROJECTION** FOR THE FINAL PHASE OF MY NARRATIVE.
THE INSTITUTE'S VOTING TOOK PLACE DURING THE **SOLAR CONJUNCTION**, WHEN MARS CANNOT BE SEEN FROM EARTH.
EARTH
MARS
HOW DOES **THAT** CHANGE ANYTHING? WE'LL BE ON THEIR **RADAR** AGAIN IN A FEW WEEKS. UNLESS YOU'VE FIGURED OUT A WAY TO KEEP THE PLANET **PERMANENTLY** INVISIBLE?
WITHOUT SUPERIOR TELESCOPES, YES...

...BECAUSE *NOW*...

WE ARE *VERY FAR* AWAY!

MY DEMONSTRA-TION HAD ONLY LEFT THEM IN A GREATER GULF OF *CONFUSION.* IF I WERE TO CONVINCE THEM, I WOULD NEED TO SHOW THEM THE *REAL THING.*

AND THE BEST PLACE FOR THAT WAS AT THE *TOP* OF OUR *BASE TOWER.*

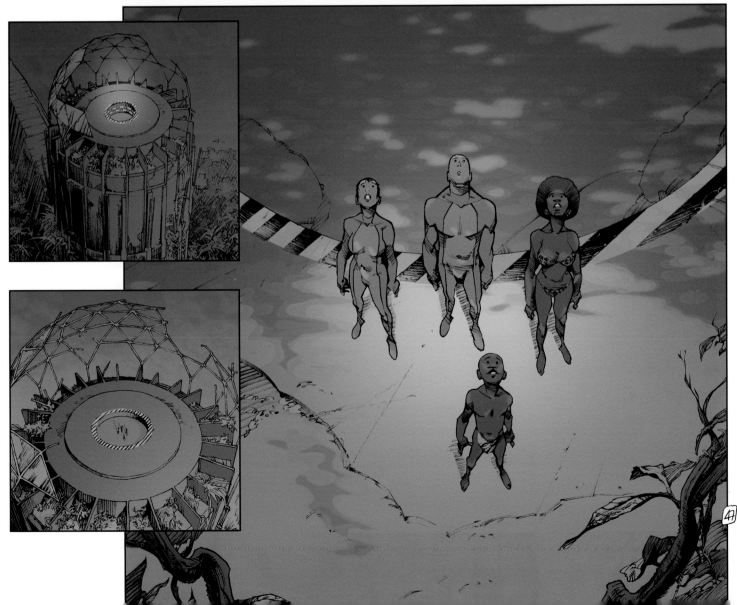

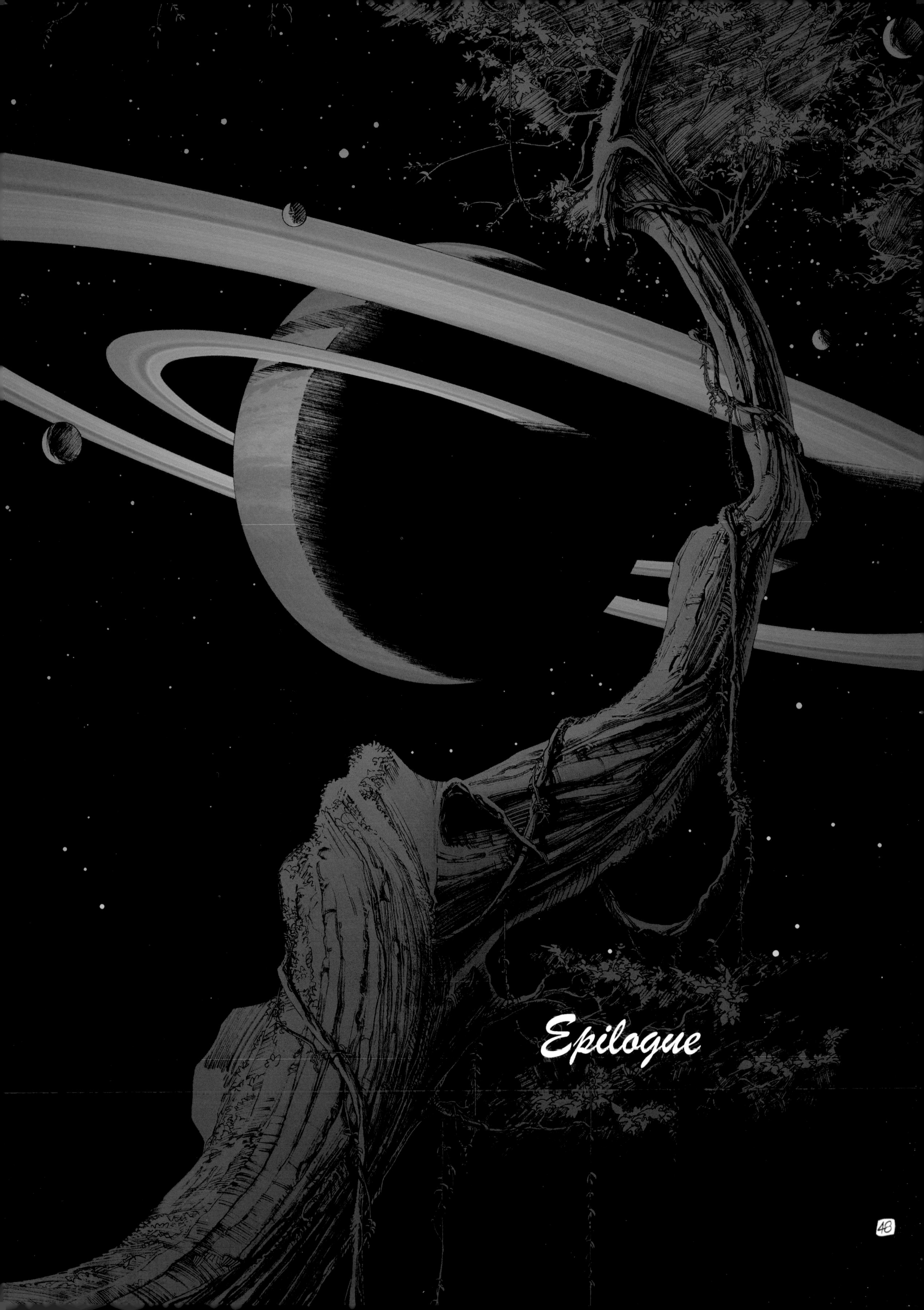
Epilogue

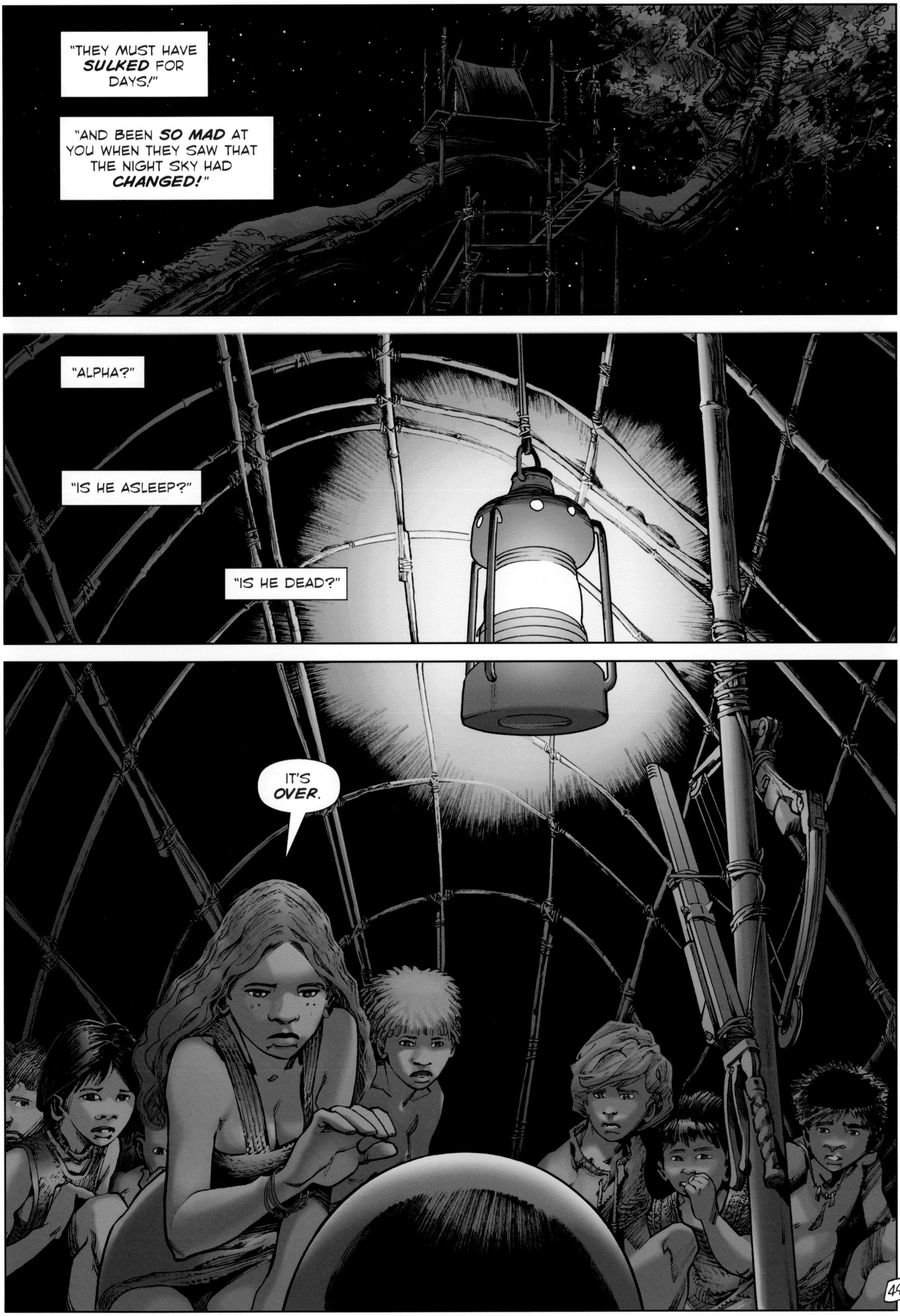
"THEY MUST HAVE SULKED FOR DAYS!"
"AND BEEN SO MAD AT YOU WHEN THEY SAW THAT THE NIGHT SKY HAD CHANGED!"
"ALPHA?"
"IS HE ASLEEP?"
"IS HE DEAD?"
IT'S OVER.

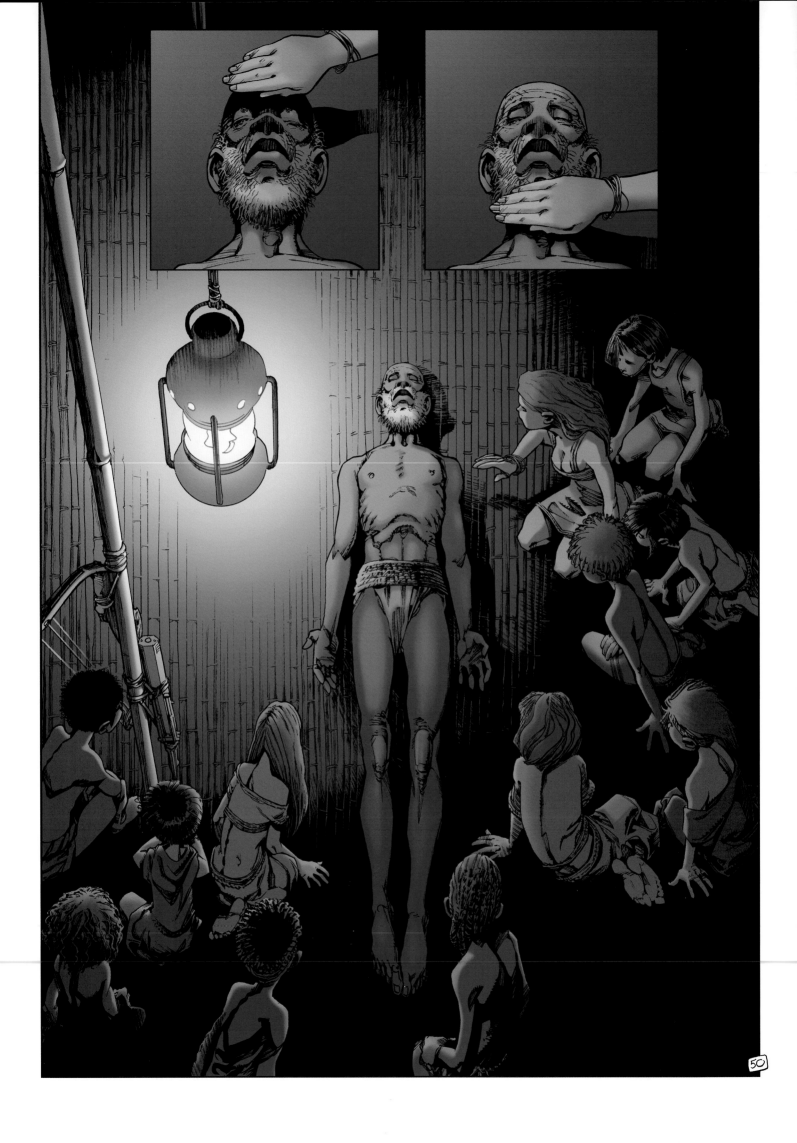

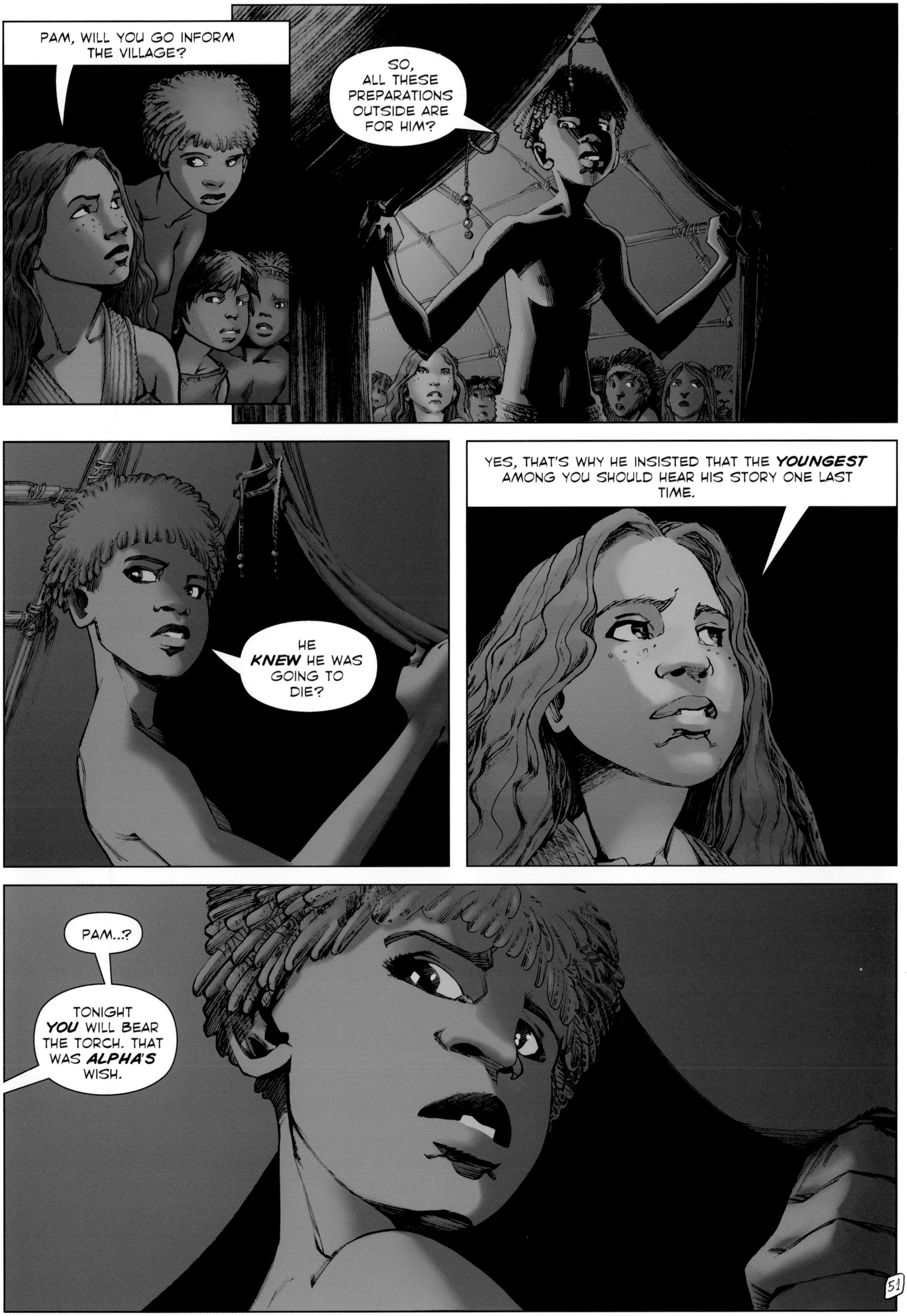

PAM, WILL YOU GO INFORM THE VILLAGE?
SO, ALL THESE PREPARATIONS OUTSIDE ARE FOR HIM?
HE KNEW HE WAS GOING TO DIE?
YES, THAT'S WHY HE INSISTED THAT THE YOUNGEST AMONG YOU SHOULD HEAR HIS STORY ONE LAST TIME.
PAM...?
TONIGHT YOU WILL BEAR THE TORCH. THAT WAS ALPHA'S WISH.

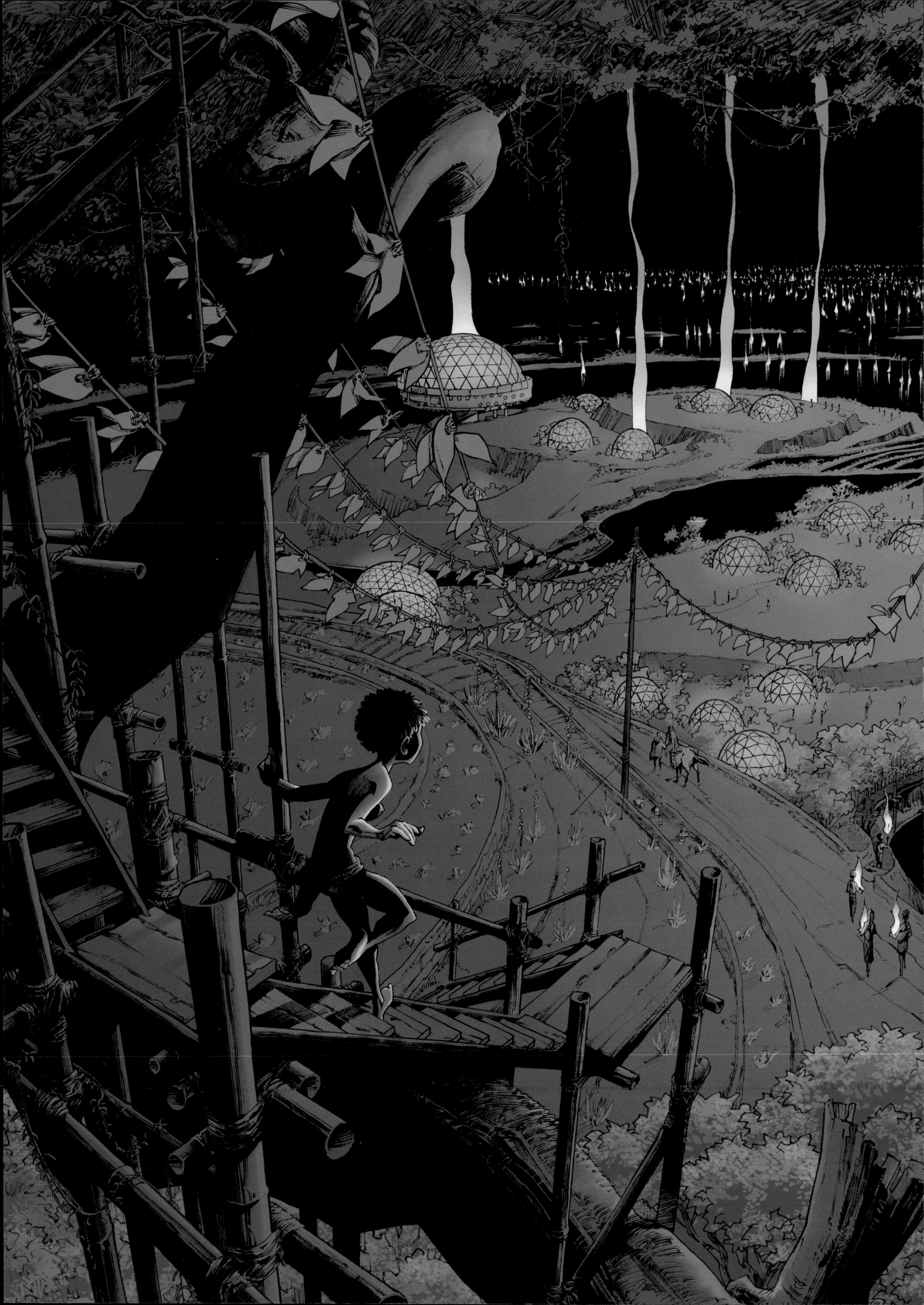

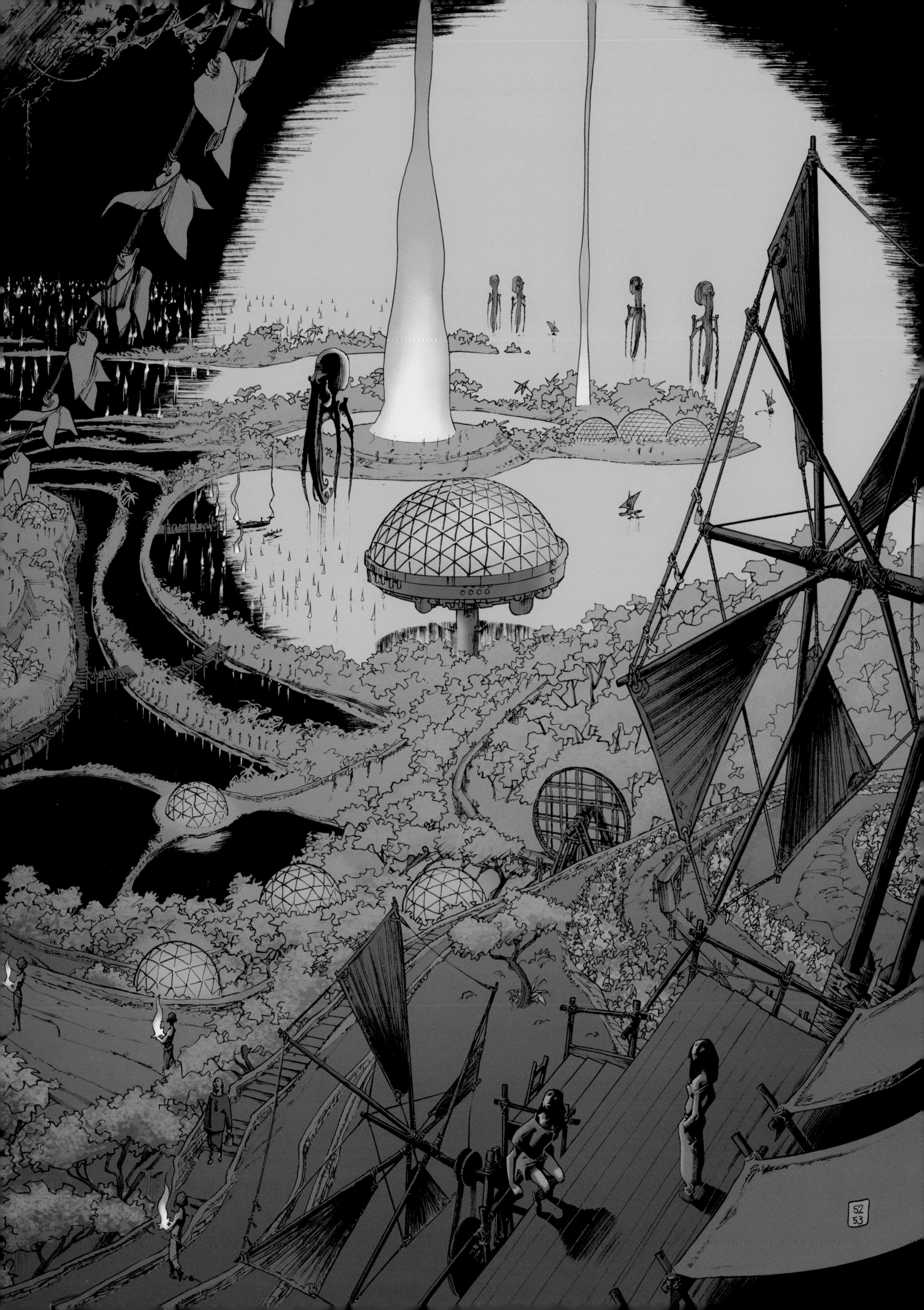
52
53

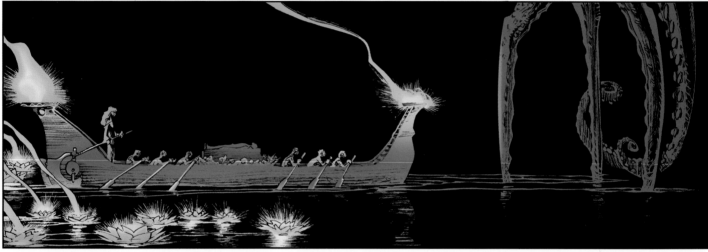

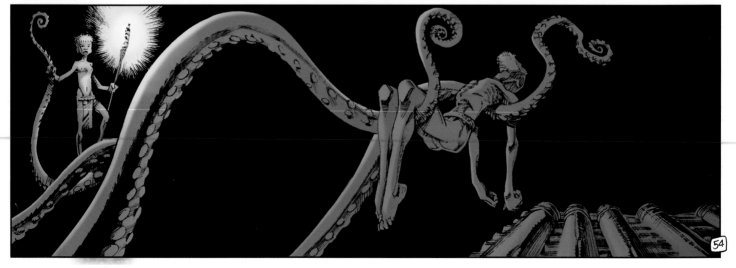

54

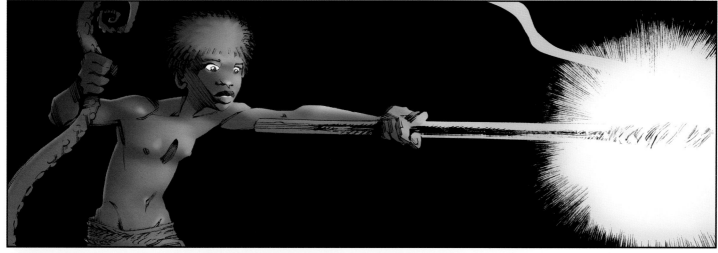

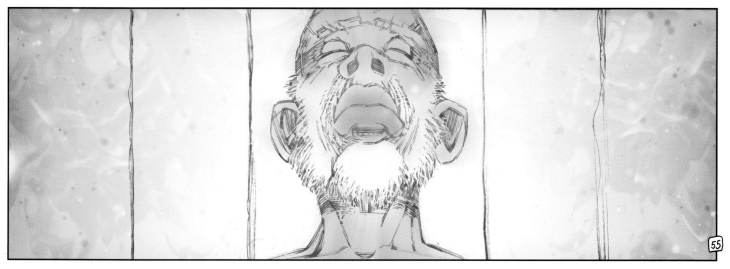

55

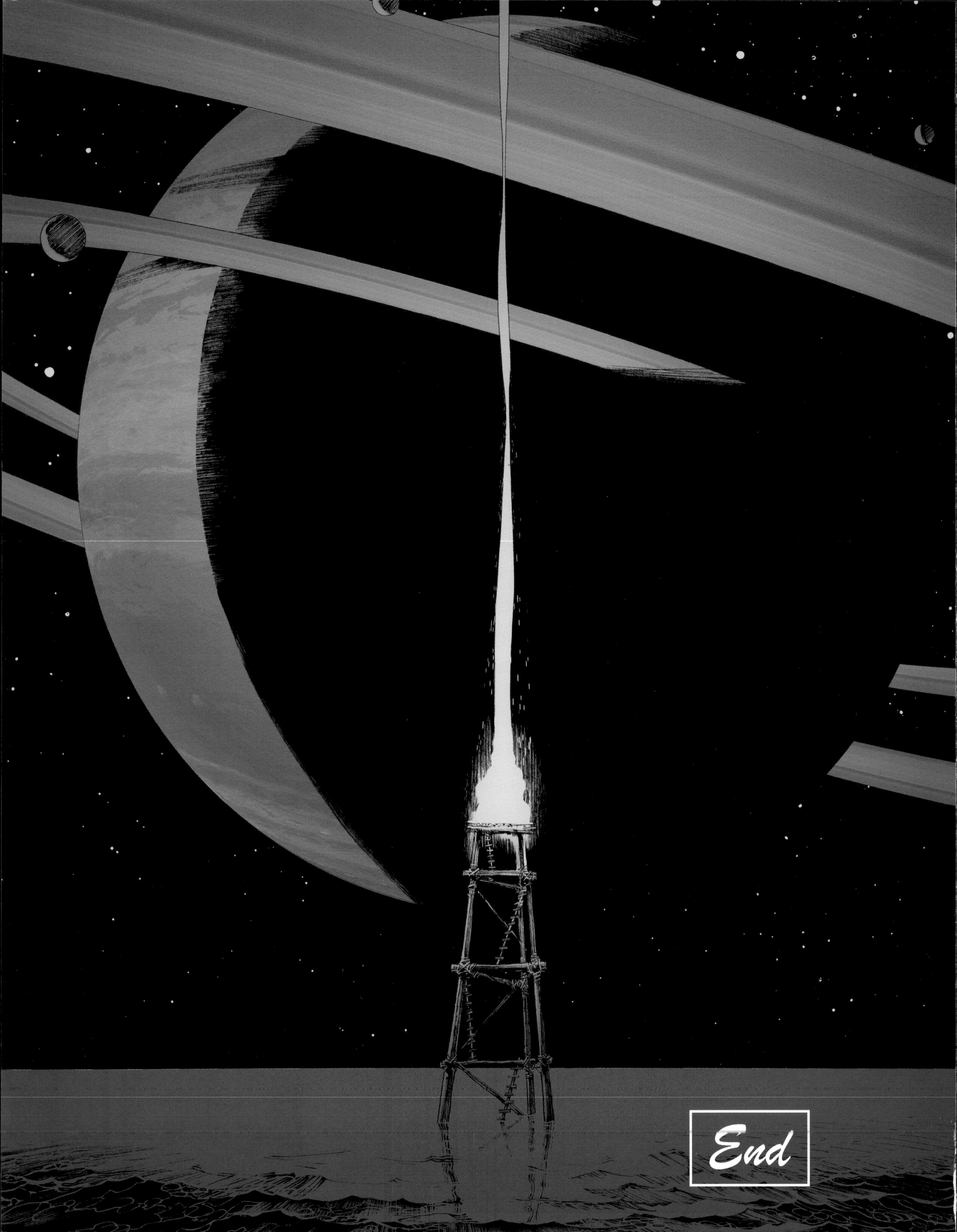
End

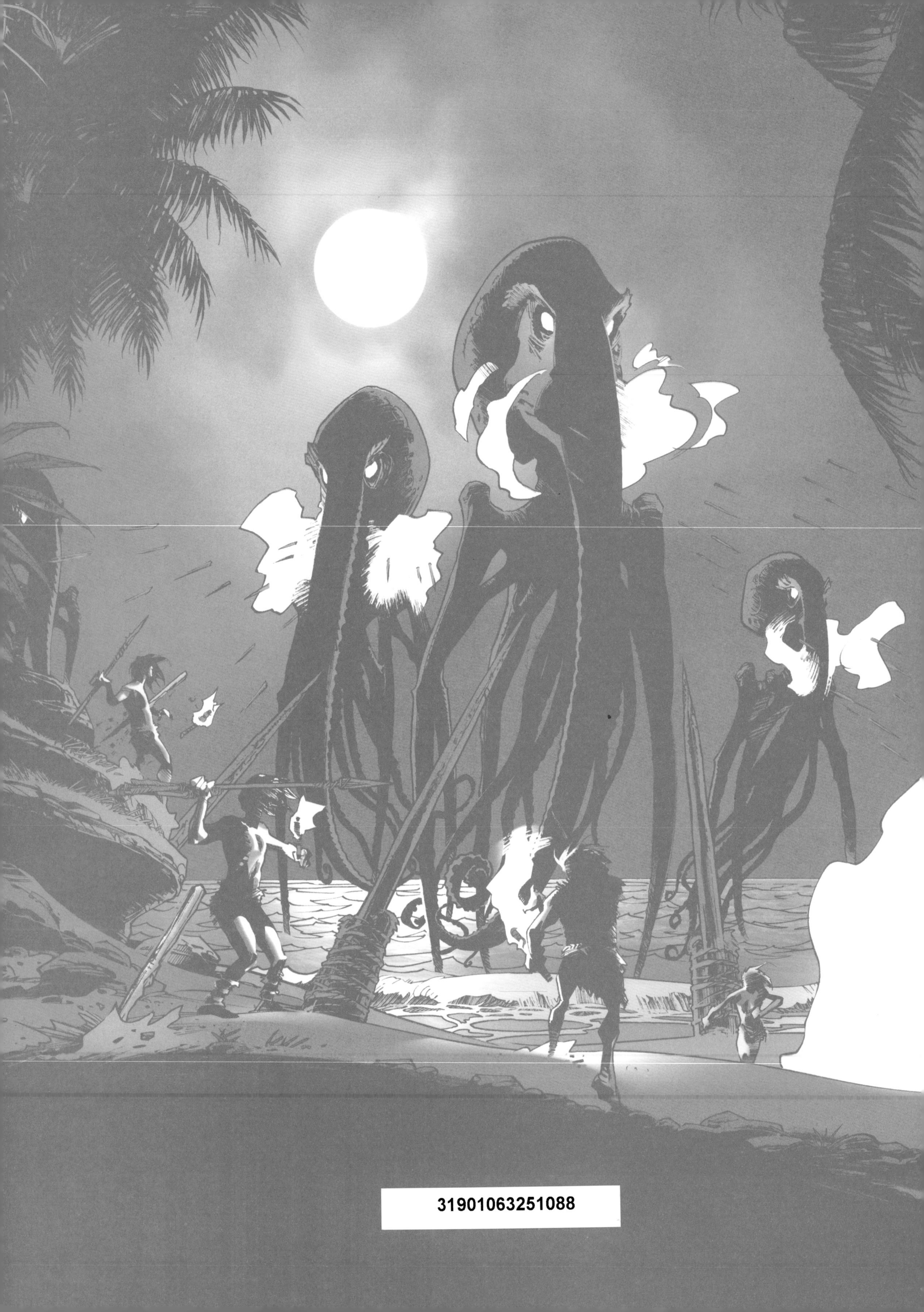